THE PRACTI(

BENJAMINS TRANSLATION LIBRARY

The Benjamins Translation Library aims to stimulate academic research and training in translation studies, lexicography and terminology. The Library provides a forum for a variety of approaches (which may sometimes be conflicting) in a historical, theoretical, applied and pedagogical context. The Library includes scholarly works, reference books, post-graduate text books and readers in the English language.

Volume 6

Alicia Betsy Edwards

The Practice of Court Interpreting

THE PRACTICE OF COURT INTERPRETING

ALICIA BETSY EDWARDS

JOHN BENJAMINS PUBLISHING COMPANY
AMSTERDAM/PHILADELPHIA

The paper used in this publication meets the minimum requirements of the American National Standard for Information Sciences – Permanence of Paper for Printed Library Materials, ANSI z39.48-1984.

Library of Congress Cataloging-in-Publication Data

Edwards, Alicia Betsy.
The Practice of Court Interpreting / Alicia B. Edwards.
p.   cm. (Benjamins Translation Library, ISSN 0929-7316 ; v. 6)
Includes bibliographical references and index.
1. Court interpreting and translating--United States. I. Title. II. Series.
KF8725.E39   1995
347.73' 16--dc20   95-15376
ISBN 978 90 272 1602 1 (EUR) / 978 1 55619 683 6 (US)   (Hb ; alk. paper)
ISBN 978 90 272 1603 8 (EUR) / 978 1 55619 684 3 (US)   (Pb ; alk. paper)
ISBN 978 90 272 8366 5   (Eb)

John Benjamins Publishing Co. · P.O. Box 36224 · 1020 ME Amsterdam · The Netherlands
John Benjamins North America · P.O. Box 27519 · Philadelphia PA 19118-0519 · USA

For My Mother and Father

About the Author

Alicia Betsy Edwards received a B.A. in History from the University of Rochester, and an M.A. in Latin American Area Studies and a Ph.D. in Latin American History from the American University. For many years she has worked on a contract basis as a translator and interpreter for the U.S. Department of State, and for the past 15 years has also interpreted in various federal courts and in D.C. Superior Court in Washington, D.C. She has been a Visiting Lecturer in Translation and Interpretation at the University of California, Berkeley, and has published numerous articles on interpreting.

Contents

To the Reader

Court interpreting can represent a satisfying vocational goal for the bilingual and bicultural liberal arts major who has the ability to interpret. Over the next twenty years the need for well-trained court interpreters will grow. This book describes the normal flow of work, how to train for it, how to find it, how to prepare for a case, how to do the work, and subsequent reading to help us improve our work. Most of the case material cited I have personally observed, while some examples have been recounted by colleagues. Names of cases and participants have been changed.

Some of the material in Chapter 2 derives from a paper given at the American Translators Association National Convention in 1982, entitled "Documents Are a Court Interpreter's Best Friend," subsequently reprinted by the Court Interpreters and Translators Association as an offset. The use of the case sheet was explained in a lecture called "Case Preparation" at the Educators' Pedagogical Institute on Court Interpreting at Montclair State College in New Jersey in 1987.

Chapter 4 originated with a paper in *The Court Manager (1988)*, entitled "Ethical Conduct for the Court Interpreter," and an article in *Capital Translator* with Attorney Lloyd Elsten, entitled "Interpreting in Criminal Court" (1982).

Chapter 5 includes comments on neologisms from an article published in *Capital Translator* (1985) entitled "Hortera Meets Empaste." Another part of the chapter was suggested by a lecture entitled "Avoiding the Pitfalls of Literal Translation/Interpretation," given at a Workshop for Federal Court Interpreters in Miami, sponsored by The Federal Judicial Center (1988).

Chapter 6 includes ideas presented at a "Workshop in Court Interpreting and Legal Translation" (1983) for the National Capitol Area Chapter of the American Translators Association (Washington, D.C.).

Chapters 7 and Chapter 8 have grown out of my work on tapes and as an expert witness, supplemented by the generous advice of Alee A. Alger-

Robbins of San Diego, and María Elena Cárdenas of Miami, with incisive comments by Irene King-Tomassini of Miami.

Chapter 9 had a modest beginning in the article "All Rise: Books on Court Interpreting" for *Capital Translator* (1982) and has been much extended and modified.

Perhaps this book can help us think about court interpreting in an organized fashion, and improve our practice of it. The book may also help attorneys, judges, and administrators better understand the role and functions of the court interpreter, to better use her talent.

Acknowledgements

It has been a privilege to work with and learn from colleagues past and present at the Office of Language Services of the U.S. Department of State, the Superior Court of the District of Columbia, the Office of the U.S. Attorney for the District of Columbia, and U.S. District Courts in Washington, D.C., Alexandria, Virginia, and some other states.

I wish to thank all the assigning officers, coordinators, editors, organizers, professors, students, and colleagues who made the interpreting, publications, teaching, and lectures possible, and who offered encouragement. I am especially grateful to: Professor Angela M. Aguirre of William Paterson College, N.J.; Alee A. Alger-Robbins, San Diego; Frank M. Almeida, Director of Court Interpreter Services, U.S. District Court, Central District of California, Los Angeles; Professor Etilvia Arjona-Tseng, Panama; Professor Arthur L. Askins, University of California, Berkeley; Edward J. Baca, Administrative Office of the U.S. Courts; Don Barnes (Ret.) and Guillermo Baserva, Language Services of the U.S. Department of State; Lynda Brown-Hall, U.S. Attorney's Office for the District of Columbia; Francis Burton, Interpreter Coordinator, Superior Court of the District of Columbia; María Elena Cárdenas, Miami; Francisco F. Campos, Benidorm, Spain; Professor Silvana Carr, Vancouver Community College; Myriam Castro-Sigler, Washington, D.C.; Professor Jerry R. Craddock, University of California, Berkeley; Ted Crump, Head, Translation Unit, N.I.H. Library, National Institutes of Health; David Foster, U.S. Attorney's Office for the District of Columbia; Dr. Deanna Hammond, Head, Language Services, Congressional Research Service, Library of Congress; Connie Landró, Interpreter Coordinator, Superior Court of the District of Columbia; Jack Leeth, formerly with the Administrative Office of the U.S. Courts; Lillian Nigaglioni, Harry Obst, and Barbara Phillips, all with Language Services, U.S. Department of State; Flora L. Phelps, Managing Editor, *Américas Magazine* (Ret.); The Honorable Milton Pollack, United States District Court, Southern District of New York;

Professor John H.R. Polt, University of California, Berkeley; Stephanie van Reigersberg, Language Services, U.S. Department of State; Professor Roda P. Roberts, University of Ottawa; Neil A. Seidenman, Language Services, U.S. Department of State (Ret.); David Sperling, Washington, D.C.; Professor Marilyn R. Tayler, Montclair State College, N.J.; Chandler Thompson, Las Cruces, N.M.; M. Eta Trabing, Fuquay-Varina, N.C.; and Wanda Tucker and Julia Zavada, Language Services, U.S. Department of State.

I also wish to thank my Father, Edward A. Edwards, M.D., who was kind enough to do two editorial critiques of the manuscript. Interpreter colleagues who critiqued the manuscript were Rose Marie Aragón of Washington, D.C., and Irene King-Tomassini, Supervisory Interpreter, U.S. District Court for the Southern District of Florida, Miami. Attorney Lloyd Elsten of Washington, D.C. and the Honorable Ricardo M. Urbina, United States District Court, District of Columbia, also read and commented on parts of the manuscript. The Honorable Colleen Kollar-Kotelly, Superior Court of the District of Columbia was also helpful. I am grateful for their detailed comments and suggestions.

CHAPTER 1

How to Become a Court Interpreter and a Brief Sketch of the Work

In its narrowest sense, court or judicial interpreting is the oral interpretation of speech from one language to another in a legal setting. Court interpreting is thus an excellent career for language and humanities graduates who have strong bilingual and bicultural abilities. Bilingualism does not guarantee the ability to interpret. A bilingual person, however, may perhaps have the gift. If one needs two languages for court work, one also needs to understand two cultures. The court interpreter must be both bilingual and bicultural.

Court interpreting is but one form of interpretation. Other varieties include conference interpreting (which is simultaneous at international conferences), and escort interpreting (consecutive interpreting done for small, informal groups). When you visit the United Nations, you hear conference interpreting. Conference interpreters usually do simultaneous interpreting into their "A" or active (usually native) language, from two or three "B" or "C" (more passive) languages. The conference interpreter who does simultaneous work usually needs only to produce correct speech into one language. She is isolated from ambient noise by a booth, she has sophisticated sound equipment provided by the conference or institution, and that sound equipment brings the sound to her on a headset whose incoming volume she can control. Her purpose is to communicate, sometimes in an elegant fashion, so she may perhaps embellish, smooth out, and fix infelicitous turns of phrase.

While court interpreting requires the ability to do simultaneous, it is more demanding than conference interpreting in that one must be able to go to and from two languages in consecutive, and into at least one language in simultaneous, usually the language that is not English. Also, one cannot fix or modify any words, because such fixing would taint the case. Because these are adversary proceedings, parties can become very angry if they sense any deviation from the formalities. The court interpreter is not isolated in a booth, and must depend on her ears and eyes to find out what is happening. Substantial court work allows the interpreter to become familiar with court terminology and to feel comfortable in the courtroom.

Who Should Become a Court Interpreter

Some interpreters are attracted to court interpreting because of its dramatic potential and excitement, while others become more lively from the experience. Translators, who work on written documents, may not always be able to interpret. They may not like interpreting even if they can do it. The life of the translator appears calm, because he is mostly involved with a computer, or else does research at the library, while interpreters move around, travel, and work before the public in exciting cases. Interpreters need to be assertive, and tend to be more outgoing, lively, and noisy than translators. Although the drama in the courtroom is that of the case, and thus belongs to someone else, we participate as actors do; we speak the lines created by others. Thus, the profession of court interpreter is not for the shy or retiring, not for the person who likes peace, calm, or routine. It requires your full attention and devotion. One never reaches a point where one can say: "Now I know it all, now I can sit back and rest." Cases, procedures, and vocabulary require constant study. Also, one can take nothing for granted: schedules change, cases are pled out instead of going to trial, there is constant movement between courts, jails, the offices of attorneys and others. No schedule is sacred, and one needs to be able to jump fast both mentally and physically.

Interpreters believe that other colleagues are "real" interpreters if they derive most of their income from interpreting. Many professionals derive almost all of their income from interpreting or a combination of interpreting and translating.

A court interpreter must love language, words, the history of words, and the interplay between language and culture. It helps also to like action, to be dismayed at the prospect of a nine-to-five job. Because most interpreting work is done on a free-lance or independent contractor basis, one needs a number of clients and work in various courts to survive. While the field offers no guarantee of economic security, skilled people can build an interesting life with a reasonable income. Court interpreting is never boring; there are few professions of which that can be said. The court interpreter will never lead a life of quiet desperation.

There is more than one way to acquire a working language. Some people may be born abroad, study English, and then move to the U.S. where they learn more English. Others are born in the U.S. of parents who speak another language at home, in which case they may take courses in both languages and spend time in the country of origin of their parents or in a country of that same language. A third route is to be born in the U.S. of English-speaking parents. In this case, it is possible to study the foreign language in school, then reside and study abroad to learn that language more fully and immerse yourself in that language and culture. Along the way, constant reading in both languages helps, as does travel. A classic ploy was to meet a boyfriend or girlfriend who spoke the language to be learned. Friendship is a great promoter of language learning.

The first goal of the prospective court interpreter is to become thoroughly bilingual in the languages he plans to use. Language courses are offered at many U.S. universities and may be supplemented by a junior year abroad, graduate work abroad, summer study abroad, or work abroad. European universities offer wonderful summer courses for foreigners in language and culture and many have full-year programs as well. Spain, Portugal, Italy, and France offer excellent teaching in an environment that obliges the student to speak the language. When you travel to Europe to study, take a vow not to read newspapers in English. You want the news, the action, read the local papers and watch local television. The classified section of the Madrid newspaper *El País* of Aug. 6, 1994, for example, has one section under "Services" entitled "Relax," which includes a "*Circulo Erótico*" or Erotic Circle where you can meet people and girls can join for free. The add explains that this circle will introduce you to relationships that are "*libres de compromiso* ," that is, with no strings attached. This no strings could be an excellent start.

Formal Training for Court Interpreting

Because interpreting involves the manipulation of two languages that one already knows, most of one's language study should have been completed before taking an interpreting course. Serious courses on interpreting and translating require the prospective student to demonstrate bilingual ability. An entrance test may also be required to see if a person can interpret or translate at a preliminary level. An interpreting course is not the place to brush up on a working language. How many years of school one needs to do the work properly is up to the individual doing the work. The creators of the federal certification exam for Spanish court interpreting (of which more shortly) say that one needs at least 14 years of schooling in English to understand the English used in court. Competent interpreting requires a solid liberal arts foundation, a foundation best acquired at a university here or abroad. I recommend at least a B.A. or B.S. degree, while an M.A. or a Ph.D. in the language, literature, history, or art of an area can be helpful. Study does not end with the acquisition of a degree or certification; the last chapter of this text suggests further reading and practice to enhance understanding of the legal process and our place in it.

William M. Park's book *Translator and Interpreter Training in the USA: A Survey* (8) provides the names of schools in the U.S. that offer courses in interpretation and translation. Interpreting schools in Europe include the University of Geneva, the University of Paris, and the University of Trieste; these schools are geared to train conference rather than court interpreters. Once you have some work experience, you may be tempted to sign up for courses in forensic sciences to better understand the analysis and discussion of physical evidence. For criminal cases, the more you understand about forensic sciences generally, the better off you will be. Any university that teaches Spanish and other languages and also offers forensic sciences could be in an excellent position to put together an innovative program in court interpreting.

Training on the Job

Much of your learning will be on the job, because the best way to learn is to do, and because so many local variations of practice affect our work. The laws differ in each state, each court has its own rules and procedures, and no case is the same. To learn on the job means you have to ask a lot of questions and observe a variety of cases. Once you have begun work, your observations will be more valuable because you will have a better idea of what you are seeing and what you need to concentrate on.

The fact that the profession is still relatively open allows beginners to obtain valuable practice. Most cases that court interpreters work on are criminal cases; the bulk of such cases are heard in state courts. State courts tend to have the most interesting cases in terms of human drama. While openness at the state level permits beginners to work, the concomitant disadvantage of an open or unregulated system is that some state courts may provide no supervision, which leaves interpreters pretty much on their own, with no official guidance.

With some exceptions, both state and federal administrators evince a natural bureaucratic reluctance to train free-lance people. The reluctance is more than budgetary. Some administrators believe that to train interpreters may place an office under the obligation to provide free-lance people a certain amount of work. One institution, not a court, which employs both free-lance and permanent interpreters, when approached about training for free-lance people, replied that it had neither the time nor the budget to train its own permanent staff interpreters, so naturally free-lance training could not even be considered. With some few exceptions, the general lack of in-house training and supervision for court interpreters means that the burden falls on us to seek and create our own training.

Training at Professional Meetings

Once one has begun work, perhaps the most useful training is at professional association meetings. The California Court Interpreters Association (CCIA) (12) and the American Translators Association (ATA) (11) are the two professional groups that offer the most training. CCIA training, offered at local meetings and at a yearly conference, may be the most helpful to court interpreters. While CCIA is mainly a California group, it is possible to join CCIA if one lives outside California, and one may also attend the meetings. The ATA holds a national conference yearly, and also has local groups that may have monthly meetings that are worthwhile attending. Interpreters may join the ATA, membership is not limited to translators. The National Association of Judiciary Interpreters and Translators (NAJIT) (13) is becoming more active in training. CCIA, ATA, NAJIT and some local ATA groups publish bulletins and newsletters that are good sources of information. At national and local meetings one may hear or present papers, meet colleagues, discuss the work, and sometimes obtain work. The contacts are invaluable; you will meet specialists who will become friends, and whom you may approach for their wise counsel.

Finding Work

A state court may have a coordinator of interpreters who may be an administrator or an interpreter, and it is the coordinator whom one approaches for
case assignments. If a state has no organized system for interpreters, the
interpreter may inquire of the office of the clerk of the court, and sometimes at
the office of the prosecutor as to need for interpreters. You may also approach
local probation and public defender offices. Most of the work will be free-
lance or independent contracting, so that is what one should ask about. Case
volume depends on the linguistic communities represented in the area, the
degree to which their activities are noticed by the judicial system, and the
willingness of court systems to believe that interpreting is necessary for
defendants or witnesses.

Once you have decided where you want to live and work, contact local
court interpreter coordinators, and some law firms. You may also wish to
contact commercial agencies that use interpreters or translators. These agencies provide valuable experience for the beginning court interpreter. Their
costs are high, what they pay the interpreter can be less than half what they
charge a client, so eventually it may be better to be on your own. As you read
the newspapers, keep in mind that where there is an indictment, there may be
work for you. Every serious interpreter should have an answering machine,
beeper, or cellular phone, some reliable means of contact.

Requirements for the Federal Courts

In 1978 the federal government passed the Court Interpreters Act (see Appendix 1), subsequently modified by Amendments in 1988 (see Appendix 3). The
law basically said that certified people would work in the federal courts, and
that the Administrative Office of the U.S. Courts was to set up certification
procedures. That Office has created an examination for Spanish that has been
given since 1980, and now offers examinations for the Haitian Creole and
Navajo languages. As of 1995, full federal certification will also be offered
for Cantonese, Mandarin, and Korean. There is also a procedure to determine
what is called "otherwise qualified status" for the federal courts for Arabic,
Polish, Italian, Russian, Mien, and Hebrew. Information about federal certification and otherwise qualified status may be obtained from the Federal Court
Interpreter Certification Project, at the University of Arizona (14).

A federal court may have one or more staff interpreters who are federally certified for Spanish. A court with many cases might have a permanent staff of interpreters, as well as a supervisory interpreter, who does interpreting and assigns free-lance work to other certified people, or to other competent interpreters for languages that are not Spanish. A small federal court may have only one interpreter on permanent staff. When a federal court does not have a staff interpreter, the office of the clerk may have a coordinator of interpreters who may be approached for work.

For Spanish, the federal courts are generally required to use federally certified interpreters. They hire permanent staff and free-lance interpreters from the list of certified interpreters published by the Administrative Office of the U.S. Courts. That office, in Washington, D.C., has contracted the certification process to the University of Arizona. The first part of the Spanish exam is written, and if one passes it, one may take the oral part. An excellent study aid for the written English is the sample exam for the Graduate Record Exam (GRE), English Aptitude part, available in most university bookstores. For Spanish, look for the Spanish GRE, although that exam has parts that deal with substantive knowledge of Spanish literature, which is not at issue in the federal exam.

The advantage of federal certification is that once certified, an interpreter may then seek work in any federal court in the U.S. Another advantage is that once one is on the list, one receives all announcements of permanent Spanish interpreter positions for the various federal courts as they open, nationwide. As of 1994, there were 558 interpreters federally certified for Spanish. Many federally certified people prefer to work as independent interpreters because they enjoy the variety and flexibility that independent work offers. To quote Jack Leeth, formerly with the Administrative Office of the U.S. Courts, the exam tells the courts that the certified person is capable of doing the work of a court interpreter. While federal certification suggests a certain level of ability or potential, it is only a beginning. The interpreter who wishes to distinguish herself needs constant study to stay abreast of current terms and events. To be respected, one also needs integrity. We discuss interpreter ethics in Chapter IV; it is ethics that regulate our conduct in and out of the courtroom.

When the federal examination for Spanish was first established, its validity was challenged in federal court in New York, in *Seltzer and Torres-Cartagena v. Foley et al.*, and upheld in a decision by Judge Milton Pollack (see Appendix 2). Judge Pollack's opinion explains in detail why such an exam was felt to be necessary, how it was put together, and what it seeks to determine.

State Certifications

California has a certification program, Washington has one of more recent vintage, and New Jersey is phasing one in. The District of Columbia uses federally certified people for Spanish, or interpreters who have passed one of simultaneous interpreting exams given by the U.S. Department of State. Other states, counties, and municipalities are beginning to recognize the need for quality interpretation in their courts. The National Center for State Courts in Williamsburg, Virginia, is currently studying the use of interpreters in the state courts. Quality interpretation depends on certification examinations, use of certified people once those people have been selected, in-service training, good working conditions, and proper remuneration. Finding and using quali- fied people costs money; financially-squeezed state administrators may not wish to take the steps necessary to guarantee quality. Those agencies and courts that do things properly attract the best, most serious people, and of course have a right to demand excellent work, which they do receive. Courts that ignore proper standards choose shoddy work.

Free-lance v. Full-time Work

Free-lance or independent work is satisfying because it allows one to move around, it provides a variety of work settings, cases, and flexible schedules. This means that if you wish to take the summer to study in Europe, you may. If you wish to teach or write, you need ask permission of no one. It will take several years to get up to speed, to get good at the work, to become known, but this holds true for any profession. Meanwhile, if the financial rewards at the beginning are modest, eventually one may have a good volume of work.

Diversification is the key to success as an independent interpreter. It is dangerous to depend on one major source of work, because something can happen to that source. Get in touch with federal, state, county, and municipal courts in your area. Contact also law firms, arbitration associations, workmans' compensation and other administrative boards. There are two issues in a successful free-lance career. One is doing the work well, which is what this book discusses. The other issue is finding the work or marketing your services. The marketing program you design for yourself should obey your own needs, interests, abilities, and time and transport constraints. Suppose you have a car and are willing to travel up to 30 miles each way to work. Take a map of where you are, draw a circle of a 30-mile radius with the center at your area, and research and contact every possible source of work within your defined area. On the other hand, if you travel only by subway, bus, bike, and foot, determine your parameters within the subway-bus-bike-foot zone, and market yourself within that area. Successful diversification, i.e., building a solid client base, depends on your drive and interests. It also depends on changing circumstances. Newsletters and journals of the professional associations, as well as newspapers such as *The Wall Street Journal* and *The New York Times* will keep you aware of shifting demographic patterns, new crimes, new laws, and, thus, demand. Flexibility is part of a happy independent work pattern. If you define your own interests, you will then see how those interests fit into changing demand patterns.

The advantages of full-time work include some financial stability and predictability as to income flow as well as the fact that it is flowing at all. An individual supporting children on one income is well-advised to seek a permanent post that provides health and life insurance, and pension benefits. Children or no, if, for your own peace of mind, you need to be able to predict what you will earn each month and when you will be paid, then a full-time job may be desirable. A predictable work schedule has some advantages. The free-lance person must spend a good deal of time hustling for work or "arranging the schedule." For the interpreter who just wants to interpret, full-time work can be an excellent choice. A full-time person must also know how to work peacefully within a bureaucracy, how to defend the territory (working conditions and budgets), and how to be happy within a large structure.

Where Court Interpreters Work and What They Do

Geographical Area

The greatest need in the U.S. is for Spanish, though other languages may also require interpretation. The great port cities that saw the most immigration in the last century still draw large immigrant populations. Further movement in this century created a spillover effect, think of New Jersey in relation to New York. Areas along the border with Mexico provide a great deal of work, as does Florida.

While the U.S. has naturally attracted immigrants, the wars that the U.S. has waged in this century have brought new groups to the U.S.: for example, many Salvadoreans fleeing war in El Salvador settled in the Washington, D.C. area. Sometimes immigrants are attracted by economic opportunity and the presence of friends and relatives, or the presence of people from the same village. Sometimes it is ease of transport that plays a role; many Dominicans now find the New York area congenial. People from the Azores may settle near Boston or Fall River, Mass. Population patterns shift, so look around and ask questions. I was recently surprised to learn that outside of New York there are substantial numbers of Portuguese speakers, for example. In the case of court work, you need certain linguistic populations. Your actual contacts to obtain the work, however, should be with courts, other governmental agencies, and attorneys. Look closely into the area where you live to see who is there. If you plan to move or have to move, contact the local chamber of commerce and the state development agency. If you plan to set up your own court interpreting business, they may be able to provide information.

Settings and Duties

Before trial, interpreters may work at grand jury and in the prosecutor's office for the government, and at line-ups. The defense may call the interpreter down to the jail, or the court may ask the interpreter to interpret forensic interviews where a psychiatrist determines the defendant's competence to stand trial. In the courtroom interpreters work at arraignments, preliminary hearings, plea bargains, status hearings, trials, sentencings, and motions. Most interpreted proceedings are criminal cases. Other matters that may require interpretation could include bankruptcy proceedings, child support matters, divorce, juvenile proceedings, civil protection orders, mental health hearings, traffic court, landlord-tenant, small claims, and other civil cases. Work in state courts of general jurisdiction is advantageous for the court interpreter, because one learns to interpret a variety of cases all the way up to serious felonies. Different subjects stretch your abilities as an interpreter, exposing you to the wonder and horror of the human condition. A wide range of work builds competence and makes you a better interpreter.

In personal injury cases, the interpreter may work primarily at interviews and depositions. After a deposition, parties to civil cases may decide to settle out of court so that for interpreting purposes, a deposition is as close to trial as a case may come. Thus, the attorneys involved will treat it with the seriousness of a trial. A hysterical woman at deposition who sobs over the trauma of an auto accident, trauma that caused her and her husband to lose their conjugal enjoyment of each other, is not the sort of witness an insurance company wants to put in front of a jury. After the deposition the company knows what it is up against and may be inclined to settle.

Civil cases may also include hearings on administrative, workmans' compensation, disability, or labor union matters. You may see commercial arbitration. If one company has inadvertently sold another some inferior goods and if their contract calls for arbitration in case of a dispute, an interpreter may be required if some parties or witnesses do not speak English.

Both civil and criminal cases may generate documents that require written translation. The criminal case may have letters to the judge, written against the advice of counsel or letters in aid of sentencing, telling what a great fellow the defendant is. Or the victim or his family may write the court describing the impact of the crime on their lives. Letters of this sort may be presented for an immediate, spoken translation, that is, a sight translation. When a government seeks extradition of a suspect, in a case involving two dead bodies and an emerald of large size, you may have to prepare a written translation of those extradition documents. You may be asked to prepare written translations of correspondence, wills, powers of attorney, and reports. A court interpreter may also be asked to prepare translations of depositions taken in another language, elsewhere, now in document form.

Major drug cases today may involve tape recordings such as phone tapes, body tapes, room tapes, and even tapes made in cars with the engine running. The tapes must be transcribed and then translated. Even divorce cases may include tapes. If the wronged spouse has a tape-recorder running in his briefcase that tape may pick up the voice of the wife yelling: "Get out, never darken my door again." The tone of her voice and her words make her insistence on a tough settlement difficult, because the tape shows her to be less than a jolly companion. Tapes for criminal cases may contain long conversations about the "merchandise," a white crystalline substance which, upon being field-tested, turns out to be cocaine.

When an interpreter presents written translations or tapes in court that she has transcribed and translated, she comes into court as an expert as to those translations or tapes, and will be questioned as to her work, its accuracy, and her work methods. On other occasions, she may be asked to testify as an expert about the accuracy of written translation or tape work done by others.

By her functions, then, and depending upon settings in which she works, the court interpreter may interpret, do sight translations, written translations, tape transcriptions and translations, and testify as an expert witness, either as to her own work, or as to that of others. Each one of these functions requires a different set of skills, and the compleat court interpreter hopes to master all of them. If well done, court interpreting provides an important service to the courts and the justice process.

The following chapters describe how to prepare for the work, how it may be done, and further reading to improve our understanding of the legal setting. Each chapter has its own list of Further Reading. There is a Bibliography at the end of the book. The Appendices provide some documents that may be otherwise difficult to obtain, which may interest interpreters. The foreign language used for examples will be Spanish.

Expressions Used in This Text

Expressions that will come up frequently in this text include **target language, source language, simultaneous interpretation, consecutive interpretation,** and **interpreting team**.

The **source language** (SL) is the language from which you take speech or a translation, while the **target language** (TL) is the language into which you interpret or translate. Either term refers to the direction of the process, so that if you interpret from Spanish to English, Spanish is the **source language** and English the **target language**. When you go from English to Spanish, then English is the **source language** and Spanish the **target language**.

In **consecutive interpretation,** the interpreter waits while the speaker says several phrases, and then interprets what has been said into the target language. Consecutive interpretation takes time, because the interpreter must wait for one speaker to finish, and the speaker, before he can continue, must wait for the interpreter to finish. It may be helpful to take a few notes as to names, dates, and numbers. Some colleagues feel that the extensive notes of the sort taken for conference-level consecutive can be distracting, and that it is best to rely on memory and take only an occasional note on the witness stand. **Consecutive interpretation** tends to be used at the witness stand, in depositions, arbitrations, interviews with attorneys in offices and cell blocks, forensic screening, probation and other interviews.

Simultaneous interpretation is done at a speed that is, according to Professor Danika Seleskovitch, thirty times greater than the speed of written translation (9). The listener is provided with earphones, the interpreter speaks into a microphone, and is about half a phrase behind the speaker. The interpreter follows the speaker almost immediately, the speaker does not have to stop, the interpretation proceeding at the same time the speaker is talking, thus its name, simultaneous interpretation. This is the sort of interpretation you hear at the United Nations and international conferences. With simultaneous interpretation the defendant can hear every word that the judge, the attorneys, and witnesses are saying, to follow the case and aid in his own defense. For example, when an FBI witness holds up a bloody jacket and says: "This was Juan's jacket," the defendant, Luis, hearing this through the interpreter, can tap his lawyer on the shoulder and say: "No, that is wrong, that was my jacket," and indeed, it does show the cut corresponding to the the the stab that Luis himself had received in the struggle.

Every defendant at trial needs to have the entire case interpreted simultaneously to him. When the defendant is on the witness stand, questions to the defendant and the defendant's testimony may be rendered in consecutive. The testimony of other English-speaking witnesses will be done simultaneously by the interpreters. Should the testimony from the stand be in the language of the defendant, the defendant may hear what the interpreter on the stand is saying through the floor microphone, or through other sound equipment.

When a matter does not exceed 30 minutes, one interpreter may be sufficient, but **if the interpreting time exceeds 30 minutes, an interpreting team of two interpreters or more is required**. Because simultaneous interpretation is so speedy, and because such concentration is required to capture each word and render it into the target language, there should always be at least two interpreters for simultaneous, working together, who switch off every thirty minutes or so, be it a single or multi-defendant case. The United Nations has determined that the limit of efficiency for simultaneous interpretation is about 30 minutes. This standard is followed by the United Nations, the U.S. Department of State, the federal courts, the Superior Court of the District of Columbia, and those state courts that wish to provide competent interpreting services.

On major cases with many foreign-language witnesses one might have a team of three interpreters, all of whom may switch around. On the witness stand, interpreters may decide to change every 20 minutes, unobtrusively, during natural breaks in the case such as bench conferences, or between questions asked of a witness. Interpreters develop their own hand and eye signals for these switches. When working at the defense table, the interpreter on break is still a member of the team, should sit next to the team member who is interpreting, and be prepared to hand her documents, a copy of the indictment if it is being quoted from, or to pass notes. The notes may consist of a word that has slipped the mind of the interpreter speaking, or suggestions for rendering of words. A good team works smoothly together, and parties to the case soon become accustomed to the unobtrusive switching between interpreters. Chapter IV discusses procedures for interpreters and how to determine the number needed for a case. It also discusses in some detail the sound equipment that an interpreter uses.

Further Reading

1. Bell, Susan J., compiler. *Full Disclosure: Do You Really Want to Be a Lawyer?* Princeton, N.J.: Peterson's Guides, 1989.
    • Introduction to the different settings in which law is practiced. Written for potential lawyers, it can help the court interpreter define the sorts of places and firms he may wish to approach for free-lance work.

2. Bowen, David and Margareta, eds. *Interpreting - Yesterday, Today, and Tomorrow.* American Translators Association Scholarly Monograph Series, vol. IV. Binghamton, N.Y.: State University of New York at Binghamton (SUNY), 1990.
    • Good overview of the history of interpreting as a profession.

3. Crump, Ted. *Translations in the Federal Government: 1985.* Privately printed. Out of print.
    • Describes translating and interpreting positions available with the federal government in 1985. If you can obtain it, remember that it has not yet been updated. It

does, however, provide an idea of which agencies one might approach for work. Popular demand suggests that Mr. Crump prepare a new edition.

4. de Jongh, Elena M. *An Introduction to Court Interpreting: Theory and Practice*. Lanham, Md.: University Press of America, Inc., 1992.
    • New. Includes a history of court interpreting in the U.S., the interpreting process, language and culture, interpreting non-standard language, interpreting in court, and court interpreting as a profession.

5. "Federal Court Interpreters Manual, Policies and Procedures." Administrative Office of the U.S. Courts, Washington, D.C. In press.

6. González, Roseann, Victoria Vásquez and Holly Mikkelson. *Fundamentals of Court Interpretation: Theory, Policy, and Practice*. Durham, N.C.: Carolina Academic Press, 1992.
    • New. Includes discussion of historical antecedents, legal overview, utilization of interpreter services, management of court interpreter services, language and the interpreter, interpretation theory and practice, practical considerations and tasks, and professional issues.

7. Herbert, Jean. *The Interpreter's Handbook: How to Become a Conference Interpreter*. Second Edition Revised and Enlarged. Geneva: Librarie de l'Université, 1968.
    • The great classic on conference interpreting, valuable insights for simultaneous interpreting.

8. Park, William M., *Translator and Interpreter Training in the USA: A Survey*, Second Edition. Arlington, Va.: American Translators Association, 1993.
    • The place to start to find out which universities offer interpreting and translating programs. Inquire also of your local universities, which while they may not have degree programs, may offer occasional courses and seminars. Look for interpreting courses taught by professional interpreters.

9. Seleskovitch, Danica. *Interpreting for International Conferences: Problems of Language and Communication*. Translated by Stephanie Dailey and E. Norman McMillan. Washington, D.C.: Pen and Booth, 1978. Available from: Pen and Booth, 1608 R St., N.W., Washington, D.C. 20009. The publisher contemplates an updated edition.
    • Basic for a discussion of simultaneous interpreting. Seleskovitch stresses that one should go for the core idea rather than sticking to the words themselves.

10. Trabing, M. Eta. *Manual for Judiciary Interpreters English-Spanish 1979*. Houston, Texas: Agri-Search International Inc., 1979. Out of print.
    • The granddaddy of the field, very useful. Includes good terminology, excellent remarks on interpreting in the courtroom, and sample court documents for the federal courts and Texas state courts in both English and Spanish.

Professional Associations

11. The American Translators Association
    1800 Diagonal Rd., Suite 220
    Alexandria, Virginia 22314
    USA

12. California Court Interpreters Association
    P.O. Box 5035
    Garden Grove, California 92645
    USA

13. The National Association of Judiciary Interpreters and Translators
    531 Main Street, Suite 1603
    New York, N.Y. 10044
    USA

For Information about Federal Certification and Otherwise Qualified Status you may write to:

14. Dr. Roseann Dueñas González, Director
    National Center for Interpretation, Testing, Research and Policy
    Federal Court Interpreter Project
    Modern Languages Building, #67, Room 445
    The University of Arizona
    Tucson, Arizona 85721
    USA

CHAPTER 2

Case Preparation - A

Context and Documents

Purpose of Information

Much as a musician would like to read a score before playing a piece before an audience, the interpreter needs to ask certain questions and examine certain documents to prepare to do a good job. If we know what sort of a case we are to work on, we will have an idea before the case starts of what it may sound like.

Although simultaneous interpreting takes place at great speed, we need not be the victims of that speed or of the unpredictability of speech if we are prepared. The more the interpreter learns beforehand about names, places, relationships, dates, statements already given, issues involved, and potential expert testimony, the easier it will be for her to receive and assimilate the new material spoken in the courtroom, and thus correctly interpret what she hears. All this prior knowledge falls under the heading of context. Understanding the context allows us to understand different terms as they come up. Our motto should be "No surprises." There will still be surprises, but to the extent we have mastered the basics of a case, we will be freer to handle the surprises successfully.

To prepare well, we need a general understanding of the trial process in the area and court where we work, as well as some specific information about a case. Our research and preparation for a case *in no way* involve questions as to the merits of a case. We need not concern ourselves with the question of "who really did it." We have no interest in the outcome of the case. We want concepts and words; our only concern is with language and the ideas that underlie those words. All prior study of a case must take place under the guarantee of secrecy and confidentiality to those who allow us to study their documents and answer our questions. This is both a legal and moral obligation, of which more in Chapter IV.

We do have some control over how much information we need for each case. First we must understand the nature or the framework of any given proceeding. This text provides a general outline of what happens in a criminal trial and in a plea bargain proceeding. There are books called trial manuals, and one may be available for your area from the public defender service (7). If there is no such service where you work, consult the law librarian at the courthouse. As for other matters, for each jurisdiction you may find books written for local lawyers who specialize in the practice of, say, juvenile law, landlord-tenant disputes and such (10, 8). Those books explain the structure and process of such proceedings in your area. The more we understand of the general context, the fewer questions we need to ask about any given case. The study of trial manuals will give you a better idea of what to expect and will keep you from feeling too lost.

Sometimes you may ask the prosecutor, defense counsel, or courtroom deputy (the clerk) for a copy of the indictment or document of accusation. This document should be available to you without question. If there is a problem, speak to the judge and request that she order copies for the interpreters. Perhaps you are the first interpreter who has ever asked for it. This should not deter you. Simply explain that you need it to prepare for the case to do a proper job. Or, one of the attorneys may have an extra copy available. Interpreters wish to know facts and names beforehand to do a proper job, but some attorneys who do not understand the interpreting process, or those who do not know us personally, may be reluctant to answer our questions. Our job is then two-fold at this stage, to obtain the information we need, but also to keep the peace. Keeping the peace is more important. It is worth repeating that our desire for information proceeds only from our desire to do a good job. There is no other purpose.

The remarks that follow are based principally on my own observations derived from fifteen years' interpreting in several U.S. District Courts (federal courts) and in the Superior Court of the District of Columbia (D.C. Superior Court). Our hypothetical trip through a case follows what might happen in the Superior Court of the District of Columbia. It is important to stress that this is only one jurisdiction, but similar principles apply in other jurisdictions, even though other jurisdictions may be so ill-advised as to call things by different names, or to do things slightly differently. On a recent visit to a state court in Kansas City, Missouri, interpreting for foreign visitors, not for defendants, I found it difficult to quickly understand their system. That experience provided rapid insight into how a foreign defendant may feel when faced with any system in the U.S. that is so different from the legal system in his country of origin. Several states have certain courts for less serious offenses, which may also handle the beginning of larger cases; cases are then shifted to a second court. In Washington, D.C. we have what is called a "unified" system, everything is in one courthouse. While a hearing commissioner may handle certain traffic and non-jury criminal matters (7), and the beginning of a criminal case, a judge of that same court will handle misdemeanor and felony jury trials, so that serious cases do not have to move to another court. While you will notice some differences among federal courts in different places, there may be some commonalty of custom and practice between federal and state courts in a given city or region.

No-Paper

Some cases stop short of trial. If the police have arrested someone and the prosecutor decides that the case is less than promising, the case may be dismissed on the first day of court or **no-papered**. The defendant is immediately released. This happens in a certain number of cases.

The Structure of a Felony Proceeding

The courtroom is like a theater. We are not the actors in the event, but we must follow the actors as they play out their roles. At a criminal trial, the prosecution (which I will sometimes call "the government"), attempting to convict someone, must go through certain steps. While these steps may differ in different jurisdictions, there is a common sequence. The interpreter needs to know at which stage he enters the proceeding. Paul Bergman's book *Trial Advocacy* (1) provides an excellent description of the attorneys' role at trial and the stages of a case; it allows the reader to see what the attorneys are trying to do.

First, a crime has to be committed, or someone has to believe that the acts complained of constituted a crime. It was John Mortimer who remarked that the criminal helps support the whole judicial system (3). That system includes the entire panoply of police, courts, jails, lawyers, judges, clerks, interpreters, marshals, guards, probation officers, psychologists, social workers, experts, and jury consultants. A lot is riding on this criminal who commits or is charged with committing the crime.

A complainant calls the police who respond to the scene. Or, the police may already be there if the case is an undercover narcotics buy. The first responder may take a statement, and then hand the case over to a detective. The detective may take a statement, will interview potential witnesses, and then will take the case down to the "papering division" of the court, a branch of the District Attorney's (D.A.'s) office or the Office of the U.S. Attorney. The detective may have **arrested** the defendant. The defendant then has his **presentment** (or **arraignment** if it is a misdemeanor), the initial appearance where he is informed of the charges against him, bail may be set, and an attorney provided. In some courts before an initial appearance the defendant may be interviewed by a **pretrial services agency** to determine if he may qualify for a court-appointed attorney, and to see what ties, if any, he has in the community, with regard to the need for bail. The D.A. may decide that this is a **felony**, a serious crime, and may want to hand the case over to the grand jury. Before he does so, he may schedule a **preliminary hearing** before a judge to allow the judge to decide if there is enough evidence to believe that a felony was committed, and that the defendant before the court was the one who did it. **Probable cause** for such belief having been found by the court, the judge may **bind the case over** to the **grand jury**. Before testifying at grand jury, complaining witnesses and police officers talk with the prosecutor, and then appear before the grand jury and tell what happened. The defense is not usually there, and these proceedings are secret. The interpreter who interprets at grand jury must swear to keep secret all that is said. Even if the prosecutor leaks that same testimony to the press later the same day, the interpreter must still remain silent as to what happened at grand jury. When the interpreter is not actually interpreting, she must not be in the grand jury room. Even if it is a short matter, of waiting while an English-speaking officer gives a few minutes of testimony, the interpreter must leave, lest her unneeded presence at that moment invalidate the entire proceeding. If the grand jury decides to accuse the defendant formally, they return an **indictment** against him, some-times called a "true bill." The indictment is then handed to the defendant at what is called a **felony arraignment**.

The case may then be set for a **status hearing** or **status conference** to discuss possible motions and other matters preparatory to the trial itself.

Next is the period known as **discovery**, when each side must provide to the other certain relevant information. The government must turn over statements made by the defendant to the police, police reports, possible exculpatory material, medical records and test results, and make photos and tangible objects available for examination by the defense. The defense must also turn over certain information to the government, and if it has tangible evidence, make it available for inspection by the prosecutor. While the defense is especially concerned with statements to the police by the defendant, each side wants to know if potential witnesses have a police record, especially prior felony convictions. Prior convictions of the defendant are important to the defense attorney, because the defendant may be less than candid about his past when he speaks to his attorney. Sometimes the government has what it calls a **discovery package**, certain data it plans to turn over to the defense. But the meeting between prosecutor and defense attorney to exchange information may be difficult to schedule, the defense typically complains that the government is hard to reach, and has not cooperated fully with the defense. The defense may also be dilatory or hard to reach, because it may have something it wishes to produce dramatically at trial, say, the knife that the dead man first attacked the defendant with. The interpreter will interpret bitter complaints about the defense's inability to get discovery, and the D.A., like a little angel, will respond: "But counsel, that document is right here, and for the record, I now hand it to you."

All along the defendant is presumed innocent, and wishes to go to trial rather than plead guilty. This may be for any of four reasons: it is his right; it is good defense strategy; he may actually be innocent; or, he may not accept a plea, even though his lawyer advises him to do so, because he thinks that he can outsmart the law.

At the **status hearing** both sides indicate how many witnesses they have, how much time they propose to use, which discovery problems are pending, the best trial date, and potential evidentiary motions.

Evidentiary hearings may be held well before the trial date, or in the days or hours just prior to trial. The purpose of an evidentiary hearing is to see what kind of evidence will be allowed in at trial. The defense goal is to suppress damaging evidence, while the government hopes to present such evidence to the jury. If there has been a lot of material seized such as medical

records, school records, old laundry bills, recipes for making bombs, works of
Marx and Lenin, and lists of co-conspirators, then the defense may fight to
keep that material out. In the above case, it seems that many defendants were
perusing an article with the endearing title "The Alienation of Marxist-
Leninist Group Therapy." Copies of this article had been repeatedly seized,
and the title was constantly mentioned. If the co-conspirators are numerous
and the number of documents seized great, then evidentiary motions could
continue for more than a year prior to the actual trial itself.

In a drug case the defense wants to exclude the drugs from use as
evidence. If the defense can convince the court that the evidence was seized
in violation of the constitutional prohibition against unreasonable searches
and seizures, then perhaps the government cannot admit the drugs at trial.
Such exclusion could mean that the government has no case. Say Carlos Iluso
arrives on a flight from Lima, Peru to Dulles Airport with two bags of cocaine
taped to his legs under his Levis. He is searched and the cocaine found,
whereupon the defense says that the search of his person was unconstitu-
tional. When the judge rules that the search was proper, the defendant may
plead guilty. When Mr. Iluso enters the plea, he says that in Lima, whence he
was asked to carry the drugs, he had been afraid that he would be caught, so
he consulted a *vidente* [seer or psychic], thoughtfully provided by the same
man who wanted the cocaine carried to the U.S, and this *vidente* looked into
her crystal ball and said she foresaw no problem with U.S. Customs. He
received a sentence of two years federal incarceration for this offense.

Assume the criminal case goes to trial. If it is to be a jury trial, a **jury**
must be **selected** from a **venire** or **panel** of prospective **jurors**. Assume a jury
of 12 citizens and two **alternates** for a total of 14 jurors. The process of
choosing the jury is called the **voir dire**. The purpose is to remove those who
would bring undue prejudice to the case, either by their own beliefs or
experience. Do they know the defendant? Will they be so disgusted or
antagonized by other characteristics of the case that they could not sit fairly
and impartially? On a case where two men were on trial for robbery, the judge
asked potential jurors already seated in the jury box if there was any reason
any of them could not serve on the case. One woman raised her hand and said
she was self-employed and to serve on the case would mean she could not
attend to business.

The Court:	And what sort of work do you do, Madame?
Juror:	I am a psychic.
The Court:	Please approach the bench.
[At the bench]	
Defense₁:	Do you have any feeling about my client?
Juror:	Oh yes, they're guilty.
The Court:	You may return to the jury lounge.

Here we have a juror who has pre-judged the case. This juror was dismissed for cause, because she based her opinion on something other than evidence to be duly admitted in the case, even before opening arguments.

Voir dire, like other parts of a case, may vary from jurisdiction to jurisdiction. Voir dire in Washington, D.C. includes questions intended to show areas of potential juror bias such as: have you ever been the victim of a crime, are you related to a police officer or have you served as one, are you an attorney, do you live near the crime scene, do you know any of the parties, do you have strong opinions about the use of drugs that would make you unable to decide the case impartially, and so on.

In a state court in New York I have seen a voir dire that by strictly limited Washington, D.C. standards was liberal. Questions to the jurors included: where did you go to school, what degrees do you have, which publications do you subscribe to, are you married, what does your spouse do. All this in open court, the jurors preening themselves on their accomplishments, the wonderful grades their children were earning at Columbia University and so on, an attorney's dream. The best part was that the government almost tried the case on voir dire. The trial involved a man accused of stabbing a woman. It was delicately suggested that both were junkies and that the woman was a prostitute, and an ill-spoken one at that. The Prosecution: "Would any of you be offended by a witness who uses foul language? Would any of you find yourselves unable to believe the testimony of a lady of the night?" No, of course not. By this time the jury was slathering with curiosity to see this prize government witness. In another voir dire at a federal court in New York, the questions asked of the jurors such as what magazines they subscribed to, and the specifics of their education, were similar.

Some jurors may be dismissed or **stricken** from the jury panel **for cause**, say a person belongs to a religion that forbids one to sit in judgement on another human being, or the potential juror has a health problem, is a close friend of the defendant, believes that anyone who has anything to do with drugs should suffer, or, like the psychic mentioned earlier, has already reached a decision. The number of strikes for cause is theoretically unlimited. Ideally, if an attorney does not like a juror, he would try to have him stricken for cause, because that way he would not use up his own limited number of peremptory challenges. Much of the discussion of who is to be stricken for what reason can take place **at the bench,** that is, close up to where the judge is, with the judge and attorneys conversing, and the court reporter taking notes, all of the sound masked by a machine that creates white noise so that the jury does not hear what is said. Conversations at the bench are usually not interpreted, but sometimes an attorney will call the interpreter up to interpret bench conferences for his defendant, which one can do quite readily if one has wireless sound equipment, of which more in Chapter IV.

Each side also has a limited number of **peremptory challenges** or **strikes,** that is, it may take a certain number of people off the jury without saying why it wants those people off the case. In the middle of a three-co-defendant drug case one defense attorney may rush over to the others, when they have one peremptory challenge left between them, and say: "Never, never put an engineer on a criminal jury." Engineers are apparently bad joss. The defense attorney may ask his defendant to take a look at the jurors assembled in the jury box and indicate if there is a juror he does not like. If the defendant says yes there is, that person will be taken off, assuming the defense still has a peremptory strike left. Jury selection is an art, and there are even special consultants for the purpose, though one presumes that they would appear on retained cases where the defendant had enough money to pay for his attorney himself. On cases that have received extensive pretrial publicity or in cases where there are many defendants, it may take several jury panels to find a jury of 12 plus the necessary alternates. Depending on the case and the judge, jury selection could last from about an hour up to a week, though a week would be extreme.

At trial, after the voir dire, **the swearing in of the jury**, and some introductory remarks and **preliminary instructions** by the judge, each side presents an **opening statement**, although the defense may **reserve** its opening, and use it or not later. The Prosecution goes first: "Ladies and Gentlemen, it is Spring, and I have an empty chair by my side because Juan Arrecho will never see another Spring, all because this vicious man Luis Pitoncito, murdered Juan Arrecho in cold blood on June 27...." The defense: "Ladies and Gentlemen, we will show that it was Juan Arrecho who started the fight by stabbing my client in the back, in his own home...." The prosecution begins by putting on government witnesses; their testimony when they are questioned by the D.A. is called **direct examination**. When the defense questions them, that is **cross-examination**. This is followed by **redirect examination**, the prosecutor wrapping up some details, and sometimes **re-cross examination** by the defense.

After the government has put on its **case-in-chief**, it is said that **the government rests**, meaning it rests its case. Then counsel may approach the bench and the defense may **move for a judgement of acquittal**, arguing that in the light of all the evidence so far presented, and viewing that evidence in the light most favorable to the government, a reasonable jury could not possibly convict. This motion is frequently made, and almost as frequently denied.

If the defense has reserved its opening until after the government's case-in-chief, it may now choose to present an opening statement, though it is not obliged to do so. The defense case may or may not include witness testimony and other evidence. Often the defendant does not testify, because if he does, the government may be able to ask him about his prior felony convictions, and other troubling questions. The defense may not wish to let the government know if the defendant will testify until just before that happens, to keep the government off balance. If the defendant testifies, his lawyer will begin questioning him on **direct examination**, then comes the government with **cross-examination**, and so on.

When a witness testifies, attorneys may **object** to certain questions, or to the phrasing of a question. If the **objection is sustained**, that is, if the judge rules that it is valid, the witness is not to answer. If the **objection is overruled**, the witness is to answer. Sometimes attorneys ask questions that they know will be objected to, but their purpose is to raise an issue with the jury, although the court may tell the jury that they "must not speculate at to what the answer would have been"(6). If an answer is given despite an objection having been sustained, the court may instruct the jury to "disregard both the question and the answer" (6). The instruction to disregard the answer has, according to attorney Lloyd Elsten, somewhat the same effect as saying: "The jury will ignore the large, pink elephant sitting directly behind it." After the case-in-chief of both sides, there may be **rebuttal** witnesses for the government and, possibly, **surrebuttal** witnesses for the defense. If the defense feels it has totally torn apart government witnesses on cross-examination, it may put on no witnesses at all, in which case, after the government has put on its case-in-chief and rested, one may simply hear "**the defense rests**." This can be a good tactic for the defense, especially if the government has saved its most damaging witness for rebuttal. Without defense testimony, there is nothing to rebut, and thus the rebuttal witness cannot be heard. If the defense puts on evidence, it will rest after the presentation of its evidence.

Because the government must prove guilt beyond a reasonable doubt, the government may speak twice in **closing arguments**. First the government speaks, then the defense, and finally the government again. At closing each side may only argue facts in evidence. After closing arguments, the defense may again move for a judgement of acquittal. Assuming the motion is denied, the judge then gives **instructions to the jury**. As explained later in this chapter, jury instructions include some formal, standard material, as well as specific reference to the case in hand. In some courtrooms no one may enter or leave the room when the jury is receiving final instructions, a marshal will be at the door of the courtroom to enforce that rule, so it is wise not to linger in a courtroom not your own. After instructions, the jury retires to **deliberate**, and may return with **notes,** or **questions**, which sometimes necessitates return of the parties.

After deliberations that may range from hours to days, the jury usually returns with a **verdict**. In a **bench trial** where the judge alone hears the case, the judge decides the case. Following a **verdict of guilty**, there will be **sentencing**, either at once or at a later time. State court sentencings are governed by entirely different rules and procedures than cases in U.S. district courts (federal jurisdiction). Under the new federal **sentencing guidelines**, a federal sentencing may require several days. With the **verdict of not guilty**, the defendant may be freed, or handed over to Immigration, if that agency wants him, or sent back for trial to another state if he has a pending matter elsewhere, or held on other charges possibly pending in the same court.

This is, in broad outline, the structure of a felony trial. **Misdemeanor** trials are similar, except that the steps of preliminary hearing and grand jury are not included, and the crimes are defined in Washington, D.C. as carrying a potential prison sentence of one year or less. The document of accusation for a misdemeanor may be called an **information**. Some areas use juries of fewer than twelve people for some misdemeanors (also for some civil cases). Some cases are heard only before a judge. Other cases or situations give the defendant the right to demand a **jury trial**. A defense attorney may prefer a

bench trial before a judge alone because although the defense attorney believes his client guilty, the client insists on telling his side of the story to convince the judge that he, the defendant, is right. Judges are fond of bench trials because they save time and money.

The Plea Bargain

Most criminal cases that flood major urban court systems could never be tried even if the number of available judges and juries were increased substantially. The system functions because the central fact of criminal practice is that up to 90% of the defendants resolve their cases without trial by pleading guilty. The defendant **enters** or **accepts a guilty plea** or what is often called a **plea**. The prosecution, to save time and money, says that if the defendant pleads guilty to a lesser included offense, the prosecution will drop the more serious charge or perhaps other pending charges. A defendant may also simply plead straight up to the indictment. The defense would generally prefer to plead to a lesser included charge, or to a less serious charge. On a rape charge the prosecution may offer a plea of attempted rape. Or if it is Murder II while armed (murder in the second degree while armed), the prosecution may offer manslaughter while armed. Pleading guilty to the lesser charge generally carries the risk of less jail time, and some judges announce that they have a policy of considering early pleas when they impose sentence. Plea agreements may result from a series of negotiations between the prosecutor and the defense attorney, the prosecutor sometimes consulting his supervisor. The defense attorney should always explain offers and seek authorization to negotiate from his client. If the client does not speak English, interpreters will often be needed to interpret plea negotiations, offers and counteroffers.

A plea agreement may also contain a clause requiring the defendant to **cooperate** with the government, often against other defendants in a conspiracy case. When a defendant becomes a **cooperating witness**, he may need special protection because those against whom he is cooperating or "collaborating" as one says in Spanish, consider him a dangerous snitch.

For a **plea bargain** the interpreter needs to know the charges, and the elements and language of the **plea offer**. At the moment of the plea, both parties may change their terms, each alleging he had understood something else in the original negotiations. Sometimes disposition hearings fail to produce the entry of a valid plea. That is, the plea **breaks down.** The plea agreement may require the defendant to admit that he committed the crime and that he knew it was a crime when he committed it. The judge says: "Listen carefully Mr. Valcárcel, the government will tell us what its evidence would have shown had this case gone to trial, and I will then ask you some questions about it." The government then recounts what it would have been shown, and this part is called the **statement of facts**. The judge then says: "Well, Mr. Valcárcel, is that what happened?" For guilt to be admitted, the defendant would have to say "Yes that is correct," or "Yes I did it," or some phrase admitting to the facts. But the defendant may answer: "Well, not exactly." Defendants are often reluctant to admit guilt; they want to have the benefit of the plea bargain without admitting their conduct was wrong. Should the **plea** really **break down**, the judge may become impatient and say: "This man claims he is innocent. I can not accept this plea. Counsel, we will set this case for trial." The defense attorney may then ask the judge to pass the case briefly to allow him to explain once more to the defendant the benefits of a plea, and then the plea may be entered later. Or, the case may simply be set for trial if the defendant finds he cannot admit his guilt.

Another reason a plea may break down or not be accepted by the judge, is that the defendant may not understand his constitutional and procedural rights as explained to him by the court. This is a special problem in cases that are interpreted. The law requires that the defendant understand those rights and also understand which rights he is waiving or giving up by pleading guilty, because after a plea there will be no trial and (usually) no appeal. The judge must make sure that the defendant understands that he, the defendant, has a right to trial; that at that trial the government would be obliged to produce the evidence and witnesses against him; that the government, to obtain a conviction, would have to prove the case beyond a reasonable doubt; that through his attorney he would have the right to cross-examine witnesses; that he could take the stand himself should he so wish, but that no one could force him to testify; and that when he pleads guilty he will waive all these rights, and waive also the right to appeal, unless it were to appeal an illegal sentence. Some judges explain these rights in such a soft tone that the defendant believes perhaps the judge is suggesting that the defendant go to trial instead of take a guilty plea. At other times questions as to understanding of constitutional rights are phrased in such an abstract fashion that the defendant does not understand them. When the court explains defendant rights in short, simple sentences, the defendant is more likely to understand them.

At the time of a plea the court is also required to ascertain on the record that the guilty plea is not the product of improper promises or pressure. The judge asks if anyone has promised the defendant what sentence the judge will give. Sometimes the defendant becomes confused and says "Yes." "What kind of sentence have you been promised" asks the court. "One year" says the defendant, thinking of the amount of time his attorney has said is the maximum for the offense. The court commonly asks what the agreement is. Then the judge may ask if any other promises have been made to the defendant. But if the word "promise" has not been used by the court in describing the plea agreement, the defendant, not used to thinking in abstract terms, may again become confused, and typically say "Yes." He does not understand what he is saying "Yes" to. If the court were to say: "Now, Mr. Valcárcel, this agreement between yourself and the government that we have just described constitutes a sort of promise. Have any other promises been made to you?" With this phrasing, the defendant is less likely to become confused. When there is one defendant in a case, much of the agreement may be spoken in open court and not necessarily written down. The purpose is to get the defendant to plead guilty and to dispose of the case in an expeditious manner.

In a larger case, with a whole slew of defendants, a plea agreement with one co-defendant, while disposing of that person's case, may also serve as a vehicle to bop the remaining defendants who prefer to go to trial. In a large federal case, let us say *U.S. v. Testaferro et al.*, the government may convince various members of a conspiracy to plead guilty and cooperate with the government by testifying against other members of the group, especially against Mr. Testaferro. In such a case the government may have drawn up a written plea agreement that sets forth the terms of the agreement; a statement of facts, the charges the defendant is pleading guilty to and those that the government will ask to dismiss, and the requirement for cooperation against a co-defendant. Furthermore, the prosecution may also agree to ask the judge to lower the potential sentence of a defendant, if his testimony against his former co-conspirator has been especially helpful in convicting the main man. The judge will review the written agreement point by point with the defendant to make sure he understands it. When this same defendant later testifies at trial against Mr. Testaferro, Mr. Testaferro's attorney will try to discredit the testimony, on the basis of that same written plea agreement. **Impeachment** or discrediting of a witness centers on an attempt to demonstrate that he has such a strong bias or motive to lie or fabricate testimony that he should not be believed. This could happen typically at cross-examination of the cooperating witness now testifying against the co-defendant. The defense attorney for the co-defendant will lean heavily on the promises made to that cooperating witness in exchange for his helpful testimony. The witness is an ex-drug pilot, one Mr. Toneladas. The defense says: "Now, Mr. Toneladas, when the government said it would make every effort with the Immigration and Naturalization Service to obtain resident visas in this country for your wife and daughter, did you understand by that that they would help your wife and daughter to come to this country?" Of course that is what Mr. Toneladas understood, but this question calls the issue forcefully to the jury's attention. The subtext is that Mr. Toneladas has a very strong motive to testify to anything the government wants because so much is at stake for him personally. The attorney for Mr. Testaferro wants to horrify the jury into thinking it is not enough that Mr. Toneladas is here in this country, but the government wants to bring his family over too, evoking the vision of future generations of drug pilots among us. Of course all plea agreements that include the obligation to testify or **cooperate** against co-defendants require **truthful testimony**. Mr. Testaferro's attorney will seek to discredit the witness and challenge the wisdom and fairness of the entire prosecution of his client, whose presence in the courtroom may have been obtained at significant cost.

Another cross-examination mode of attack is to ask the witness **who decides** if the cooperation or testimony has been really helpful to the government. Well, it is the prosecutor, who decides how helpful that cooperation has been. This allows the defense to point out to the jury that the cooperating witness may fashion his testimony to please the prosecution. In a case with more than one defendant, a plea can have many uses and may take on a life of its own.

While a **plea offer** may be open up to a certain deadline, perhaps until the last status conference, a person may be allowed to **plead to the indictment** any time before the verdict, even several days into trial.

After a defendant has lost a case at trial or has entered a guilty plea, he has a **conviction** on his record. The case will proceed to sentencing. If the court accepts the plea, or after a defendant has lost at trial, the court may **sentence** an individual immediately (smaller, or non-federal cases), or else may request a **pre-sentence report** from the probation office. Sentencing will be set for a later date after the pre-sentence report has been prepared and forwarded to the court.

Documents and Information

When you are assigned the case, ask what it is, is it a trial, a plea, motions, what? Once you know what sort of a proceeding it is, you will want more specific information about the case.

To obtain the necessary documents and information the interpreter must develop rapport with counsel. One must explain one's neutrality and the need to see documents to ensure smooth interpretation. Diplomacy may be required. When an experienced attorney sees you appear for his case he may hand you the indictment, police report, autopsy report, and so on, without your having to ask.

For a **plea on a misdemeanor**, the interpreter needs the names, the police report, the terms of the plea agreement, and to know how much time or what fine the defendant can get on the charges, because the judge and the attorney will review this information with the defendant. Also one needs to what sections of the law have been violated. All of this will be spoken at great speed in the courtroom, so prepare beforehand.

For a **felony plea**, or **felony trial**, you also need the **indictment**. The indictment sets forth the charges; it may be followed by a **superseding indictment**, one modified in the light of new information or in the light of second thoughts by the prosecutor's office. You also need the **police report** of what was said to have happened. If there is a **written plea agreement**, you would like a copy for your use.

The indictment may also reveal each **a/k/a** (also known as) or **alias** of the defendants. On large cases defendants may have used a variety of codenames to speak on the phone, to speak to third parties, or to discuss a deal or plan. The indictment helps keep the cast of characters straight.

On **civil matters**, request the **names of all parties involved**, also the names of boats, official agencies, or whatever other element may be involved. Also, you want documents as to the **original suit** or **complaint**, and **answers**, **motions**, and **oppositions to motions**. Just as the indictment in a criminal case indicates the parameters of the case, the complaint and the answer indicate the beginning parameters of a civil action. The issue usually concerns private property. On a criminal case, it is helpful to know how many years someone can get on the charges. For civil, you want to know what relief the plaintiff seeks.

Turning back to a criminal case that is going to trial, you have the charges, either the information if it is a misdemeanor, or the indictment if it is a felony. Let us say the case is Murder II. Where a homicide has been charged, an **autopsy report** usually exists. Obtain a copy of this report, preferably before trial, because the testimony of the medical examiner, which you will have to interpret simultaneously into the language of the defendant, will be based largely on this document that will be full of technical, medical expressions. Once you have the autopsy report, prepare a written translation of it into the target language, so that when the case starts, you have a copy of both the original and the translated version in your hands. This will help your interpretation of the medical examiner's testimony.

If a gun was used in an assault, the jury may hear testimony from a **ballistics expert**. That testimony may include the name of the gun, its description, the results of test-firing if the police obtained the gun, and details of markings on the bullet. You cannot totally predict what the ballistics expert will say, but a good text on ballistics or on forensic evidence can help. Not all experts have the term "Dr." preceding their names. A police officer who has spent fifteen years working on ballistics may qualify as an expert in the field, so when you see the **witness list** from the prosecution with the names of various police officers, ask if they or any one else will offer expert testimony on any subject. Particularly with regard to technical expressions, we must understand the concepts behind the words. Indeed, concepts or ideas are more important than the actual words because if we have the idea, we can explain it, but if we miss the idea, no amount of preparation will save us. If a man is jailed on a rape charge and the government has **DNA evidence** against him, an interpreter may be called to the jail to interpret for the attorney who wishes to discuss the weight of the evidence against that defendant. The interpreter will wish to know DNA concepts and terminology in English and Spanish to be able to properly interpret the attorney's explanation of it. Was **alcohol** found in the blood of the participants? Read about alcohol blood levels, and about what is considered the standard for sobriety in your area.

Place names can figure in a case. At a trial in Norfolk, Virginia, counsel asked the Captain of a marijuana boat into which port his boat had been towed by the Coast Guard. His answer: "Boh Boh." The interpreter asked the Captain to repeat, which he did: "Boh Boh." By this time both judge and jury were smiling broadly, all of them having understood the witness to say "Portsmouth." Take a map with you and study it. In a city where you usually work, you will become familiar with how witnesses pronounce the names of streets: for Spanish-speakers in Washington, D.C., "La Juan" turns out to be Swann Street, and "La Barc" is Park Road.

Knowing where witnesses are from will also alert you to dialect varia- tions in their speech that may be predictive of their educational level and potential precision in the use of their own language. Spanish varies between countries, and rather large countries such as Argentina and Bolivia have regional speech variations within them. In some places underlying Indian or African languages affect both vocabulary and pronunciation of Spanish. From Cuba, for example, some of the people who came over on the 1980 Mariel boat lift spoke what we might call a black Spanish, which presents some of the difficulties that certain forms of black English present for the uninitiated. We may not necessarily hear any language used to perfection in court. We often work with the verbal equivalent of the blurry Xerox copy that translators are familiar with. We should be prepared to hear and deal with imperfect speech in all our working languages.

Jury Instructions

You know the charges, you know where the witnesses are from, you have enquired as to the sorts of expert testimony coming into the case. The next concern is **jury instructions**. These are the instructions that the judge reads to the jury at the end of the trial, as to the law to be applied to the case. Some states have these instructions in books, both for civil and criminal trials (5, 6), as do the federal courts (2). At the state level, purchase the book that your local the court uses. With some experience, you may study the instruction book and imagine which instructions you would request if you were trying this case. Some instructions are general, such as to the function of the judge, the function of the jury, reasonable doubt, and may be used in almost any case. Others will be more specific, such as the definition of different degrees and types of homicides, which include the elements of the crime to be proved.

If you have the instructions in front of you, you may do a sight translation as the judge reads the instructions. Take care, however, because the judge may paraphrase or move away somewhat from the written text. Some people find it easier to follow the judge entirely and do straight simultaneous of what she says. In any event, study the written instructions at leisure to better understand them. Some instructions are not clearly written in English or are full of arcane legalisms. If you review the instructions before trial, you will see that the instructions include the **elements of the crime** to be proved. The prosecution wants to prove each and every element of each offense, while the defense does not want to have them proved. Some defense attorneys in discussing a case with a client may ask the interpreter to sight translate for the client the jury instructions for the offense with which the defendant is charged, so the defendant can see what the government must prove. Thus, the jury instructions have many uses; consult them with the frequency needed.

Physical and Verbal Evidence

Whenever possible the interpreter should view **photographs** before trial. At trial, counsel may present photos of a crime scene to the witness, and ask: "Was this the claw foot hammer that you threw at the deceased?" "Was this the electric saw with which you attacked the Immigration Agent?" Crime scenes can have a lot of **tools** and weird objects scattered around the floor. If you see the pictures beforehand, take notes. For objects you do not recognize, make a sketch of them; your dictionaries at home may have drawings to help identify them. Look also at the **autopsy photos**, and **crime scene photos** of the body, to overcome your revulsion and shock before trial. Photos are handed to witnesses and the jury at trial, but this is too late for the interpreter to study them, nor will they be handed to him for study. To the extent that you can concentrate on the interpreting at trial and have emotions suspended, you will do a better job. A glance at gruesome photos beforehand can begin to inure you to them.

Ask what **other objects, clothing, knives, machetes, guns**, and the like will be presented as evidence in court, to get an idea of the color and description to prepare the right terms. The objects themselves may not be available for you to see before trial, because they may be at the police evidence locker, but the prosecution or defense should be able to describe them to you. Keep secret the fact that you have seen the photos, seen the knife, or had objects described to you. Each of the lawyers has his own evidence discovery procedure he must follow, while we have our own preparation to do. Our information is only for ourselves. If the indictment mentions a ladder at the scene of the crime and you ask the prosecutor if he has a photo of the ladder, when he tells you "there is no ladder," that is one less issue for you to have to deal with by way of terminology preparation. The defense, however, must never hear from you that there is no ladder. If the defense has the knife that Luis Arrecho stabbed Juan Pitoncito with and describes it to us before trial, but the government has not yet seen it, we also keep that secret. We do not reveal our information to any one. Any information we obtain is for us alone, to enable us to understand the case better and to prepare our terminology.

Ask if there will be **other medical evidence** besides that of the medical examiner. If one man was killed and two others wounded, the attending physician may testify as to the condition of all three when they arrived at the emergency room. Find out what wounds they sustained. For civil cases, inquire what **physical damage** the plaintiff sustained, especially for workmans' compensation. Orthopaedics, trauma, and neurology are helpful in civil work, while knowledge of bullet and knife wounds, alcohol or drug involvement, serology, and DNA are helpful in criminal work.

When the **grand jury** meets to decide if it will **indict** a **felony**, the testimony is kept secret. Testimony is taken down by a court reporter, and that testimony is provided, as part of the **Jencks material**, to the defense when that witness has testified at trial. In some federal courts the material may be provided to the defense a few days ahead of time as a courtesy. The interpreter may learn the content of grand jury testimony because he may have interpreted for the witness at grand jury, or the prosecutor may ask the interpreter to review that material with the government witness just before trial. No matter how you learn about what was said to the grand jury, you must never reveal that knowledge, and the easiest way to do that is to tell no one that you did grand jury interpretation, thus no one will be tempted to ask you about it. If a defense attorney asks the prosecutor just who is interpreting for a grand jury against his client, and she tells him, and if he then asks you: "Well, has María Correveidile already finished her testimony?", your answer may be: "Even if I were working in grand jury, interpreter ethics would not allow me to answer you." Meanwhile, what the defense doesn't know is that the prosecutor is still waiting for María Correveidile to show up. The prosecutor has said there is a "problem with the witness." Often a problem with a witness means that someone does not wish to get involved, or has been intimidated, or had urgent matters to attend to up in New York. Such information is part of the prosecution case, and must not to be revealed to anyone. By the same token, if you work for the defense at a jail or elsewhere, what is said there, what you learn, must also be kept secret. More of this in Chapter IV.

In civil suits one side may have **deposed** the other before trial, that is, taken a sworn statement from a witness in front of attorneys for both parties, with a court stenographer present who makes a transcript of the deposition. Attorneys may be willing to let you read the **deposition transcript**. Once you have read it and taken notes, make some time to talk to your witness before trial, to check words and terms with him from the transcript. What you have is a backtranslation, let us say he spoke at deposition about some governmental agency in his country, but the transcription has only the English, you may ask him what he calls it, and so, when questions are put to him on the witness stand, you will use the correct name or acronym for that agency and thus be more precise and faithful to the meaning intended. Attorneys on civil cases may have enough experience to realize that you should have a chance to talk with the witness before trial, and may offer you the time; if not, request it, saying that you would like to meet with them at the courthouse about 15-30 minutes before trial, if convenient.

We do not want our questions to be intrusive, but the more we know about a case, the more faithfully we will be able to interpret. The issue of information may be summed up in the rule that if the interpreter understands the case, the defendant will understand it.

A Case Sheet

To remember what questions to ask, and to organize the information obtained, it helps to prepare a check sheet for a case. Feel free to copy and modify the following case sheet form to fit your own needs. A case sheet allows you to track what is happening, where you have to be and when, as well as other data. With it you can take down information quickly over the phone when you are assigned to the case, circle or check items, and fill in the blanks. If you save the sheet after a case, when that case comes up again, you will not have to ask an attorney or clerk to repeat information provided three months previously. The case sheet serves as a good beginning for the subsequent terminology research.

A detailed explanation of abbreviations follows this case sheet.

Case Sheet

1. Date _____   Time _____

2. Case Number _____   Case Name _____

3. Sp Ct/FedCt/Jail/Lorton   D.C./Alex/Office

   _____

4. Equipment Yes/No   Second Int _____   Third Int _____

5. [Court] Room N _____   Next Date _____   Next Time _____

6. For: C_1, C_2, C_3, C_4/ D_1, D_2, D_3, D_4 Estimated Trial Time _____

7. Judge _____   Certified Out to _____

8. Client[s] _____

9. Type: Arriagn/Prelim/Deten/ GJ/ Motions/Stat/Pretrial/ Dep/Trial, Plea/
   Diversion/ BRA/ Pre-sent/Sent/Foren (MH)/Land-Ten/Family/Arbitra/SC

10. Origin: El Sal, Cuba [Mariel], Col, DR, _____

11. Male/Female   Charges _____

    _____

12. Plea: Accept _____   Nolle _____

    Waive/Reserve   Step-Back, Allocu/Repeat/Release/Life   INS Det.

13. Wired   Co-D _____

14. D is: In/Out:PR/Surety/3rd Party/Cash Ref: DC/Fed Ct/AUSA/CJA/PDS/Ret

15. Date Assigned _____   Who _____   Phone_____

16. AUSA/DA _____   Phone_____

17. DC _____   Phone_____

18. Documents: Indic/Informa, PD 163, Motions, Statements, Deposit
    Reports: Autopsy, Autop Photos, Other Photos,
    Jencks [Wit List, Md reports, Other]

19. Experts: Medical [Examiner], Ballistics, Blood, Prints, Chem, DNA, Psych

20. Story: _____

Explanation of Abbreviations
(Note: Terms differ in different courts)

I.   Date   Time
Date scheduled at court, and time.

2.   Case Number   Case Name
The **case number** is that number officially used by all concerned. In D.C. Superior
Court, for example, the number F-1325-94 means the case is a felony, and it was 1325
in order in the 1994 year. M-10082-93 would mean a misdemeanor, one that was
initiated as a case in 1993. If you see CR-81-94 that may be a federal criminal case,
initiated in 1994. CA-22-93 might be a federal civil action. Numbering systems may
differ by area and jurisdiction. In a criminal case the **case name** is Prosecution v. One
or More Defendants. If you see a case captioned *The Commonwealth of Massachusetts v.
Tia Tula*, you know that it is a state case and there is one defendant, the aforementioned
Tía Tula. If, however, you see *U.S. v. Tia Tula et al.*, you know that this is a federal case
and that a number of other people are charged along with the aforementioned Tía Tula.
The "et al." means et *alii* , "and others" (useful when there is a raft of defendants). In a
civil case it is usually the names of One Party v. Another, *Cristina Boba v. Juan Listo.*

3.   Sp Ct/ Fed Ct/Jail/ Lorton   .... D.C./Alex/Office
Sp Ct = Superior Court. **Fed Ct** = Federal Court. **Jail** where defendant is kept.
Lorton, which is the District of Columbia prison located in Virginia. Location of those
courts might be Washington, **D.C.**, or **Alex**andria, Virginia. **Office** could be that of
prosecutor or defense attorney. The line underneath is provided for the specific address
of where the interpreter has to be.

4.   Equipment Yes/No   Second Int   Third Int
Will the interpreter need to bring her sound equipment. My own practice is always to
bring equipment to court, even for one defendant. Names of second and third
interpreter when names available.

5.   [Court] Room No Next Date   Next Time
Which **court**room or **room** for the process. **Next date** if the matter is to continue.
Next time on that continued date. Depending on how interpreting services are
organized at any given court, it may or may not be the same interpreter who works on
the next part of a case. A coordinator may wish to know the next date, sometimes
called the "return date," to make sure interpreting service is provided. If you are to
continue on the case, you need to know when it is next up.

6.   For: $C_1C_2C_3C_4$/$D_1D_2D_3D_4$ Estimated Trial Time
The **for** means for whom one is interpreting C_1, C_2 etc. would be first complaining
witness, second complaining witness etc. D_1, D_2 would be first defendant, second
defendant and so on. **Estimated trial time** is possible duration of the trial, a figure,
usually in days, provided by the person who hires you, perhaps the court clerk or

interpreter coordinator. During the trial itself that estimate may change. Marshals and court reporters tend to have a good sense of the length of a case once it is underway.

7. Judge   Certified Out To

The name of the **judge** may be known at the time of referral, or any time thereafter. If the trial judge has a very busy calendar, once the case is before her, she may tell counsel she is going to send the case to another judge that same day. The clerk of the court may then inform the parties who that new judge will be. When a case is moved in this fashion it is said to be **certified out** to the new judge.

8. Client[s]

The **client** name and the case name are not necessarily identical. For example, let's say that María Andapesos, who does not speak English, had her purse grabbed by John Snatcher. The case is perhaps captioned *Commonwealth of Virginia v. John Snatcher*, but your client is María Andapesos. Or, a client may be, and is most likely to be a defendant, in which case you will see the client's name in the case caption or title, *The State of Righteousness v. Mario Inocente*. For crimes of violence or family matters, witnesses on both sides of a case may require interpretation, so this is something to ask the attorneys about.

9. Type: Arraign/Prelim/Deten/GJ/Motions/Stat/
Pretrial/Dep/Trial/Plea/Diversion/BRA/Pre-sent/
Sent/Foren(MH)/Land-Ten/Family/Arbitra/SC

Type here means what sort of a proceeding one is called to interpret. **Arraign** = arraignment. **Prelim** = preliminary hearing. **Deten** = detention hearing. **GJ** = grand jury. **Motions** = motions. **Stat** = status hearing. **Pretrial** = a conversation with the government or the defense with its witnesses prior to a trial. **Dep** = deposition. **Trial** = trial. **Plea** = a plea of guilty. A plea of innocent sets in motion and culminates in the trial itself, unless a plea of innocent is changed to a plea of guilty at some time in the process. In some courts a guilty plea is therefore referred to as a "change of plea." Originally, if a defendant has an attorney, when he is arraigned, the defendant, once the charges have been read, may be asked how he pleads, and his attorney will say "We waive further reading of the charges, plead innocent and demand a speedy trial." **Diversion** = Diversion. In Washington, D.C., a program for some first offenders that allows them to do community service in lieu of a sentence if they admit guilt to a prosecutor but not to a judge. Eventually, should the diversion program be successfully completed, the defendant's record may be wiped clean. If diversion is not completed successfully, the defendant may plead out before a judge, or go to trial. **BRA** = Bail Reform Act violation. In Washington D.C. if a man is released on bail or on his own recognizance and subsequently fails to appear for trial or his next court date, it will be said that he has a BRA violation: he will be sought on a bench warrant (an arrest warrant issued by the judge) and once found, detained until he has a hearing on the new charge of failure to appear. I also use this term to refer to probation violation. **Pre-sent** = pre-sentence interview with the probation officer and the defendant, or, a reading of the pre-sentence report with the defendant and his attorney just prior to sentencing. **Sent** = sentencing. **Foren** = forensic screening, an interview where a forensic psychiatrist or psychologist speaks with a defendant to determine if a defendant is competent to stand trial. **MH** = mental health hearing, at which a client petitions the court to leave a mental health facility where he has been confined. **Land-Tent** = Landlord Tenant Court. **Family** = Family Court. **Abritra** = arbitration proceedings which may take place outside the court system, an approach often stipulated by contract in commercial undertakings. **SC** = Small Claims Court.

10. Origin: El Sal, Cuba [Mariel], Col, DR, _____
Line 10 represents places of origin of clients, and the places cited here are those from which the Hispanic clients in Washington D.C. courts most frequently come: El Salvador, Cuba, Colombia, and the Dominican Republic. The notation [**Mariel**] appears next to Cuba, referring to those Cubans who came to the U.S. during the 1980 boatlift, some of whom have with different speech patterns than earlier Cuban immigrants. The line _____ is for other countries of origin. Colleagues working in California or Texas, for example, might wish to add Mexico as a place of origin to indicate potential speech patterns.

11. Male/Female   Charges
The first notation refers to the sex of the client. Charges means the charge or charges pending against the defendant.

12. Plea: Accept   Nolle
On a proposed plea bargain agreement, if the defendant agrees or accepts to plead guilty to a certain charge [**accept**], the government will **nolle** (short for *nolle prosequi*) or not prosecute certain other charges, actually asking to withdraw certain charges if the defendant pleads to others, sometimes also known as "nol pros." As part of the government's armamentarium in urging a defendant to plead guilty, it has other bargaining chips along with the offer to plead to reduced or fewer charges. The government may **Waive/[or]Reserve** some other privileges. If the government waives something, it means it will not exercise that privilege. If, on the other hand, it reserves it, it means that the government will make use of that privilege. Part of the plea negotiation process that the defense goes through with the government involves negotiating each one of these items that may be applicable. For example, **Step-Back**, in Washington, D.C., refers to the government's ability to ask the judge to detain a defendant after conviction and before sentencing. Thus, in a plea bargain, if the government **waives step-back**, it will not ask that the defendant be incarcerated pending sentencing. But if it **reserves step-back**, it will ask that he be incarcerated for that period. Mind you, the government can ask or not ask, but it is still the judge who has to decide such matters. It is possible for the government to waive step-back but if the court feels that a defendant is especially dangerous to the community, or will not appear for sentencing, the court may **step the defendant back**, that is, lock him up until the day of sentencing. **Allocu** = allocution here refers to the government's ability

to speak just before the judge pronounces the sentence. When the government allocutes, it usually does so to point out the badness of the defendant, and the need for a harsh sentence. Thus, should the government **waive allocution** this will give the defendant an advantage. **Repeat/Release/Life** all refer to certain sentencing enhancement papers that the prosecutor may file with the judge, called repeat papers, release papers, life papers. **Repeat papers** tell the judge that the defendant has one or more prior convictions in any jurisdiction that are the "same as or necessarily include[s] the current offense." (7). To simplify, this means that the defendant did it again, whatever he had previously been convicted of. **Release papers** tell the judge that the defendant committed the present crime while he was on release status in another case. **Life papers** may be handed to a judge when the case at issue is a felony, and that "before *committing* the current offense, the defendant had been *convicted* of at least two felonies." (7) These are considerations in a plea bargain in D.C. Superior Court. Other courts and jurisdictions may have similar enhancement provisions that apply at this stage. The role of these papers in a plea is that the government can promise not to hand them to the judge (waive), as part of a plea bargain. On the other hand, if the case continues to trial, such papers may indeed be handed to the judge just prior to jury selection, thus calling the judge's attention in a formal fashion to provisions that allow for a harsher sentence, should the defendant lose at trial. **INS Det** = Immigration and Naturalization Service Detainer, a request that the Immigration Service lodges with the court whereby once the court is through with that person, the Service wishes to detain him for possible deportation or exclusion action. It is an issue that attorneys might mention in the case of foreign nationals, especially those who are illegal immigrants, and is on this line for convenience. It is a separate matter from plea issues.

13. Wired   Co-D
Wired means that in cases with one or more co-defendants, the government will only allow a guilty plea if all defendants plead guilty. When the government wires a plea offer, it may throw confusion into the ranks of the defense. If one defendant wishes to plead and the other does not, the one who wants to plead may try to convince the government to unwire or sever the plea, but the government may be unwilling to do so. **Co-D** refers to the names of co-defendants in the case.

14. D is: In/Out:PR/Surety/3rd Party/Cash
Ref: DC/Fed Ct/AUSA/CJA/PDS/Ret
D is: = defendant is **In/Out** of jail. If he is **In** he may be in one of various places that we need not know unless we are going to interpret for him there. You definitely do not want to know precisely where he is if the government is holding him at a secret place in a high-threat trial. If by chance you learn where he is, you do not repeat the information to anyone. **Out** means the defendant is out of jail, possibly on **PR** = personal recognizance, **Surety** = on a surety bond, that is, one posted by a bail-bond company, **3rd Party** = in third-party custody, or **Cash** = out on a cash bond.
The information about whether a defendant is in or out of jail is usually only for the

purpose of helping you predict his presence in the courtroom. If he is in jail, he will likely be brought to court, though that is not always certain, because there are times when the defendant is not on the list to be transported from the jail, and the marshals do not bring him up. If he is out on personal recognizance, he may not show up. If he has a surety bond, the bondsman may help him appear in court, because it is in the financial interest of the bondsman to do so. But on personal recognizance, the defendant could have fled to Miami, to Los Angeles, or back to his native country in certain cases. Until you see the defendant sitting next to you in the courtroom, nothing is certain. If you have reserved three weeks of your time for this trial, and turned down other work, if a defendant out on bond does not show up for trial, you lose. The defendant now fled to Miami will be apprehended, some time later. He will then have the additional charge of bail violation, which means he will likely stay in jail until trial. But you may have lost three weeks' work.

Ref = The office that referred the case to you, and the office which you will bill. **DC** = Superior Court of the District of Columbia; **Fed Ct** = Federal Court, properly called U.S. District Court; **AUSA** = Office of the United States Attorney; **CJA** = billing under the Criminal Justice Act that provides for individual attorneys to defend the indigent. **PDS** = Public Defender Service, again, a group of attorneys who defend the indigent. **Ret** = retained, a privately contracted case where no government agency is paying but rather a private individual, company, or law firm.

15. Date Assigned = date you were assigned the case. **Who** = by whom. **Phone** = phone number of person who assigned you the case.

16. AUSA = Assistant United States Attorney, sometimes called "The Assistant" meaning the prosecutor in a federal court. If he represents a state he may be called the **DA**, (District Attorney) or Commonwealth Counsel, depending on the state. If the case is handled by municipal authorities, it may be the Corporation Counsel who prosecutes. In civil cases this spot could be for counsel for the plaintiff. **Phone** = phone number of prosecutor.

17. DC = Defense Counsel.   **Phone** = phone number of defense counsel.

18. Documents = documents you need: **Indic/Informa** = Indictment/The Information. The **indictment** is the charging document on a felony that originates with a grand jury. The **information** is the charging document for a misdemeanor. **PD 163** = police department form number 163 which, in the District of Columbia, tells what happened from the police point of view. **Motions** = motions. According to *Black's Law Dictionary*, a motion is "an application made to a court or judge for purpose of obtaining a rule or order directing some act to be done in favor of the applicant." **Statements** = what the defendant was said to have said when talking to the police. **Deposit** = depositions, usually in civil cases. **Reports =** reports you need to see. **Autopsy** = autopsy report from medical examiner's office; **Autop Photos** = photos of autopsy that the prosecution has; **Other Photos** = other photos that the prosecution might have. **Jencks** =

Jencks material which includes **Wit List** = witness list, **Md reports** = medical reports, and **Other** = other material.

19. Experts = while it is unnecessary to see most reports beforehand (the autopsy report is an exception and the defense should already have it), simply knowing that there will be expert testimony in a given field alerts us to the need for special preparation. Such fields may include **Medical [Examiner], Ballistics, Blood, Prints** = finger prints; **Chem** = DEA-7 or other report of chemical analysis of evidence; **DNA** = deoxyribonucleic acid, specifically, "DNA fingerprinting," a method of analyzing genetic material taken from a suspect, to match it to that found at the crime scene. DNA evidence may require special terminology preparation on the part of the interpreter. Such evidence, where admitted, is sometimes used in rape, murder, and paternity cases. **Psych** = psychological or psychiatric evidence.

20. Story = what happened, assembling of important information in your own words. Should include dates and addresses of alleged crimes, names of case participants and what supposedly transpired.

Further Reading

General

1. Bergman, Paul. *Trial Advocacy.* 2d ed. St. Paul, Minn.: West Publishing Company. Nutshell Series, 1989.
    • The author describes what attorneys try to do, and provides a good idea of the structure of a felony trial. Lucid writing, good humor, excellent.

2. Devitt, Edward J., Charles B. Blackmar, Michael A. Wolff, and and Kevin F. O'Malley. *Federal Jury Practice and Instructions, Civil and Criminal.* Fourth Edition. 3 vols. St. Paul., Minn.: West Publishing Co., 1992. Three Vols.
    • Check with attorneys in the area where you work, or with the clerk of the court to see which federal jury instruction pattern book is used in the area where you practice.

3. Mortimer, John. "Rumpole of the Heavy Brigade," *Rumpole of the Bailey.* New York: Penguin Books, 1978.

4. Wellman, Francis L. *The Art of Cross-Examination: With Cross-Examination of Important Witnesses in Some Celebrated Cases.* Fourth Edition, Revised and Enlarged. New York: Collier Books, 1962.
    • A reprint of the 1936 Fourth Edition, the book provides concepts and examples of good cross-examination from cases in the early part of this century.

Legal Texts for the District of Columbia

For the District of Columbia the following books are listed as examples of the sorts of things that may be available for your jurisdiction

5. *Civil Jury Instructions: District of Columbia.* 3d ed. Young Lawyers Section of the Bar Association of the District of Columbia. Washington, D.C., 1981. Supplement, 1985.
    • Good book to have if you work on a lot of civil trials.

6. *Criminal Jury Instructions: District of Columbia.* Edited by Barbara E. Bergman. 4th Edition. Young Lawyers Section of the Bar Association of the District of Columbia. Washington, D.C., 1993.
    • The judge may read selected instructions to the jury from the book of instructions. Criminal jury instructions are highly recommended to get a feeling both for the law itself and for the language of the law and the court.

General remarks about jury instructions

West Publishing Company of St. Paul, Minn. publishes instructions for a variety of states. In some cases West has both civil and criminal instructions, in other cases, it might be one or the other. The states are: *Arkansas, California, Colorado, Connecticut, Louisiana, Illinois, Minnesota, Mississippi, Missouri, Nebraska, Tennessee, Virginia and Washington.* West's phone number for ordering books is: (800) 328-9352.

Jury instructions are occasionally updated as the underlying laws change. Request the most recent edition when you purchase a set of instructions. Specify whether you want criminal or civil instructions, which may be included in different volumes. Ask your local bar association who publishes jury instructions for your state if you are unsure.

7. *Criminal Practice Institute: Trial Manual.* Young Lawyers Section Bar Association of the District of Columbia, Public Defender Service for the District of Columbia. 2 vols. Washington, D.C., 1993. Updated yearly.
    • Details court rules, stages of trial, social service agencies and rehabilitation programs for *criminal* proceedings in D.C. Superior Court. Explanations, for D.C. Superior Court, of what "Gerstein Proffer" and the like are. When you hear about "Brady" and such, requirements that stem originally from case names, some of those cases may have been federal cases, and others may have been from a local state or jurisdiction. Thus, if you work in courts of various states, you may expect to hear different names you need to know to understand the process. Ask your local bar association if it publishes a trial manual for criminal cases, or ask the Public Defender Service or Legal Aid in cities large enough to have a big, active office.

8. Cunningham, Lynn E., Esq. *Neighborhood Legal Services Program Manual of Landlord and Residential Tenant Court Practice and Procedure, March, 1978 Edition*. Washington, D.C.: District of Columbia Neighborhood Legal Services Program. Bound manuscript, 1978.
   * Helpful to prepare for landlord-tenant cases in D.C. Superior Court.

9. *The District of Columbia Practice Manual*, Third Edition. The District of Columbia Bar and The Young Lawyers Section of the Bar Association of the District of Columbia. Washington, D.C., 1994. Two Vols.
   * Helpful brief descriptions of different sorts of cases and procedures. Read the chapter on criminal cases before plunging into the much more detailed (7).

10. Mlyniec, Wallace J. and John Copacino. *Juvenile Law and Practice in the District of Columbia: Representing Children and Parents in the Juvenile and Intra-Family and Neglect Branches of the District of Columbia Superior Court Family Division*. Washington, D.C.:
    * The District of Columbia Bar, 1988.

11. *Second Annual Neglect/Delinquency Practice Institute, March 30 and 31, 1990*. Washington, D.C.: Young Lawyers Section The Bar Association of the District of Columbia. Spiral bound.

CHAPTER 3

Case Preparation - B

Terminology, Reference Books and Dictionaries

Terminology Preparation

Once you know what sort of procedure you will handle, and once you have some of the specifics of a case, it may be time to complete your English word list and to prepare a Spanish list of those same words. A useful bilingual word list will contain new technical words, as well as other words to be used in the case that you already know but wish to remind yourself of. In civil cases, because we have requested documents available in both languages, when they exist, it may be possible to peruse English and Spanish documents and match up the words. After you have done this there may still be some words in both languages for which you have not yet found matches in the documents, in which case you need to turn to other sources. For most of our work, criminal cases, there may be no documents in original Spanish, so that we begin with the English word list we have created.

Forensic Reference Books

Before turning to dictionaries, you may wish to consult technical books, such as those on forensic pathology, to gain an understanding of the concepts involved. Textbooks allow us to imagine what an expert might say, not so much the content of his pronouncements, as the language in which they will be couched. Your local law library should have books written for attorneys on physical evidence. Some books provide a brief overview of physical evidence (7, 9). Or, you may prefer a large general volume on forensic evidence that includes chapters by many specialists on blood alcohol, death by drowning, stab wounds, auto-accident marks, fingerprint analysis, handwriting analysis, etc. (10). Cause of death is detailed in books of forensic pathology (11). More specifically, you may find a text on the varieties of gunshot wounds (4). University medical school or law libraries may have such books. Experts have written on every sort of physical evidence. Such books will give you, in English, the basic concepts and more of the terminology of the subject matter. The term "forensic" includes much more than medical-legal matters. For example, "forensic engineering" would concern testimony about physical defects in a building which has fallen down and killed people. When a man murders 4 coeds and leaves bite-marks on two of the victims, the testimony that will convict him may come from "forensic dentistry."

Kinds of Dictionaries

You may now turn to dictionaries and glossaries. The term "dictionary" embraces a whole range of books, each of which has something different to offer. Each of the languages you handle in court may, if you are lucky, be represented by at least one large, **comprehensive monolingual dictionary** that attempts to include most of the words in the language. Because language changes, such dictionaries can go through various editions. Some, such as the multi-volume *Oxford English Dictionary* (55) include in their entries the changing use of words at different dates, to provide a historical overview of a word's growth and development. Others, such as the "Webster's II International" (66), are simply excellent dictionaries that one can more easily own and handle.

Because the large dictionaries may not include all the technical words specific to each field, we may need to seek specialized dictionaries that may be monolingual. Sometimes these may be called dictionaries, or they may be called glossaries, compendia, encyclopaedias, or handbooks. They may provide specific definitions, and with luck can include drawings and illustrations.

If you do not find good medical dictionaries, or, a good, large bilingual dictionary for the languages you need, you may use two monolingual dictionaries side-by-side. For example, it is possible to use the *Black's Law Dictionary* (18), with a monolingual Spanish legal dictionary (22, 28, 57), and achieve the result you want. A large specialized bilingual dictionary while ideal, may not always be available. Unavailability of dictionaries seems to come about in at least three ways: the dictionary you want simply does not exist; or it does exist but is out of print; or it is relatively new, you have not studied it to see how good it might be, but it costs $65.00 in paperback and the bookseller may or may not be able to get it to you in three months' time.

For glossaries without illustrations, Penguin (56), for example, has a series in English, that includes computers, geology, economics, and the like. Another good dictionary series in English is published by Barron's (14, 15); it includes dictionaries on finance, accounting, and real estate. A monolingual dictionary may be intended for novices in a field of work or study, so that it can be most helpful to those of us who are not economists, real estate brokers, or accountants.

The Spanish publishing houses Pirámide (39) and Rioduero (33) publish small monolingual dictionaries on various subjects. Be careful, however, when you look at what you believe is a monolingual dictionary in another language; check to see if it is a translation from German, English, or French. If the dictionary itself is a translation, proceed with more caution.

Other specialized dictionaries concentrate on regional expressions or regionalisms, such as Spanish as spoken in Puerto Rico (27), or Lunfardo, or Panamanian expressions, etc. These are useful, if difficult to obtain, because the original press run was 2,000 copies, the edition is now sold out, and the publisher has no intention of going back to press with it.

Bilingual dictionaries come in two sorts: there are the large general dictionaries, which attempt to cover most of the language, and there are the smaller, technical dictionaries, which may be bilingual, or go heavily in one direction.

Not every bilingual dictionary does justice to its purpose. Still, there are instances where one book is much used because there does not seem to be a better one readily available. For example, Robb's *Diccionario de términos legales: español-inglés e inglés-español* (58), a leading Spanish-English, English-Spanish legal dictionary, is outdated, incomplete, confusing, much-maligned, and constantly used. The great challenge of re-writing the Robb has been assiduously avoided by prudent colleagues for the past twenty years. The more experience you have, the more you see the wisdom of this decision which seems to spring from the collective unconscious of the court interpreting corps. Robb needs more terms from criminal procedure in both English and Spanish, and could offer more detail on the appropriate use or context for each word provided. No matter what is said of the Robb, it is very useful.

Some *glossaries* are not in book form, but may be found *in government and scientific publications*. History books especially can also be useful. For example, a monograph on the sale of political office in the Spanish Indies may append a bilingual glossary on economic terms in use at the time in Spain and the Americas.

Monolingual glossaries are often embedded in articles on scientific or governmental subjects. *Legislation* is also a fruitful source of monolingual glossaries; some laws or sets of regulations have definitions in their opening or closing pages. Legislation is also helpful as to technical terms generally. For example, if you have to translate Mexican pesticide registration requirements into English, look at U.S. pesticide legislation, because many of the concepts and the words are already there in English. While the terms may not always be totally equivalent, they will at least get you in the neighborhood of the problem that the regulation tries to solve or avoid.

For new medical terms consult articles on the pertinent subject in *medical journals*. Medical school libraries may have on-line bibliographies of articles on certain subjects, or they may have foreign medical journals in their libraries. Certain newspapers may also have good medical coverage. For example, the daily newspaper *El País* of Madrid sometimes runs stories on medical matters from *The New York Times* service so that new medical terminology is immediately available in Spanish to a translator or interpreter.

If legislation is a good source of terminology for administrative, civil matters, it is also helpful for criminal and civil procedure. The *rules of civil and criminal procedure* from various countries may be available at law libraries or bookstores. These books are to be read or skimmed, and the terminology noted. At times one looks for specific words, at other times one reads for new words generally. Read newspapers and magazines to find out new ideas and terms that are bound to come up in court interpreting. Write down the new English or Spanish as you find it, and then you can look for the term in the other language as you go along in your reading.

Encyclopaedias can provide information about a subject, and may contain terminology that a dictionary does not have. The large *Enciclopedia universal ilustrada europeo-americana* (Espasa-Calpe) (35) is good for technical specialties and for items such as the history of Spain in North Africa and the New World. If you want to see how certain Arabic words go into Spanish, that is where you may find them, assuming they have not yet been accepted into the *Diccionario de la Lengua Española*, published by the Real Academia

Española (32). Special problems are created by the adoption of foreign words into a language. Comprehensive dictionaries and encyclopaedias will have solved older terms; more ingenuity is needed for newer words. When new immigrant groups begin to learn English, they may first incorporate loan words from English into their native speech, so that the interpreter does not always face a pure Spanish word. Thus, in certain parts of the U.S. the "foreign" language is greatly corrupted. There are some specialized dictionaries for this purpose (38, 43), and if the language group is small, there are university dissertations available on microfilm that may contain glossaries as to the language in question, and its adaptations in the U.S.

How to Buy a Dictionary

If a dictionary is technical or highly specialized, it may be the only one in its field, in which case the decision is to buy or not to buy. If the words look new to you, if you see interesting solutions to linguistic problems you have or believe you may have, and if the price is not outrageous, buy it. When the book in question is a monolingual legal dictionary from any country that speaks your target language, you may wish to acquire it to be able to rove through it at leisure to find more satisfactory solutions to constant questions. This is especially true for Spanish. Let us say that you cannot find a Spanish-Spanish legal dictionary from El Salvador, but you find a Spanish-Spanish legal dictionary from Argentina that provides good words to deal with criminal procedure. You may wish to purchase such a dictionary because it may offer more terms or different terms than does a Spanish-Spanish legal dictionary from Spain. Dictionaries sometimes overlap in their coverage, so that having more than one dictionary for a single subject is helpful, especially when the subject is law, science or computers. The question is how helpful will the book be to you in the long term. As to purchase of dictionaries for translation work, it is common for translators to purchase specialized dictionaries and texts when they receive a long translation assignment, if they do not already have the required books in hand.

When a bookstore has a selection of large monolingual or bilingual dictionaries, and you are not familiar with those books, ask the merchant to place on the counter three or four of his best in that category, and use some test words to compare the books. The test words ought to include both older words and newer expressions. Each dictionary treats a word in a different way. The difference in treatment helps you decide which approach you prefer. Look also at the copyright date on a dictionary. The publisher may bring out a book that was originally copyrighted in 1958 and has not been significantly revised. See if what you have in hand is the 12th printing, or a really new edition. Read the author's introduction to see when the first edition came out, how many words, if any, have been added since the original publication, and if there have been other modifications or revisions. Publishers take care to inform the reading public of the glories of what is truly a new edition, and the introductory material, as well as the dust jacket, may contain the data you need. This is not to say that books with an older copyright are useless. Some may actually be preferable to a new edition, and others may have had only one edition and be classics that the well-rounded interpreter feels she must own.

For certain books, then, one may compare and choose the best of a selection, mainly with large monolingual and bilingual dictionaries. Other dictionaries are well-known and seem necessary, so the question becomes is it affordable now. If a dictionary is technical and relates to some work you are doing or might do, and if it is fairly new or not easily available where you live, buy it. On your travels, when you find a local dictionary of Spanish slang or legal terms, snap it up immediately. You may not see it again at any price, and certainly not for the price on offer in Madrid or Mexico City, because the book importer also has to send his kids to college and pay for their orthodontia. Direct purchase when you travel abroad is preferable to exclusive dependence on book importers.

What to Do When a Word is Not in the Dictionary

Pray. This will set the right tone for the proceedings. Divine Intervention in the form of a bright idea or a felicitous meeting may result from serious prayer. The final step, which is easy but not sporting, is to call a colleague. In between you have to do the work.

After you have consulted your dictionaries you may visit a library to see if they have some dictionary that you do not have, or if they have other texts. A library has handbooks, annual reports, and technical texts and journals. Furthermore, some large universities, besides having two or three large libraries, may also have departmental libraries that professors and graduate students consult. Government agencies and offices may also have small, specialized libraries. If you plan to visit such a library, call first. Introduce yourself and explain that you are looking for some words and need to consult reference material. Find out the name of the librarian or person in charge of the collection. Find out the hours the library is open and make an appointment to go in to talk to them. The librarian is your best friend. The extra time all this takes is worth it, because you will find useful words. Even if those words do not come up in the case, they will come up in another case, so no research work is ever wasted. Proper preparation will enable you to do a great job for the client, and look real smart.

If a word is very technical, as it usually is, you may wish to consult an expert in the field. An expert in the field can be anyone who knows more than you do about it. An expert may be monolingual or bilingual. Either can be helpful. For industrial machinery and equipment, foreign companies selling equipment in the U.S. can provide brochures and catalogues in more than one language, as may a U.S. company selling equipment abroad. Trade and industrial associations have people who know the details or vocabulary of their trade, who may be able to explain concepts and definitions to you. A search for a sugar term for a translation led to the Beet Sugar Association in Washington, D.C., to ask them who handled cane sugar. They referred me to the Florida Sugar Cane League. The Washington, D.C. office of the League referred me to their Florida office, where a woman suggested a friend of hers who worked at a Florida sugar mill who was happy to tell me that *azúcar blanco de la plantación* was not "white sugar from the plantation," but, simply, "plantation white." Intuition will often tell you when a term is incorrect, so that you may seek a better solution. The goal is to produce in the target language a version that sounds right to a technical person in the field. We mentioned context for interpreting, to help us understand what is said. For translations as well, knowledge of a field or subject clarifies context and meaning, and thus the words.

Call people, visit them. If there is a recalcitrant technical translation, call a specialist and ask if you may come in to see him. People from governmental agencies are especially helpful when the translation you are doing is for another governmental agency. While the phone is still an efficient work instrument, a few visits to experts can clarify the mind wonderfully. Ask questions of the lawyers, if there are any special or slang words that the client is using in the case, and find out exactly what they mean to the client.

From your questions and study you have an idea of what kind of a case it is. You have also prepared a word list, done further reading, and finally have chased down all the words you want for trial, so that you have now made a complete bilingual word list of all the tough words you believe will be used in a trial. The more complete your bilingual word list, the more ready you are to deal with other terms as they arise, and the better you will understand the general context into which they fit. It is always preferable to over-prepare than under-prepare for any case. To be under-prepared may simply mean that there is one word that you do not know. When there is one word you do not know in a case, that word will be repeated at least five times during one proceeding, so that the lack of it presents more than a momentary problem.

Further Reading

General

1. Murray, Katharine Maud Elisabeth. *Caught in the Web of Words: James A.H. Murray and the Oxford English Dictionary.* Preface, R.W. Burchfield. New Haven: Yale University Press, 1977.
   • Because you will prepare your own word lists, it is good to know something about the making of dictionaries. This excellent biography describes the life and work of James Murray who created the great Oxford Dictionary.

Forensic Reference Texts

2. Carper, Kenneth L., Editor. *Forensic Engineering.* New York: Elsevier, 1989.
   • Includes chapters on fire investigations, industrial accidents, traffic accident reconstruction, transportation disaster investigation, and the engineer as expert witness.

3. Conway, J.V.P. *Evidential Documents.* Springfield, Ill.: Charles C. Thomas, 1959.
   • Lucid introduction to questioned documents including handwriting analysis. Very clear illustrations.

4. Di Maio, Vincent. *Gunshot Wounds: Practical Aspects of Firearms, Ballistics, and Forensic Techniques.* New York: Elsevier, 1985.

5. *Genetic Witness: Forensic Uses of DNA Tests.* Congress of the United States, Office of Technology Assessment. Washington, D.C.: U.S. Government Printing Office, 1990.

• Introduction to the principles of DNA testing.

6. *Gray's Anatomy of the Human Body.* 30 Edition. Ed. Carmine D. Clemente. Philadelphia: Lea & Febiger, 1984.
    • Helpful if you believe there will be medical testimony as to which tendon was cut, which nerve affected, and so on, especially for cases involving murder, malpractice, or personal injury. Excellent illustrations and descriptions.

7. *Handbook of Forensic Science.* U.S. Department of Justice, Federal Bureau of Investigation. Washington, D.C.: U.S. Government Printing Office, 1994.
    • Discusses collection and examination of physical evidence, and notable characteristics of each kind.

8. Hilton, Ordway. *Scientific Examination of Questioned Documents.* Revised Edition. New York: Elsevier Science Publishing Co., Inc. 1982.

9. Jaffe, Frederick. *A Guide to Pathological Evidence.* Toronto, Canada: The Carswell Company Limited, 1976.
    • Brief general introduction to varied pathologies. Good place to start.

10. Saferstein, Richard, Editor. *Forensic Science Handbook.* Englewood Cliffs, New Jersey: Prentice Hall, Inc., 1982.
    • Includes chapters on investigations involving glass, human hair, arson and explosives, bloodstains, paint, gunshot residues, alcohol, soils, and questioned documents. Also forensic applications of liquid chromatography, mass spectrometry, and biochemical markers of individuality. Remarks on expert testimony.

11. Wantanabe, Tonio, and Michael M. Baden and Milton Helpern. *Atlas of Legal Medicine.* Philadelphia: Lippincott, 1968.
    • Excellent color photos with clear explanations of the various modes of death that a forensic pathologist may refer to. Outstanding.

Dictionaries and Glossaries
Legal dictionaries marked with an asterisk*

12. Alonso, Martín. *Enciclopedia del idioma: diccionario histórico y moderno de la lengua española (siglos XII al XX) etimológico, tecnológico, regional e hispanoamericano.* Primera Reimpresión. Madrid: Aguilar, S.A. de Ediciones, 1968. Three Vols. Spanish.
    • Good for historical uses of words and regional uses or expressions common in Latin America but not in Spain. Includes words not always "accepted" by the Royal Academy.

13. *ARCO English-Spanish, Spanish-English Motor Vehicle Dictionary: Diccionario ARCO del automotor.* Edited by Robert F. Lima. New York: ARCO, 1980. Eng-Sp/Sp-Eng.

• Helpful for traffic cases or depositions in insurance cases when a vehicle is involved. Good for any criminal case that includes obsessive questions about vehicles.

14. *Barron's Dictionary of Accounting Terms.* Joel G. Siegel and Jae K. Shim. New York: Barron's, 1987. English.
   • Helpful for work with financial statements.

15. *Barron's Dictionary of Finance and Investment Terms.* Illustrated. Second Edition. Jon Downes and Jordan Elliot Goodman. New York: Barron's, 1987. English.
   • Illustrations include such things as a "head and shoulders" pattern on a stock chart.

16. Bartlett, John. *Familiar Quotes.* 15th and 125th Anniversary Edition Revised and Enlarged. Emily Morison Beck, Editor. Boston: Little, Brown and Company, 1980. English.

17.* Benmaman, Virginia, Norma Connolly, and Scott Loos. *Dictionary of Criminal Justice Terms-Bilingual (English/Spanish).* Binghamton, N.Y.: Gould Publications, 1991. English-Spanish.
   • Provides some good suggestions for Spanish and a range of definitions of English legal terms depending by state. Because the English is so well-researched, the book may help all court interpreters learn more about the English of the courtroom.

18.* Black, Henry Campbell. *Black's Law Dictionary.* 6th ed. St.Paul, Minn.: West Publishing Co., 1990. English.
   • The standard legal dictionary for the U.S. May be used back-to-back with monolingual legal dictionaries from other countries.

19. Bragonier, Jr., Reginald and David Fisher, eds. *What's What: A Visual Glossary of Everyday Objects - From Paper Clips to Passenger Ships.* New York: Random House, Inc., 1981. English.

20. ——. *Qué es Qué: What's What. Enciclopedia visual bilingüe español-inglés.* Barcelona: Ediciones Folio, S.A., 1988. Spanish-English.
   • Bilingual edition of (19). Both excellent for visual identification of common objects and their parts. Includes some weapons.

21.* Cabanellas de las Cuevas, Guillermo and Eleanor C. Hoague. *Butterworths English Spanish Legal Dictionary: Diccionario Jurídico Inglés Español Butterworths.* Austin, Texas: Butterworth Legal Publishers, 1991. Two Vols. Eng-Sp/Sp-Eng.
   • Some useful terms but the next item (22), while only in Spanish, has more detailed definitions. One would still like to see a bilingual dictionary that takes U.S. criminal practice seriously.

22.* Cabanellas de Torres, Guillermo. *Diccionario jurídico elemental*. Buenos Aires: Editorial Heliasta S.R.L., 1988. Available from: Editorial Heliasta S.R.L., Viamonte 1730 - 1er P. -C.F. 1055- Buenos Aires, Argentina. Spanish.
   • A thoughtful book, good, lengthy descriptions of terms, interesting varieties. The sort of book to read at leisure to see which Spanish terms provide the closest match to the English of the courtroom. Highly recommended.

23. Cabrera, Luis. *Diccionario de aztequismos*. México: Ediciones Oasis, S.A., 1980. Spanish.
   • Especially good for plants and animals.

24. Casares, Julio. *Diccionario ideológico de la lengua española: desde la idea a la palabra; desde la palabra a la idea*. Segunda Edición, puesta al día. Barcelona: Ediciones Gustavo Gili, S.A., 1959. Spanish.
   • Almost half of the book is a thesaurus, providing lists of associated words. The second half is an alphabetical list of words not easily found elsewhere. Helpful for someone writing Spanish or doing written translation into that language.

25. Cobos, Rubén. *A Dictionary of New Mexico and Southern Colorado Spanish*. Santa Fe: Museum of New Mexico Press, 1983, Spanish-English.
   • Cobos indicates that the Spanish he studies grew in relative isolation for about 300 years, and so it would not be the same as Chicano Spanish, but rather an older version of Spanish itself, somewhat frozen in time.

26. Deive, Carlos Esteban. *Diccionario de domicanismos*. Santo Domingo: Politecnia Ediciones, 1977. Spanish.

27. Del Rosario, Rubén. *Vocabulario puertorriqueño*. Sharon, Conn.: The Troutman Press, 1965. Spanish.
   • Words collected from conversations held on the Island from 1945 to 1964.

28.* De Pina, Rafael. *Diccionario de derecho*. Décimoprimera Edición, Aumentada y Actualizada. México: Editorial Porrúa, S.A., 1983, Spanish.
   • Written within the framework of Mexican law, also provides some basic legal definitions applicable to Spain and other Latin American countries.

29. *Diccionario de frases célebres*. Recopilación y Selección por Jorge Síntes Pros. Quinta Edición. Les Fonts de Terrassa, Barcelona: Editorial Síntes, S.A, 1981. Basically Spanish.
   • A useful dictionary of quotes, we might say a Spanish equivalent of Bartlett (16) including quotes from the Bible, Shakespeare, and others up to the early twentieth century. When the original quote is in another language such as English, the English is given along with a Spanish version. Helpful to dip into and have ready when attorneys wax eloquent.

30. *Diccionario enciclopédico University de términos médicos, inglés-español.* México: Editorial Interamericana, S.A., 1981. English-Spanish.
   • Outstanding dictionary, contains a plethora of terms.

31. *Diccionario moderno español-inglés, English-Spanish Larousse.* Dirigido y realizado por Ramón García-Pelayo y Gross y Micheline   Durand.   New   York: Ediciones Larousse, 1976. Eng-Sp/Sp-Eng.
   • Generally referred to as "The Larousse," favored by some as a good bilingual general dictionary.

32. *Diccionario de la Lengua Española,* Real Academia Española. Decimoctava Edición. Madrid: Espasa-Calpe, S.A., 1956.

33. *Diccionarios Rioduero: Países de la Tierra.* Versión y adaptación por Walter Strobl. Madrid: Ediciones Rioduero, 1978. Spanish.
   • A translation of a 1976 book originally published in Germany, provides a lively description of different countries, their major products, geographical areas and characteristics. Good reading.

34. *Dorland's Illustrated Medical Dictionary.* 28th Edition. Philadelphia: W.B. Saunders Company, 1994. English. Useful in conjunction with (30).

35. *Enciclopedia universal ilustrada europeo-americana.* Madrid: Espasa-Calpe, S.A. 1958. 70 Vols. with supplemental volumes [which cover years after 1958]. Spanish.
   • The *Suplemento Anual* for 1985-1988, for example, has a nice article on espionage, another on military arts with pictures and descriptions of some new warplanes, one on geology, including plate tectonics, and another on chemistry. The articles are written by specialists and do what the *Encyclopedia Brittanica* used to do in English. Informative and rich for Spanish terminology. Often spoken of as "The Espasa."

36. Espina Pérez, Darío. *Diccionario de cubanismos.* Barcelona: [n.p.], 1974. Spanish.
   • More emphasis on individual words than on sayings.

37. Frías-Sucre Giraud, Alejandro. *Diccionario comercial español-inglés - inglés-español: el secretario: compilación al día de todos los términos y expresiones para la correspondencia comercial.* Nueva edición [cuarta], revisada y ampliada. Barcelona: Editorial Juventud, S.A., 1981. Eng-Sp/Sp-Eng.

38. Galván, Roberto A. and Richard V. Teschner. *El diccionario del español chicano: The Dictionary of Chicano Spanish.* Silver Spring, Maryland: Institute of Modern Languages, Inc., 1975. Spanish-English.
   • Helpful to understand some Spanish-speakers resident in the U.S. who use Anglicisms in their speech.

39. Garmendia y Miangolarra, J. Ignacio. *Diccionario de Bolsa.* Segunda Edición. Madrid: Ediciones Pirámide, S.A,, 1979. Spanish.

- Provides Spanish versions for such words as "bearish" [*bajista*] and "bullish" [*alcista*]. Good place to begin.

40. Gööck, Roland. *Enciclopedia de "Hágalo usted mismo"*. Traducción del alemán por Joaquín Rodríguez Monteverde et al. Dibujos de Holmold Dehne. Segunda Edición Madrid: Espasa-Calpe, S.A., 1978. Spanish.
    - Useful for construction, houses, and tools.

41. *Grant & Hackh's Chemical Dictionary*. Roger and Claire Grant. Fifth Edition. New York: McGraw-Hill Book Company, 1987. English.
    - A comprehensive work, covers both organic and inorganic chemistry.

42. Harrap's Spanish Idioms: *Harrap's Diccionario de expresiones idiomáticas: Dictionary of Idioms*. By Louis J. Rodrigues and Josefina Bernet de Rodrigues. London: Harrap Books Ltd., 1991. Eng-Sp/Sp-Eng.
    - Nicely presented, easy to use, about 9,000 idioms in a format that depends on the "most important word" in each idiom. One regrets that literal translations are not supplied, but space is always a consideration in a work such as this.

43. Kemiji, Steve C. *Glossary of Unusual Words and Phrases Frequently Encountered by ALRB Interpreters*, Ed. Robert F. Escudero. State of California, Agricultural Labor Relations Board, 1982. Available from: Steve C. Kemiji, Supervisor, Language Services, Agricultural Labor Relations Board, 915 Capitol Mall, Sacramento, CA, 95814. Eng-Sp/Sp-Eng.
    - Excellent book, lots of Anglicisms and other slang used by witnesses who appear before the Agricultural Labor Relations Board of the State of California. For example, we see the literal "*planta de huevo* ," also given as the more correct "*berenjena* ," for "eggplant." While Anglicisms used by Spanish speakers vary by region in the U.S., and perhaps by place of origin, there is enough overlap so that this book can prove very helpful if you happen to be working in the cities of the East Coast, or in the Western part of the country (anything West of the Hudson River).

44. Köhler, Josef and Rudolf Meyer. *Explosives*. Fourth, revised and extended edition. New York: VCH Publications, 1993. In English, but includes occasional French and German terms.
    - Describes a variety of military and industrial explosives, as well as blasting techniques. Helpful also for understanding improvised explosive devices. Outstanding.

45.* Lasca, R. and I.D. Bustamante. *Diccionario de derecho, economía y política: inglés-español, español-inglés*. Madrid: Editorial Revista de Derecho Privado, Editoriales de Derecho Reunidas, 1980. Eng-Sp/Sp-Eng.
    - Especially good for matters of contracts, business, and trade law.

46. Lender, T. and R. Delavault and A. Le Moigne. *Diccionario de biología*. Traducido [del francés] por Mercè Serrano y Ferran Vallespinós. Barcelona: Ediciones Grijalbo, S.A., 1982. Spanish.
   • Good for details of DNA terminology. Carefully done, an exception to the caveat about translated dictionaries. Detailed explanations of terms make it resemble a mini-encyclopaedia.

47. León, Víctor. *Diccionario de argot español y lenguaje popular*. Madrid: Alianza Editorial, 1980. Spanish.
   • More useful than the Umbral book (59). Particularly good entries for "*hostia* " and "*huevo* ." Should you need to interpret vulgar expressions from English to Spanish, appropriate equivalents will be readily found here. Amusing reading.

48.* Mazzucco, Patricia Olga and Alejandra Hebe Maranghello. *Diccionario bilingüe de terminología jurídica, inglés-castellano, castellano-inglés*. Buenos Aires: Abledo-Perrot, [1988]. Eng-Sp/Sp-Eng.
   • Very helpful, good supplement to the Robb (58).

49. Mejía Prieto, Jorge. *Así habla el mexicano: diccionario básico de mexicanismos*. Cuarta Edición. México: Panorama Editorial, S.A., 1987. Spanish.
   • Explanations of Mexican terms and their origins. Some of these words are also used outside of Mexico.

50. Moliner, María. *Diccionario de uso del español*. Madrid: Editorial Gredos. 2 vols. 1981. Spanish.
   • Perhaps more complete than the *Diccionario de la Lengua Española* (22), and somewhat more accepting of words. Good for usage.

51. *Multilingual Dictionary of Narcotic Drugs and Psychotropic Substances under International Control*. New York: United Nations, 1983. Multilingual.
   • Languages include English, French, Russian, Spanish and some terms in Arabic and Chinese.

52. Muñiz Castro, Emilio G. *Diccionario Terminológico de Economía, Comercio y Derecho Inglés-Español/Español-Inglés: Dictionary of Economics, Business and Legal Terminology*. Madrid: Editorial Fontenebro, 1990. Eng-Sp/Sp-Eng.

53. Orellana, Marina. *Glosario internacional para el traductor: Glossary of Selected Terms Used in International Organizations*. Con la Colaboración de John D. Chadburn. Tercera edición revisada y aumentada. Santiago de Chile, 1990. Available from: Waldenbooks, 1700 Pennsylvania Ave., N.W., Washington, D.C. 20006. Eng-Sp/Sp-Eng.
   • Excellent organization, many expressions helpful to the interpreter as well as to the translator. The sort of book to read at leisure and to consult for specific words. Includes also some "Common Stock Phrases" in both English and Spanish.

54. *The Oxford English Dictionary.* Second Edition. Prepared by J.A. Simpson and E.S.C.
     Weiner. 20 vols. Oxford: Clarendon Press, 1989. English.
     • What the editors have done is to put on the computer all the entires in *The
     Oxford English Dictionary*, the First Edition by James A.H. Murray, and combine it
     with what was called *A Supplement to the Oxford English Dictionary*, and to make
     some corrections and further additions. The First Edition has for some time been
     available in a two-volume photo-reduced version sold with a magnifying glass. The
     Second Edition is also now available in a photo-reduced edition, comprising one
     very large volume.

55. *The Penguin Dictionary of Computers.* Third Edition. Anthony Chandor with John
     Graham and Robin Williamson. New York: Viking Penguin, 1985. English.
     • Cited as an example, Penguin has a wide range of monolingual dictionaries and
     in Europe one sees that some have been translated into other languages. It looks as
     though Penguin conceived the idea of a series of monolingual paperback dictionar-
     ies, by field. And it also looks as though Barron's has now caught up with the idea.
     Penguin is heavy on arts, sciences, and history, while the Barron's series seem
     heavier in finance, economics, and law. There is some overlap, and both are
     valuable series.

56.* Ribó Durán, Luís. *Diccionario de Derecho.* Barcelona: Bosch Casa Editorial, S.A.,
     1987. Spanish.
     • Presents more than six thousand legal terms defined as they are understood in
     Spain in accord with Spanish law. Well-written, well-made book. Very helpful.

57.* Robb, Louis A. *Diccionario de términos legales: español-inglés e inglés-español.* Mexico:
     Editorial Limusa, 1978.Eng-Sp/Sp-Eng.
     • Available in the U.S. in hardcover or paperback, a basic place to start for a
     bilingual legal dictionary.

58. Saiz Viadero, J.R. *Diccionario para uso de raqueros.* Santander, Spain: Ediciones
     Tantin, 1983. Spanish.
     • Some uses of Spanish in Spain (Santander). One of the most interesting words
     is "*raquero*." A "*raquero*," now meaning a petty crook, was originally a personage
     who heisted goods from wharfs and boats.

59. Sánchez-Boudy, José. *Diccionario de cubanismos más usuales (Como habla el cubano).*
     Miami: Ediciones Universal, 1978. Spanish.
     • Cuban sayings and expressions.

60. *Simon and Schuster's International Dictionary: English/Spanish, Spanish-English.* Tana
     de Gámez, Editor in Chief. New York: Simon and Schuster, n.d. Eng/Sp-Sp-Eng.
     • A large general bilingual dictionary favored by many colleagues.

61. Suárez Gil, Luis. *Diccionario técnico marítimo: inglés-español, español-inglés.* Segunda
     edición revisada. Madrid: Editorial Alhambra, S.A., 1983. Eng-Sp/Sp-Eng.

• Includes labelled drawings of maritime engines.

62. Torrents dels Prats, Alfonso. *Diccionario de dificultades del inglés.* Barcelona: Editorial Juventud, S.A., 1976. English-Spanish.
• Concentrates on individual words, and the variety of meanings they may have in English. Considered from the point of view of the interpreter.

63. ———. *Diccionario de inglés americano.* Barcelona: Editorial Juventud, S.A., 1983. English-Spanish.
• Presents Spanish solutions for U.S. expressions and words.

64. _____. *Diccionario de modismos ingleses y norteamericanos.* Tercera Edición. Barcelona: Editorial Juventud, 1979. English-Spanish.
• Torrents dels Prats addresses interpreter concerns. Here he provides solutions to problem phrases: "to carry coals to Newcastle" becomes *llevar leña al monte* [to carry firewood to the forest], and "fresh as a daisy" becomes *fresco como una rosa* [fresh as a rose]. A fine demonstration of the idea that languages do not always have exact equivalents. Presented so that the reader is inspired to add new expressions and solutions.

65. *Websters' New International Dictionary of the English Language.* W.T. Harris, Editor in Chief. Springfield, Mass. G. & C. Merriam Company, 1933. English.
• Popularly referred to as "Websters' II International," the book, which includes more than 400,000 words, can sometimes be found in secondhand bookstores and at estate sales. The wise writer, translator, or interpreter will not easily relinquish a copy once she has managed to secure one.

66. Webster's *Third New International Dictionary of the English Language Unabridged.* Philip Babock Gove, Editor in Chief. Springfield, Mass.: Merriam Webster Inc., 1986. Principal Copyright 1961. English.
• One of the appropriately 450,000 words included here is "ain't," shocking to people of delicate sensibility who realize that linguistic corruption goes hand in glove with moral decay. Those who wish to retain their values and sense of good English style will prefer (65).

67.* *West's Spanish-English/English-Spanish Law Dictionary: Diccionario Legal Español-Inglés/Inglés-Español,* Gerardo Solís and Raúl A. Gasteazoro, Jr. St. Paul, Minn.: West Publishing Company, 1992. Eng-Sp/Sp-Eng.
• The authors provide the meanings of more than 12,000 terms. Explains some terms of art more clearly than Black's (18). Civil terms predominate. Good to browse through.

68. Umbral, Francisco. *Diccionario cheli.* Barcelona: Ediciones Grijalbo, S.A., 1983. Spanish.
• Umbral, a humorist, uses this book as a vehicle for social observation of the *jeunesse dorée* of the Madrid of 1983. He presents a few words, and spins glorious

essays on each. Umbral is a great stylist, somewhat after the fashion of Henry Miller.

69. Urquía Gómez, Antonio de. *Diccionario técnico militar inglés-español, español-inglés.* Madrid: Ediciones Agulló, 1980. Eng-Sp/Sp-Eng.
  • Excellent. Offers terms that can be readily understood by Latin Americans as well as Spaniards. Good on weapons, also explosives and the vocabulary of how they are to be dealt with. English into Spanish section slightly longer than Spanish into English part.

70. Villate, José T. *Dictionary of Environmental Engineering and Related Sciences: Diccionario de ingeñiería ambiental y ciencias afines.* Miami: Ediciones Universal, 1979. Eng-Sp/Sp-Eng.
  • Villate, himself an engineer, has gathered words in use, and studied technical journals to find more words. Good for environmental engineering, also helpful for some aspects of construction, agriculture, and hydrology.

CHAPTER 4

In the Courtroom

Ethics, Roles, Procedures

Our goal is to make a full and faithful interpretation of courtroom speech. If we interpret for the defendant we interpret all proceedings for him. If we interpret only for some witnesses, we simply interpret testimony from the witness stand. Either way, our goal remains the same: full and faithful interpretation of speech. To achieve our goal we must enter the courtroom already prepared, with the correct information (Ch. II) and terminology (Ch III). Once in the courtroom, we must know what ethical standards to follow. We must also know who the other participants are, the role of each and our relationship to each actor. We also need to know what procedures to follow. And because sound equipment is so helpful to our work, we need to know what equipment to use and how to use it. Then we come to the interpreting itself, our position to see and hear, and what we do in simultaneous and consecutive modes. At the end of the chapter are remarks for judges as to how their direction of the proceedings may promote the best possible interpreting.

Ethics

Because the interpreter may be the only person in the courtroom with a full command of both languages being used, she has enormous power. It is the function of a code of ethics to tell us how to wield that power responsibly. The ethics will be the unseen basis of our courtroom behavior. By following a good ethical code, we earn the respect and trust of all parties to a case, which we need to work effectively.

Secrecy

Each side wants to know what the other is doing, thinking, planning. You are privy to conversations, such as at grand jury, where you swear to keep what you have interpreted secret. When working with defendants, the same pledge of secrecy applies, although you take no oath at that time. In criminal cases, you may work for the prosecution at grand jury, as well as for the defense at the jail. You should tell neither side where you have been, and mention no details of what you have learned. Your knowledge is for yourself, for your understanding of the case and the preparation of terminology.

Lawyers ask questions and police ask questions, but there is no such thing as an innocent question from an attorney, a detective, or an investigator. Sometimes it is best not to be around people at certain stages of trial, so that when a police witness excluded from the courtroom asks: "How is it going?" you do not have to pretend you do not know what he means. Take your break elsewhere.

For large civil cases, you may be hired not by the court, but by one party or another, in which instance, limit your contacts to the side that hires you. In a civil case, the attorney for the other side may call and ask you for "just some information about the work you have done" for "your" side. You may tell him that all questions about your work should be directed to the attorney who hired you. The attorney on the phone may become angry. Allow him the freedom of his anger. He may say "Well, we may have to depose you," which is fine, but you still tell him "Please direct all questions and requests to the attorney who hired me." By way of an aside, a colleague has said that there are four possible answers that an interpreter should give if he is deposed: "Yes," "No," "I don't know," and "I don't remember." This was said in jest, but it may be prudent advice.

Impartiality and Having No Opinion

Interpreters expend a good deal of emotional energy remaining impartial, because we do not want to hold an opinion in the case, lest that opinion subconsciously color our interpretation. It is the duty of the court or the jury to decide the case. It is the duty of counsel to decide if they believe their witnesses or not. Our duty is to remain impartial. Several advantages accrue from impartiality. It is easier to concentrate on the interpreting, on language and meaning, when you do not have to look at the content of the message in terms of what it means for the case. Also, counsel, defendants, and jury can read attitude and body language. If an interpreter feels that a man is guilty, she may let this attitude be seen in her body language, which says: "Yeech, I am sitting next to a murderer." Such an attitude will get you thrown off the case. The defense will pick up on it quickly, because the vibrations can influence the jury and make the defendant uncomfortable. Impartiality has to do not only with not taking sides, but with not forming a judgement, not reaching a conclusion about the case. We have enough to do in reaching conclusions as to the meaning of words and phrases without having to worry about the outcome of the case. No matter who hires the interpreter, he must always do his best to remain impartial.

The interpreter must also take care not to compromise the appearance of impartiality. Thus it is well not to chat with defendants or witnesses during breaks, or the jury may think that one side is "cooking something up." There may be times when it is necessary to speak with witnesses to clarify certain words or phrases, something perhaps done in a witness room, out of the sight of the jury, and **with the permission of counsel**.

We hold no opinion about a case and we express no opinion. Three situations came to mind where one must take special care. A defendant may ask you "what are my chances?" You may tell the defendant that that is a question he needs to ask his attorney. You have no opinion. Or, a defense attorney or prosecutor may ask you if you believe that a certain witness (usually at the pretrial stage) is telling the truth. Again, you need to say you have no opinion. It may be tempting to comment, but you should refrain. Another question you might hear from prosecutor or defense is what you think their chances are with the jury. You have no opinion. And you certainly have no opinion or comment about the work of attorneys or judges. Professional interpreters can get all riled up when judges and attorneys intervene erroneously into their work with either misguided orders or criticisms. Rightly or wrongly, interpreters may see any comment, other than those from another interpreter, as unwarranted intrusion. By the same token, anything we say about other participants may be seen as intrusive and offensive. Just as non-interpreters may have little understanding of our work, so too, we have little understanding of the work of other functionaries. Thus, we must refrain from any remark. When attorneys, judges, witnesses and defendants know that they can trust us to say nothing, either about the contents of the case or about our impression of their performance, they will feel more comfortable working with us. An interpreter is an extra person, a necessary evil not normally present. By not commenting on what others do, we create a comfort zone around us that facilitates our work.

Remember also that anyone in any profession can have a bad day. For us that might mean inadequate concentration, inability to catch the flow and direction of a case, or forgetting some words. We ourselves know how well or how poorly we have worked. It may be in the morning on a case you feel your work is not as good as you would like it to be, but by the afternoon session you have hit your stride and are doing brilliant work. Of course we would like all of our work to be brilliant all of the time. Much as we would like others to give us the benefit of the doubt, we should extend it to others in the courtroom.

Keeping Out of the Case

Being impartial helps us keep out of the case. We should have no prior personal connection to a case, and no interest in the outcome. If you are related to or close friends with one of the parties, do not work on the case. If you have a financial interest in the result, do not work on it. This is fairly simple and clear, and once you are off a case the problem ends. Assume, then, no prior interest in the case.

All the other aspects of keeping out of a case depend on our own attitude. We have mentioned impartiality. Impartiality helps us keep out of a case by allowing us not to be swayed by sympathy for one side or another. Keeping out of a case also means not helping, not fixing things. Frequently questions are unclear so that the answer will be non-responsive, that is, it will not respond to or answer the question asked. It is not up to the interpreter to tell the witness what counsel really meant. Nor is it up to the interpreter to suggest in court how counsel or the court might frame their questions for clarity. Counsel will have to figure that out themselves.

Sometimes an attorney may deliberately ask confusing questions. On one case, after a long involved snarled question, before the interpreter could interpret it to the witness, the judge said: "Counsel, your question is so complicated that the interpreter will not understand it, the witness will not understand it, and the Court will not understand it." Snarls are for the court or counsel to clear up. We are not there to "help" or "help out." The interpreter as advocate has no place in a judicial setting. Our best social contribution as interpreters is fidelity to the meaning of speech. Our role is humble. Grandiose desires should be fulfilled in some other arena.

Conversation with a defendant poses certain problems. Clients sometimes want to convince you, the interpreter, that they are innocent, or, in family matters, that they were right in beating the wife, the daughter, etc. The interpreter has no interest in the content of a case as such. She wants only to understand the situation as a function of what might be said. If she is to interpret for a witness, it is helpful to know more or less what the witness will say. Witnesses do not always speak clearly or coherently. In a case for child support or for a civil protection order, heard without a jury, the wife seeking support will know the names of the children involved, their birthdays, the sort of work she does, the sort of work her husband does, and how long it has been since they have been together, if they are now living apart. Because she will have to repeat all of this in court, it is helpful to obtain some data before going into the courtroom, with the permission of the attorney, if she has an attorney. It will also allow you to follow her general flow of ideas.

Witnesses are tense, nervous, and afraid, all of which causes them to speak quickly so that extra pressure distorts their speech even further. Even their unpressured speech may be imprecise. This is why we like to talk to a witness beforehand, to determine speech patterns and accent so we can understand properly and transmit accurately what the witness says. At the same time, we never ask a defendant did he really do it.

The problem at the pretrial interview stage, whether working for the defense or the prosecution, or with either side in a civil suit, is that attorneys and police have their own agenda, and there is a natural human tendency to want to help. Resist this tendency, otherwise the attorney or investigator may feel you are mixing in his case. "Helping" is dangerous and will be resented. Don't help. We must be prudent about how we work.

Prudence reminds us to never ask a defense attorney "What do you really think, did he do it, or not?" Defense attorneys are uncomfortable with that question. In any event, it is none of our affair. Their concern is what can the government prove. If each criminal defendant is entitled to a defense, and he is, then his attorney will do the best job he can. He has enough trouble justifying to himself the kind of client he must represent. Do not add to his problems by asking what he "really" thinks. By the same token, never ask the prosecution if it thinks its witness is telling the truth, even if that witness is a woman who claims to be an ex-Marine, ex-prostitute, ex-drug dealer, and during the lunch break takes a toot of some illegal substance. Don't ask.

Two more aspects of keeping out of the case are worth mention. Never talk to a juror, never talk about a case near a juror. Jurors are identified, at least in Washington, D.C., by a badge that they wear in the courthouse. The judge will instruct jurors not to talk to parties. Interpreters must not approach or talk to jurors. We also do not want to talk about a case near other members of the public. This has to do with keeping the process clean, because the jury may only hear evidence duly admitted in the courtroom.

Avoid the press. Some cases attract reporters. Do not seek out reporters. If reporters seek you out, simply refuse to speak with them, even if they catch you by surprise. Suppose you have interpreted at a hearing where the prosecution has said that "*muérete* " means "I will kill you," while the defense has said that it means "drop dead." As the interpreters leave the courtroom, a reporter jumps out and asks them what does "*muérete* " mean and all three say it means "drop dead." The next morning the local newspaper will report that "all three federally certified interpreters said that it meant 'drop dead.'" Those same interpreters will receive black looks from the clerk, and rightly so. Don't talk to the press, and don't answer any of their questions, however brief. If the judge wants an interpreter's opinion as to the meaning of an expression, she will ask the interpreter in the courtroom.

Interpreters must not practice law, offer legal opinions, or answer legal questions. Even if the interpreter is an attorney, she is not the attorney for the case she is interpreting. And most of us are not attorneys anyway, and must be very careful not to practice law without a license to do so. This means not giving legal advice, not answering defendants' legal questions. And certainly it means not pressuring a defendant to plead guilty, to go to trial, or to take any other step. The decision about what a defendant or witness will do is between that person and his attorney. We may interpret such conversations, but we have no part in their outcome. We do not know better than a defendant which course will best serve his case. We also do not know better than an attorney which line of argument will sway a jury. Some attorneys who may be very busy may ask us to explain certain legal matters to their clients. This we should not do. We are delighted to interpret an attorney's explanation, but that is it. Our role is transparent: we only interpret. It is always someone else who speaks the message.

Because attorneys are not always aware of how limited our role is, they may sometimes ask us to do things that are improper. Usually this is not out of a desire to hurt the interpreter, but if we accede to the request, the effect can be ruinous. For example, the prosecutor asks the interpreter to please take some pictures into the witness room and ask Mrs. González if she recognizes anyone in these pictures. The interpreter who agrees to do this has become an agent of the prosecution and thereby lost her impartiality and her ability to work further as an interpreter on the case. The answer should be: "I'm sorry but interpreter ethics do not allow me to do this, but I would be delighted to accompany you into the witness room and interpret for you when you ask the witness the question yourself."

By the same token, if a defense attorney asks you if from where you are sitting you can get a glimpse of Officer Jones' badge number, you simply must tell the attorney that your ethical code prohibits such participation in the case. Once you say this the attorney may apologize and immediately realize that he should not have asked you to do this. Our answer to attorneys in such situations must be soft. It is usually not their intention to set us up. If, however, an attorney becomes angry, he is free to do so. We should not answer with anger, but firmly and politely. We need to protect our impartiality, which is the same thing as protecting our ability to work. The problem with such situations is that they are usually spur of the moment and catch us by surprise, and it seems like a small favor. Don't do small favors, don't do big favors. Attention to this issue helps keep our role clear.

Willingness to Admit Error

Correct an interpreting mistake as soon as possible. It makes no difference who catches it, you, your interpreter colleague, the witness, the defendant, the judge, or counsel. The mistake should be corrected in such as way as to make it clear to the jury that it is the interpreter who is changing his version, and not the witness. For example, during testimony of the same Captain whose boat was towed into the port of "Boh Boh," the Captain provided a date in answer to a question, which the interpreter wrote down incorrectly, and began to repeat to the jury, but the Captain, seeing the note, caught the mistake and corrected it. It was then possible to change the date, and say: "Interpreter correction as to the date," so that the witness did not look as though he were fudging on the witness stand.

Another way to correct a mistake, particularly when it takes you some time to realize you have made an error, is to wait for a break, approach counsel for both sides, explain the error, and ask how they wish to correct it. Sometimes they prefer to re-ask the question, and this time the interpretation of the answer will be correct. In any event, the interpreter must always be ready to say for the record that the error was hers, when it was. If there is no break when the jury is not present, the interpreter may ask to approach the bench and explain it to the court and counsel. If both counsel have left, approach the judge or ask to speak to him in chambers. How and when a correction is to be made will depend largely on the nature of the error, when it was caught, and by whom.

More and more in the future we will see Spanish speakers serving on juries. Some judges ask potential bilingual jurors if they will swear to accept the version of the court interpreter, even if they disagree with it. Other judges take another approach. A recent example recounted by Judge Ricardo Urbina of the U.S. District Court for the District of Columbia told of a judge who asked a bilingual juror if he had any disagreement with the interpreted version of testimony to simply raise his hand. During interpreted testimony that juror did raise his hand. The rest of the jury was sent to the jury room, and the juror said that he believed that the interpreter had made a mistake, that the word interpreted as "purse" had really been "gun." The interpreter was asked about this and said "Let's ask the witness," which was done. It turned out that the witness had indeed meant to say "gun." The juror was told not to discuss what he had said to the court, and the mistake was corrected in front of the whole jury.

There are times when counsel will allege interpreting errors where none have occurred, at which point one must stand up for one's work and indicate that no error was committed. This can happen especially when counsel is bilingual and dislikes the answer that his client provides to a question. In one case, attorneys constantly alleged interpreter error where no errors were being made. Tiring of the bad-faith performance by the attorneys, the chief interpreter on the case approached the lead defense attorney and told him that if complaints of non-existent interpreter error continued, she would speak to the judge. Counsel subsequently refrained from complaining about non-existent errors.

At a deposition (a sworn statement taken in the presence of attorneys for the opposing sides and transcribed by a court reporter) where an attorney said he spoke Spanish, and did not care for his client's answer, the attorney said "I think that my client did not understand the translation." The attorney then did this a second time, at which point the interpreter said, for the record, "Perhaps counsel would like to suggest an alternate phrasing in Spanish for this question, since counsel has indicated that he speaks Spanish." The attorney had no alternate wording he wished to provide.

In depositions where more than one attorney is present from a law firm, and where one of those attorneys speaks Spanish, you may find that the Spanish-speaking attorney disagrees with the interpretation but that his disagreement is a minor one. The professional interpreter should not feel abashed or insulted at what he considers an unnecessary correction. It may be that the attorney in question is showing another member of his law firm that he is "watching" the interpreter and "checking up on him," thus bringing his own language talents to bear in the case. This is fine. Or, it may happen that the attorney has found a real error of meaning, or that he has provided a word that is slightly better than the one you used. If you think the correction is valid, you may say "the interpreter accepts the correction," and move on.

Projection of Interpreter Image

Image is important because it will be taken for the reality. Thus, for example, we should not put on a face of disgust at having to sit next to a man accused of an especially obnoxious crime. We will look lively, and pay attention even though we are not interpreting, because we might have to pass a note or documents to a colleague, or take the microphone if a colleague suddenly feels unwell.

The interpreter should dress soberly. For the women, do not get into the slit skirt, see-through blouse routine. Forget loads of bangle jewelry. Forget short skirts, no matter what is currently fashionable. Forget the Venus's-flytrap look, it does not fit on your agenda. Your agenda is to get from the other participants the conditions you need to work effectively: if you look like a bimbo, you will get bimbo conditions rather than interpreter conditions. For the men, decent grooming, a decent suit and tie, and a crisp shirt, professionally laundered project the look you want. The image the interpreter wishes to project is that of someone serious, who has interpreting and only interpreting on her mind, and who has taken the care to come in looking neat and well-groomed. Slobbovia has no place here. Your look should convey the reality of your competence.

Outside of court, at the jail or prison, for example, try to dress simply but well. Do not follow the example of attorneys who may visit the jail in Levis and T-shirts. A visit to jail is somewhat akin to a visit to a hospital. The people incarcerated there have enough problems: do not depress them further by dressing too informally. When an inmate receives visitors, both inmate and interpreter gain face if the interpreter dresses nicely. Wear something nice and crisp. The client will feel honored and better about himself, because he will conclude that the people working with him are taking him seriously. Thus, he may talk more freely and with more confidence to his attorney, social worker, or probation officer. When a client talks more freely and more honestly, the interpreter may be credited.

Need for Interpretation

While the issue of who needs an interpreter is a legal question, prudent courts provide interpretation when alerted by attorneys that interpretation will be needed. When we are called to provide interpretation, we do so unless the defense attorney or prosecutor tells us otherwise. At that point, the interpreter should ask the attorney to state for the record that his client does not wish interpretation. This protects us, because it indicates for the record that we were there to provide the service. Prosecutors or police may sometimes ask you how much English a defendant or defense witness "really" speaks. My answer to that question is: "I don't know because I do not speak to the defendant in English." The real answer is that we, the interpreters, are not in court to give English tests to defendants and witnesses. This is simply not our function, nor are most of us equipped to do so. If we are sent to a case, we presume the need, and if an attorney wishes to waive our use, he should do so on the record.

Sometimes an attorney prefers to have a witness testify without interpretation but to keep the interpreter there in case the witness has a question about what was said, in which case we make ourselves available and pay attention, so that if we should have to supply a word or a phrase, we can do so immediately.

Giving the Client Good Value

What we may charge a client is sometimes fixed by regulation, as in the federal courts, or by administrative fiat, as in some state courts. Sometimes you are free to negotiate a rate with a client. In any event, as responsible professionals, we should keep in mind that if we can advise the client so that he can save money and still receive the quality work he has a right to expect, then we are behaving properly.

A simple example would be on the written translation of a large document. Let us say that a client has a whole slew of documents to be translated. The first question is does he really need all of them translated. You may offer to go over the documents with him, and briefly describe what each one contains, to make sure that he really needs them all translated. Some clients may not wish to be questioned about their need, but it is worth checking.

Perhaps a set of documents contains one that is a copy (inadvertent) of another in the set. That copy does not need to be redone, presumably. Point this duplication out to the client and ask him. When you work transcribing and translating surveillance tapes (see Chapter 7), confirm with the client that he really needs all those tapes if it is a large set. It may happen that the client, typically a government agency, has had some tape transcriptions and translations already prepared by someone not fully qualified to do them and now, approaching trial, wants the tapes re-done or corrected for presentation in the courtroom. You may offer to review the written transcripts with the client so that he may select the tapes or parts of tapes he will actually need at trial, and only those will have to be re-done. Here you may be able to save the client money by having him decide what he really needs for trial. This will also save you time and enable you to better meet the deadline on the tapes that you actually do. While no one likes to turn down work, it is our professional responsibility not to lead a client into contracting for unnecessary work.

Neither Too Many nor Two Few Interpreters

In Chapter 1 we said that two or three interpreters are generally sufficient for a large case, perhaps four at the most, assuming the need to use only English and one other language for defendants and witnesses.

It is generally understood by the United Nations, the U.S. Department of State, the U.S. district courts (that is, the federal courts), and some other courts, that there must be at least two interpreters who will switch off every half hour or so when the defendant needs interpretation. This half-hour rule insures accuracy and helps avoid interpreter mistakes. Thus, for one defendant at trial who does not speak English, you need at least two simultaneous interpreters. If the prosecution also has witnesses whose testimony needs interpretation, then perhaps a third interpreter could be helpful, and all three interpreters could then switch around every 20 minutes or so. This would be a reasonable procedure. If two or more defendants require interpretation, you may still be able to provide excellent coverage without having to use more than two or three interpreters, by using sound equipment (described shortly). With sound equipment, each defendant receives a headset and the interpreter speaks through a microphone so that all defendants can hear equally well. It is not necessary to have one interpreter per defendant in a multi-defendant case. Indeed, any situation where you have more than one interpreter talking at once is to be avoided when possible, as the noise level will be too high to hear well. No matter how many interpreters are working, if they are not switching off every half hour, the interpretation will be inferior and inaccurate and subject to challenge. For best results, then, you want at least two interpreters and if you have more than one defendant, sound equipment is necessary. Even for one defendant the use of sound equipment allows the interpreters to hear better.

Who Is Who in the Courtroom

The **judge** controls the courtroom. The judge has other participants to contend with as well as interpreters. He has attorneys snapping at his heels, marshals demanding that he wear a bullet-proof vest, and an administrator who wants him to move cases along. Meanwhile, some of you may have learned from professors or supervisors the dictum that "the interpreter must be in control of every situation." In court, however, the judge controls, so you must work with the judge and inform him of what you need to do your job properly. When the judge arrives or leaves the courtroom, all present generally stand. We stand to show respect for the judicial process that seeks the impartial administration of justice. Another mark of respect is not to read newspapers or anything else in the courtroom. If you must wait for your case, pay attention to the other cases, because there is always something to be learned from them. It is impolite to talk in the courtroom when you are not called on to do so. Any unnecessary noise will distract the judge. If you need to talk to an attorney, or an attorney wants to talk to you, go out into the hallway for the chat. Courtroom acoustics may carry the sounds to the judge's ears, thus interrupting judicial concentration. One is a guest in the courtroom and should maintain proper decorum.

Because the job of interpreting is highly technical, there is no reason why a non-interpreter should be familiar with the inner workings of it, any more than a movie director should understand all the details of the lighting technician's specialty. But just as the movie director needs to know something about lighting, so too the judge should know something about the interpretation, because the judge is directing this movie. You may tell the judge how many interpreters you will need, and the fact, if there is more than one, that you will be switching off and presumably using sound equipment so all defendants can hear easily. You may also tell the court that Spanish needs more words to say the same thing than English, so that the speed of speech in the courtroom should be moderate.

When you arrive, let the **clerk** know you are there and for which case, because the clerk may decide which case is called and in which order. All the lawyers want their cases called first, unless they are elsewhere, in which instance, they would just as soon the case sat on the back burner. The clerk should know you are there so that when attorneys for your case show up she knows the case is ready to be called.

The **marshal** or **bailiff** is in charge of security; he protects the judge, prisoners, witnesses, jurors, and the public, and recommends on security matters to the judge as required. Let the marshal know who you are, and for whom you will be interpreting and find out if the defendant is in the lockup. When the defendant is brought in from the lockup, you will get up and stand next to the defendant, while the marshal stands behind him. The marshal needs to know who you are, because one of his functions is to protect the defendant, and an unidentified person suddenly approaching his defendant could be anyone. Marshals are trained to react quickly. If the defendant is in the courtroom, out on personal recognizance or bail, you still need to let the marshal know who you are.

In high-threat/high-profile trials, talk to the marshals to see where you will be sitting. You need always to sit or stand close enough to the source of the sound to hear and see the speakers. Because you will probably have sound equipment for your defendants, you need somewhere to place the wires, assuming you are using wired equipment. If you are using a wireless system, make sure it is properly set up. Come in early for a sound test of any equipment that the court has provided.

Some courthouses have security, but many do not. In federal courts marshals man the doors and everyone must pass through a metal detector, while briefcases go through an X-Ray machine of the sort seen at airports. On high-threat federal trials, there may be another metal detector at the door of the courtroom. Some attorneys become impatient with the searches and feel that they are somehow demeaned by being subjected to such procedures. Court security procedures exist to protect the entire process, and because the interpreter is part of the process, they exist to help protect interpreters. Cooperate with the marshals or with any other security people and do not get into power games about who is to be searched and who is exempt. We do not want to be exempt. Remember that it is forbidden to enter a federal court-house with a weapon (even pen-knives), tape recorder, or camera. Any exception may require special permission of the judge.

The **court reporter** has to hear all parts of the case, even as you are interpreting. If you are used to simultaneous interpretation in a conference booth, lower your voice when you speak into the microphone of your sound equipment so as not to interfere with the hearing of the court reporter and other members of the trial. When there is a foreign word that you need to use, spell it out for the court reporter, be it a word, a place name, or the name of a person. Sometimes at a break you or your colleagues may hand the court reporter a list of foreign words and names that have been used. Talk to the reporter about this. The interpreter is generally at the witness stand or near the defendant/s. On the witness stand, where interpretation is consecutive, that is, short phrases with breaks, the waiting time allows the court reporter to hear the English version of everything that is said. But court reporters and other participants can be troubled if the interpreter next to the defendant does simultaneous interpreting without keeping his voice down. The simultaneous proceeds at about the same space as the original speaker, and if the interpreter is not careful, the interpretation can mask the English of counsel, the judge, or an English-speaking witness. The interpreter needs to speak in a very low voice, which is one reason I recommend the use of sound equipment for the simultaneous, because one can then speak softly into a microphone. The sound will be amplified to the defendant, and the floor language of the courtroom will not be masked. Ideally, when the interpreter does simultaneous interpretation in the courtroom, the only one who can hear the interpreted version is the defendant or someone else who has an earphone of the same system. The main consideration is to keep your own voice down.

Show respect for **witnesses** and **defendants**; be polite with everyone in the courthouse. Remember that were it not for the witness or defendant, we would not have work, so right away we have an excellent reason based on self-interest to be polite. Ask yourself if you were a witness or defendant in a foreign court how you would like to be treated. The answer is, with consideration, dignity, and respect. Politeness to all parties is warranted because it helps smooth the way for the interpreter and creates a pleasant work experience. It is best to avoid personal conversation with witnesses and defendants.

Attorneys should also be treated with courtesy. The attorney has special problems: he is the advocate and wants to win. Attorneys have to psyche themselves up for trial. Part of this process involves generation of some hostility towards the other side. Attorneys can become very touchy and almost paranoid at trial. They may resent your questions. If you ask the prosecutor how many government witnesses there are, a defense attorney may accuse you of "talking about his case" with the prosecution. This you are not doing, but the attorney is having a rough time of it and lashes out at what he perceives as a threat.

Sound Equipment

When non-interpreters first see or hear about interpreting equipment they may believe that the equipment does the interpreting. It does not: it simply amplifies and transmits the voice of the interpreter to the defendant. It is the interpreter herself who does the interpreting. In the bad old days, and in some courts still, you may see an interpreter sitting next to a defendant and whispering throughout the entire trial. This is called whisper simultaneous and it not good for the voice, the posture, or the ability to hear what is being said. Also, the marshals are not fond of it in certain situations where security is an issue. It is preferable to use sound equipment to transmit the interpretation to a defendant. The use of sound equipment means that two or three interpreters can do effective interpretation for, say, eight defendants, without having to hire eight interpreters. If the court does not own such equipment, you may purchase your own. Interpreters use at least four configurations of equipment in the courtroom.

1.   **Portable Wired Equipment**, arranged like this, with the > representing the direction of travel of the sound impulse:

Microphone >Amplifier> Wire > Headsets

Portable wired equipment is fairly simple. It consists of a microphone connected to an amplifier, which in turn transmits the sound down a line or wire to a series of jacks into which are plugged earphones or headsets for the defendants. Volume control is on the amplifier so that the interpreter controls the volume, and checks with the defendants to see if the sound level is proper. The advantage of this equipment is that it is relatively inexpensive and light, has its own batteries and does not need to be plugged in. We call this portable hard-wire equipment. Hard-wire equipment is secure, not easily subject to interception or interference. Because the interpreter and defendants are all connected to a series of wires, the interpreter is limited to where she can move, so that her range of motion may only be a few feet in the area of the defense table, frequently not sufficient to hear testimony or arguments well.

2.   **Portable Wireless Equipment**, arranged thus:

Microphone > Transmitter > Receiver > Headset

Portable wireless equipment works on a radio frequency. The interpreter has a transmitter and a microphone, and the transmitter broadcasts to the defendant who has a receiver with a head-set or earphone. Both the transmitter and receiver work on batteries, and it is pleasant not to have a snarl of wires on the table. The set-up allows the interpreter to move to any spot necessary to hear the sound, because there is no direct wire between interpreter and defendant. Each receiver has a volume control knob, so that the listener can control incoming volume. The size of the transmitter and the receiver is about that of a fat pack of cigarettes. Some models come with a little pouch that slips onto the belt, convenient for the interpreter because it leaves the hands free, and convenient also for the defendant.

Either wired and or wireless equipment is easy to use and makes court interpreting more rewarding and efficient. The wireless equipment costs more than the wired equipment, but both are good and allow one to keep the voice low. The wireless equipment allows one to move around the courtroom more than the wired. You may tell the judge that the headsets your defendants are wearing are for the interpreting equipment, lest the judge believe someone is listening to a Walkman in his courtroom and wax wroth. Or, you may ask the judge for a minute to set up the equipment and in that request mention that the headsets are part of your equipment. Once judges see wireless equipment in operation, they are pleased with its efficiency. I myself prefer the wireless equipment because it allows me to position myself close enough to the speaker to hear all of what is being said. When you can hear every word spoken, you may then interpret what the speaker actually said, not what he might have said, what he should have said, or what he probably said.

3. Infrared Equipment, arranged thus:

Microphone > Wire > Infrared Transmitter Stand > Headsets

A third sort of equipment is normally used for a large number of defendants in a trial that might last for some time. The transmission is by an infrared process, and needs a plug-in power source. The microphone is connected by a long wire to the infrared transmitter, so the interpreter is somewhat limited in range of motion relative to the transmitter. The defendants are given wireless headsets, each with its own volume control. Such equipment may be useful when there are many defendants. Because of the size and expense, such equipment is typically supplied by the court.

4. Booth with Infrared System, arranged thus:

Booth
[Floor microphones] > Interpreter Earphones
Microphone > Wire >
Infrared Transmitter >
Headsets

The fourth configuration is an interpreting booth, familiar to conference interpreters, which may sometimes be set up in courtroom, by the court, for large, long trials. In a booth interpreters receive the sound they need to hear through a headset, and they have a volume control on the incoming sound, so they can make the sound as loud as they like. This may also include an infrared transmission system to transmit the sound from the interpreter to the defendants. In a booth, as at a conference, the interpreter does not have to keep her voice as low as she would with equipment used outside a booth. Interpreters are protected from ambient courtroom noise by the booth. With the first three kinds of equipment, the wired, the wireless, and infrared without booth, the interpreter is responsible for hearing what is being said in the courtroom. Attorneys are sometimes supposed to speak into room microphones, but they do not always do so, so the interpreter may have to approach the source of the sound. In the booth the sound is brought to the interpreter, but when one works without a booth, it is up to the interpreter to get close enough to the source of the sound to hear it well.

Positioning and Sound Reception

Sometimes the interpreter needs permission of the judge as to where to sit, which might be requested through the judge's law clerk before the case, or one might speak to the judge beforehand. You need line of sight and line of hearing for all speakers, not always easy. In federal courtrooms which can be very large, it is good to be fairly near the front if possible. You may have to ask the judge to ask witnesses and others to speak into their microphones so that you can hear them. To find the best source of sound, interpreters may stand near the bench, or near the witness stand, or generally move around the well of the court to hear all speakers well.

Some courtrooms and situations do not allow for much interpreter movement, but neither does the sound carry well. If movement is inconvenient, or if the witnesses mumble and do not speak into their microphones, if the judge does not have his microphone turned on, or if the courtroom has no microphones, then the interpreter may wish to purchase a small battery-operated **directional amplifier with earphones**, to hear the participants. The amplifier includes a wand to point at the speaker. Show this amplifier to the marshals or bailiffs before the case begins and explain its purpose. While a directional amplifier may help you hear better, one disadvantage is that when you receive sound through a headset, you naturally raise your voice in speaking, so while you can now hear the testimony, your own voice may not be as soft as you would like.

The interpreter needs a table to sit at. Ideally one should be seated at the same table as the defense (assuming you are not there just for witnesses), with room for your amplifier or transmitter, documents, word list, indictment, jury instructions, some water, etc. Being at the same table also allows the interpreter to quickly interpret comments between the defendant and counsel when necessary. For non-jury matters, if you use wireless equipment, it may be convenient to sit in the front row of the jury box. From this position you can hear all participants. This is especially helpful in family cases where eight different people may address the court, and where each parent holds a crying child.

Procedural Matters

Transmission of Angry Speech

There are two schools of thought as to what extent anger should be transmitted when interpreting conversation or testimony. Attorneys may simulate anger to convince a jury, or to inflame it. Another purpose is to jar the witness into a damaging admission, and in a murder or assault case, to enrage the defendant so that the jury can imagine the defendant committing the crime.

Anger is often expressed by a raised voice, a disagreeable inflection, and sometimes by vulgar language. The crude language we must transmit. Many interpreters hold that yelling is out, simply because if we do much of it, we may lose or damage our voice, and we must protect our ability to do our work, which includes protection of the voice. One should try to reproduce the tone in the target language, but it is an extra and if the speaker is going very fast, an interpreter may ignore voice inflection in favor of accuracy of meaning and speed. Of course full accuracy ought to properly include transmission of voice tone. Our colleague Francis Burton recounts that on one occasion a sign language interpreter had to interpret a meeting between a supervisor and a worker at a government agency. The supervisor was offensive, and the interpreter so accurate that the worker got mad, hauled off and slapped the interpreter. Here we must suppose that the sign language interpreter was fully accurate as to tone as well as meaning.

Doubt as to Meaning

There are times when a witness will use a word or expression that the interpreter does not know. The first step is to ask the witness to repeat the word. This can be done with a short phrase and it is clear to all what is going on. Judges hate conversation on the stand between interpreter and witness where the interpreter talks with the witness for fifteen minutes and then tells the court: "He says no." This must not happen. You may have asked a witness to repeat his statement. He has repeated, and the word is still not clear. One approach is for the interpreter to say to the judge: "You Honor, may the interpreter clarify a word?" If the judge gives permission, ask the witness about that word in a non-leading way. A question that does not lead is one that does not bear the seeds of the answer within it. Say you have a word, such as *maceta*, which can mean flowerpot, small mallet, stonecutter's hammer or large drinking glass. Chandler Thompson of New Mexico has a good solution for how the question is to be asked: when the witness says "I threw a *maceta* at him," you may ask: "What is a *maceta* used for, what does it serve for?" This will allow the witness to specify. If you ask the witness: "Do you mean *maceta* as flowerpot, or as mallet?", that might alert him as to which answer would best serve his case, something we must not do. Thus, a question as to the meaning of a word or phrase should be brief, and non-leading.

For a word at grand jury that the witness uses and cannot give a definition for, which the interpreter also does not know, the interpreter does not wish to provide an inaccurate rendition, lest the witness later be impeached through no fault of his own. Simply preserve the original word for the record, so that when the witness answers a question about what kind of a knife it was by saying "*Era una sevillana*," you may say "It was a *Sevillana* knife, S-E-V-I-L-L-A-N-A," spelling out the word "*Sevillana* " for the court reporter. You have preserved the witness' word for that knife, and he cannot be subsequently impeached on the basis of your ignorance. At trial the witness will repeat himself; the police may indicate that it was a gravity-blade knife.

There are some words whose various meanings you may know, but whose use by a witness needs further clarification. The word "*compadre*," for example, can mean friend, companion, buddy, colleague, or co-godfather. If a witness says "He was my *compadre*," you might leave "*compadre*" in the original and allow counsel to enquire further of the witness as to the precise relationship meant. Some witnesses have little verbal facility with what is supposed to be their own language, and find it difficult to provide synonyms. In any event, sometimes counsel should be allowed to clarify the meaning of a word that a witness has used.

Interpreting at Trial

In a formal proceeding such as grand jury, a hearing, a plea, or a trial, the interpreter should first be sworn by the clerk or judge to interpret faithfully and accurately to the best of her ability the words that are about to be spoken. At a deposition it is the court reporter who reads you the oath. The interpreter is given the oath before the witness is sworn. The oath may resemble the Short Oath in Appendix 4. If you are interpreting for a witness, the witness will then be sworn to tell the truth, the whole truth, and nothing but the truth.

All interpretation in legal settings takes place in the first person. What this means is that the interpreter should interpret the speakers' words in the first person: when counsel directs questions to witnesses, counsel should address his question to the witness directly, and not to the interpreter. Thus, counsel should say to the witness: "Did you see?" and not "Did he see?" The record needs to be in the first person in all proceedings. It may feel strange at first, when a male witness is asked about his day, for a woman interpreter to say: "I got up, I shaved my whiskers, and then I took out my pipe," etc., but you will get used to it, and so will the jury. If you personally need to ask a question or offer a clarification, refer to yourself in the third person: "The interpreter would like to ask if...." The "I" is reserved for the voice of the witness or other party.

For a defendant on trial who needs interpretation, most of the trial will be interpreted simultaneously. The interpreters may sit next to or close to the defendant, some may occasionally walk around to be close to the source of the sound. We have stated that at least two interpreters will be necessary to do simultaneous interpretation. We have also mentioned earlier that the interpreter must speak in a low voice so as not to mask the sound of the floor language.

Simultaneous interpretation is a big mystery to those who have not yet done it, yet for the professional interpreter, it is often easier and preferable to consecutive interpretation. To see if you have a knack for simultaneous, and to give yourself an idea of what is involved mentally, try a simple practice: turn on the radio or the television and simply repeat what the speaker is saying, as he says it, without changing a single word, in the same language that the speaker is using. This is called **shadowing** and can be a good introduction to simultaneous work. Notice the great amount of concentration you need to hear, listening to all that is said, to catch and repeat every word of it; this involves a very concentrated sort of listening. The next step is simultaneous interpretation where you repeat what the speaker says, with a lag of perhaps 3 to 4 words, now into your other working language, say Spanish. There you have it. You may wish to practice this with the television or the radio. The advantage of simultaneous is that no one has to wait for the interpretation, because it is done immediately. You create, when you do this, a process of transformation, and it is Professor Seleskovitch (2) who describes in detail how simultaneous interpretation is best done, and the considerations to keep in mind as you do it. Some writers put great emphasis on analysis and understanding of the message to be transmitted. Most of that concern is subsumed in this book under the notion of understanding the context and preparing for the case. Seleskovitch, however, has some general remarks on message analysis, and on the transformation of the idea rather than the words. As you progress in your work, you will find yourself more and more liberated from the actual words the speaker uses, more able to hew to the message or idea the speaker wishes to transmit. Professor Seleskovitch stresses the importance of not becoming enslaved by the actual words of the speaker. If you stick too close to the words you may lose the idea. As we move into good expression of the idea, we try to move into the cultural context of the target language. We cannot move too far there, but far enough to help the defendant locate himself, find his bearings. No two interpreters agree on how far to go. As you read Seleskovitch and try the process yourself, you will obtain a notion of how it is to be done. You may be fortunate enough to take a course in simultaneous interpretation, in which case your professors will provide some guidance.

Your best learning will come from your own work experience. When you return home from court, you will have notes to study and think about. As you meet more colleagues, you will have a chance to talk to them about choices they have made, and to observe their work. A good piece of simultaneous is a work of art that creates a feeling of physical exhilaration akin to good downhill skiing. Our goal is to work as artists every day.

On the witness stand, interpretation is generally **consecutive**. The interpreter waits until the witness has finished a phrase or two, perhaps take notes, and then interprets the statement. It may be necessary to ask the court to ask witnesses and attorneys to speak in short sentences, in sound-bites as it were. The process of consecutive interpretation differs from simultaneous, because you have to wait and depend on your notes or memory to transmit the whole message. This waiting means that consecutive may take twice as much time as simultaneous interpreting.

At the witness stand, place yourself so that both judge and jury can see the witness. When a witness gestures, do not imitate his gestures. If he says "The knife was this long," and gestures with his hand, you may say "The knife was this long" without the hand gestures. Or, when the witness says "I was grabbed here," pointing to his neck, you simply repeat his phrase and do not point to anything.

Attorneys do not always care for consecutive interpretation on the witness stand, because the necessary stops and starts throw them off their rhythm in direct and cross-examination. Also, they feel that the mere presence of the interpreter acts as a buffer, so that reactions are delayed, the witness is protected from fast verbal assault, and the jury cannot perceive the true essence of the witness.

Interpreters themselves may favor simultaneous interpretation at the witness stand. We do not like to interrupt witness speech, and we recognize that when the witness has to answer in short phrases, he may feel constrained and not say fully all that he had meant to say. Most uncomfortable for the interpreter is the notion that if he does consecutive on the witness stand, he may forget and thus not transmit an entire phrase or part of a phrase that the witness said. It is this missing of phrases that gives rise to attorney objections when there is interpreting from the witness stand. The interpreter's oath is to interpret fully and accurately all that is said. "Full" is sometimes lost in consecutive.

To overcome these problems, it is possible to do simultaneous from the witness stand, as well as from the defense table. In other words, one could do an entire trial simultaneously. The ability to do simultaneous from the witness stand means that the witness could provide a full, uninterrupted answer, and the interpreter could follow along and provide the full and faithful interpretation that he is sworn to do and prefers to do. Our colleague David Sperling reports that on a recent case in a family matter in D.C. Superior Court, a bench trial with no jury present, he was able to do everything including witness testimony simultaneously, much to the court's satisfaction. The court reporter was also enthusiastic about the method. Using portable wireless equipment, Mr. Sperling provided receivers and headsets to all parties, including the judge and the court reporter, and the Spanish-speaking witnesses were able to testify in an uninterrupted fashion, while Mr. Sperling did both questions and answers simultaneously. All of this was done on one channel. With the court's permission this could be done for a jury trial, if each juror were asked to use a headset when there is foreign language testimony.

On the witness stand, is is especially helpful to know beforehand what the witness might say, what the general drift of his remarks will be. If you have interpreted for the witness at grand jury, you will have an idea, or if you have been at the jail with him and his attorney, you will also know. Wise trial attorneys try to use the same interpreter for trial that they used at grand jury or at the jail, because then the story has the best chance of being fully and faithfully transmitted. If you are called to work a case at trial and have not previously interpreted for the witness at an earlier stage of the proceedings, you might ask the attorney involved if you may chat with the witness for a while, out of the hearing of the other side of the case. Some attorneys suggest this, and it is an offer that should be accepted. Naturally, whatever you hear you keep secret. As attorneys work with you and learn that you are to be trusted, they are more likely to be forthcoming and to suggest that you talk with the witness. Access depends on the confidence the attorney has in you, and on your general reputation for secrecy and confidentiality. Remember that there is the sensitive issue of whether or not the defendant himself will testify. The defense attorney may not wish to reveal his decision to the prosecutor until the defense has put on part of its own case, so if you learn from an attorney that his client will testify, this fact should be kept secret. The defense attorney will reveal it when and if he sees fit, and only he may reveal it. The same holds for prosecution witnesses, just who is to testify in the case-in-chief, and who is to testify at rebuttal, or at all.

Because an English-speaking witness on the stand hears attorney objections raised in open court, so too a non-English-speaking witness should have those objections interpreted to him simultaneously. When a judge wishes to go into the substance of objections out of the hearing of the jury, she may instruct counsel to "approach the bench." So that the jury not overhear the ensuing bench conference, she may turn on a machine that produces "white noise," or she may instruct members of the jury to talk amongst themselves. If you are at the witness stand with a witness during a bench conference, both you and the witness may be asked to step down for the duration of the conference, because even though the noise machine is on, the witness box is usually so close to the bench that one can still hear the bench conference. If you are at the defense table with the defendant, this time of the bench conference may simply represent a break for the interpreter who is "on." But it may not. In a recent case with six defendants, one attorney wanted the bench conference interpreted for her client. Using wireless interpreting equipment, the interpreter approached the bench with the attorneys and the court reporter, and was able to transmit what was said to the defendants, all of whom remained sitting in their usual places at the defense table. In most instances bench conferences are not interpreted, but if you use wireless equipment and a defense attorney requests interpretation, you may be asked to approach along with the attorneys and the court reporter. In theory, there is almost no part of a case that might not be subject to interpretation.

Comprehension

If the interpreter is well-prepared, she has a preliminary understanding of the case. She will understand the case better as evidence is presented. As we said earlier, if the interpreter understands the case, the defendant will understand it. Many defendants have not had much chance at formal education. Some may not be able to read or write in their own language, let alone in English. Their own legal systems differ from ours, and they may have little or no knowledge of those systems, less of ours. Some parts of a case, such as motions or jury instructions, can be difficult to interpret into another language, and there is a tendency on the part of some interpreters to say: "Who knows how much he really understands" of the defendant. One suspects that the interpreter does not understand, and thus cannot make it comprehensible to the defendant. The interpreter in question, Juan Zángano, may sit next to the defendant without interpreting everything. When asked why he is not interpreting a certain part of the proceedings, he will say that it is "not really important." It is not the interpreter's role to decide what is and is not important. The interpreter is to interpret everything, unless told otherwise by the judge.

When you do simultaneous for the defendant he must understand in such a way that he can aid in his own defense, and know what the witnesses against him are saying. When you interpret on the witness stand, the witness must understand in such a way that he can formulate answers to questions asked. All this understanding is predicated on the interpreter's ability to understand all of what is being said by all parties to a case. However, it is not our responsibility to make meaning clear when the source language is unclear. A reply of "Huh?" should be repeated as "Huh?" and will hopefully signal the speaker to come down a few notches.

The interpreter must understand each variety of Spanish that comes into the courtroom. It is this requirement that leads us to ask prosecutors and defense attorneys what country a witness is from, and one more reason why it is helpful to be able to speak with a witness before he testifies.

Judicial Checklist

A helpful checklist created by a judge at the Superior Court of the District of Columbia allows a judge to prepare mentally for an interpreted case.

Checklist for Establishing Ground Rules Prior to Trial
(Quoted by Permission)

1. Determine the need for an interpreter and the level of the linguistic skill in English of the party-witness.

2. Explain the role of the interpreter to the parties/witness.
    a) The interpreter is present to bridge a communication barrier.
    b) The interpreter is not a party and is not working for any of the parties, and is completely neutral.
    c) Interpreter cannot give legal advice, cannot provide other assistance, and cannot answer questions as to what is transpiring during the proceedings.
    d) If the witness and/or party does not understand the court interpreter, the judge should be informed.

3. Determine whether the party/witness requires a complete translation of everything said in the courtroom, including their testimony, or whether the party/witness will indicate to the interpreter when a translation is needed.

4. Determine whether the translation will be contemporaneous with the speaker [simultaneous interpretation], or whether the translation will be at appropriate breaks in the questions and responses [consecutive interpretation].

5. Reminder that short sentences facilitates the translation.

6. Discuss any linguistic difference which may affect the translation or create difficulties; e.g. double negatives for Spanish.

7. Remind everyone that the interpreter is to state only what is said, not add to the testimony or delete testimony or merely summarize.

8. Determine where interpreter is to sit if translating at counsel table and whether translation is to be audible.

9. Determine where interpreter is to stand if translating for witness on the stand.

10. Remind witness if on the stand that testimony is to the judge and/or jury and not the interpreter, that the witness cannot ask advice, talk to the interpreter or seek clarification from the interpreter, and that the interpreter cannot clarify questions or responses when the answer is non-responsive to the question.

11. Identify the interpreter to the jury. Swear in the interpreter in front of the jury. Explain the role of the interpreter to the jury.

12. At the end of each trial day or at the conclusion of testimony of a witness, put on record whether party/witness was satisfied with the services of the interpreter."

Author's Information for Judges

Before the interpreter can interpret, she must first hear and understand what counsel, the court, and witnesses are saying. We have some but not total control over our ability to hear and understand what is said. Hearing and comprehension improve with case preparation. We obviously comprehend technical and scientific words and names better when we know or believe they will be used, and have prepared for them. Physical hearing can be improved by our placement in the courtroom, sitting, standing or moving around, depending on the direction of the sound. If sitting we may also use an amplifier to pick up the sound.

Speed of speech, however, also affects our comprehension. First there is speech that is very fast which interpreters can interpret well, if they switch off every twenty minutes instead of every thirty, but which, when interpreted, will still be too fast for the defendant to understand.

A more serious situation is created by speed that is so great that the interpreter can neither understand nor interpret it fully. The interpreter's first step is to ask the judge to slow down, or to ask the judge to ask counsel to slow down. When the interpreter asks the judge to intervene, the judge becomes involved and has a stake in helping the interpreter do a better job. One may also approach the judge in chambers beforehand as well and ask him to speak at a reasonable pace and to have the lawyers do so also.

In certain circumstances an interpreter may request but receive no real cooperation from the court. This can happen when the judge speaks very quickly and cannot easily slow down his speech. Interpreters swear to fully and faithfully interpret all that is said, but if the speakers go too fast to be understood, even with the good preparation the interpreter has already done, then the interpretation will be neither full nor accurate. The real danger of excess speed is that it is possible to interpret half an hour of speech and still miss the real meaning and not transmit it to the defendant. This is the interpreter's worst nightmare, and the best argument for urging the court to impose a reasonable speed on the proceedings. It can happen especially in short matters such as plea bargains and short detention hearings. For the defendant understanding is crucial at such points. Judges and attorneys who speak too fast in interpreted cases invite and indeed compel less than total interpreter accuracy. On the other hand, the judge who wants to insure that the interpreting is indeed full and accurate, may do so by speaking and insisting that counsel speak at a speed that is reasonable.

Further Reading

1. Goffman, Erving. *The Presentation of the Self in Everyday Life*. New York: Doubleday, 1959.
   • An excellent discussion of life and work as a sort of theater or public perform-ance.

2. Seleskovitch, Danica. *Interpreting for International Conferences: Problems of Language and Communication*. Translated by Stephanie Dailey and E. Norman McMillan. Washington, D.C.: Pen and Booth, 1978. Available from: Pen and Booth, 1608 R St, N.W. Washington, D.C. 20009.
   • First cited in Chapter 1.

CHAPTER 5

The Rich Potential for Error

Question: How far were you standing from the car?
Answer: About three meters.
Interpreted answer: About three feet.

The courtroom can present fertile field for error. If we can identify categories and sources of error, we may be more aware of the dangers, and perhaps avoid some of them.

Errors that Originate with the Interpreter

Misunderstanding Context

If you misunderstand what is said in the source language, you may interpret it incorrectly into the target language. Depending on the context, a word may have opposite meanings. An attorney says: "When we were here last week, we pled...," which you take to mean pled guilty. The plea, however, was innocent. If a word comes up out of context, and the interpreter guesses at its meaning, the interpreter may guess wrong.

Misunderstanding Witness Speech

It is so simple to be wrong. In a setting where dogs were the main topic of discussion, a speaker said *yo traía unos peros*, which should have been rendered as "I had some doubts," or "I had some reservations." But what the interpreter heard was *yo traía unos perros*, "I was bringing along some dogs." Basically we have a one letter difference in one word: *pero* = doubt; *perro* = dog. All it takes to be wrong is to mishear one letter. In this case, the interpreter also assumed too much from context; after all they are talking about dogs, right?

The witness may mumble or speak in a slang or jargon that is very fast, or may stutter, or use a word one simply does not know. As mentioned earlier, one asks the witness to repeat, and then, if necessary and with permission of the judge, one may try to clarify that word with the witness. The interpreter may ask to speak to the witness beforehand, to obtain a sense of the person's speech patterns. It may take some time to make out what the witness is saying, especially if he stutters. This is best done before trial, and it is one reason why interpreters prefer to continue work on the same case, with the same people, when possible.

Incomplete Rendition of the Message

The interpreter must listen carefully to pick up the whole phrase. It is possible to fail to transmit some words into English without realizing one has dropped those words. The issue here is transmission of the entire message in consecutive interpreting. Counsel may call the error to your attention, and the answer itself may be repeated. Good trial preparation helps avoid this problem, good concentration on the stand, and having the witness stop every few sentences so that one can interpret the entire thought before it is lost.

Lack of Precision - Error of Meaning

There are many ways to be imprecise. Lack of precision could cover gross violations of meaning such as substituting "three feet" for "three meters," to details such as switching "this" for "that" (2).

Lack of Precision - Error of Register

Register has to do with the level of language, its degree of formality, elegance, or lack thereof. One always looks for the equivalent register in the target language. If a witness says *El señor venía hacía mí* [the gentlemen was coming toward me], he did not say "the guy," in which case it would have been *el tipo*, or *el cara*. Another example, if someone goes to jail, in Spanish, it is *la cárcel* . But if that person gets sent to the slammer, it is *la trena*. Neither is very pleasant, but jail is a more proper term, while slammer has a more vulgar tone to it, that is, a different register. Various registers might include the legal, the deliberately obscure, the academic, scientific, elegant, cultured, polite, low-rent, vulgar, and deliberately offensive. The interpreter needs to be able to identify the position of a given word in the register or spectrum of language. Because the court interpreter must be able to move freely up and down this spectrum or register in at least two languages, she must be both bilingual and bicultural. When the speaker uses a certain register, the interpreter must also use that register in the target language.

Condescension

Speakers may use speech in a deliberate effort to be polite, in which case that effort must also be reflected in the interpretation. Failure to take witness speech patterns seriously is condescension, seen most notably in the dropped honorific. If the witness says *Sí Señor*, [Yes Sir], and the interpreter only says "Yes," the interpreter has been inaccurate as well as condescending. Condescension is also revealed in how the interpreter says "you" in Spanish to the witness or defendant. Spanish has a formal way of addressing another person, so that "you" in this formal use is *Usted*. For children, animals, close friends, family members (though not always), and sometimes servants (depending on the family, the relation with the servant and so on), one may use the familiar *Tú*, or "thou." In Latin America, between people of the same age and station who do not know each other, one needs permission to use the word *Tú*. Thus, in court, witnesses and defendants are always the formal *Usted* to the interpreter. An exception may sometimes be made with child witnesses, if the child is more comfortable being addressed as *Tú*. Just because a witness has frayed cuffs and is a laborer, is no reason for the interpreter to call him *Tú*.

Errors that Counsel Help Create

Counsel and the court *should speak in the first person and address the witness directly*. Did you do, Did you see. Counsel should also use names and encourage the witness to do so, so that instead of hearing "when he told her," we hear "when Juan told María." *Use of names rather than pronouns in testimony* promotes clarity and avoids interpreter confusion as well as jury confusion.

Another creator of error is *the needlessly complicated question*. An attorney sometimes asks a complicated question to trap the witness. But the witness may become trapped in the coils of language, not mendacity. No matter what, the interpreter simply interprets all questions put to the witness, even though she knows some questions will cause confusion. If the witness does not understand, counsel will rephrase the question, or the judge will ask counsel to.

Negative constructions consistently cause special problems. In this next example, we have the use of a negative and a request that the witness think in *abstract terms*. In a burglary, where a stereo was taken, and the complaining witness has already appeared before a grand jury, the government asks at trial:

Q.   *"Did you not testify* before the grand jury that your stereo had been robbed on June 4th?"

A.   "Well, I was coming home from work, and the neighbors told me that my stereo had been robbed, and that stereo I had just gotten as a gift from my sister Amanda."

The question is as to prior testimony, but the witness, not used to thinking in abstractions, thinks the question is about the robbery of the stereo.

Another use of the negative is the question that begins with *"Is it not true that...."* It is true, or it is not true? When the witness says "yes," is he saying "yes" to the fact that something is true or is not true? By the same token, it would be helpful if counsel would avoid *"Did you not go* to the bar on Columbia Road on the night of September 5 ?" Why the "not"? Either the man went to the bar or he did not. Just ask him if he went. *Did you go.*

The Perils of Literal Interpretation

After an interpreter is sworn to fully and faithfully interpret all that is said at trial, the interpreter may hear:

The Court: Madame Interpreter, I want you to just interpret literally every-
              thing that is said.

While we want to provide a faithful rendition of the speech, we should not always be literal, because there are times when a literal interpretation is wrong. Different sorts of expressions provide different challenges. If we look at some categories of language we can be prepared for the problems that arise. Certain expressions are more susceptible of solution than others. If we examine their categories in order of ease of solution, we move from more established, orderly procedures to the more fluid or debatable. It is in such matters that colleagues often agree to disagree, and it is here that constant discussion with colleagues and others provides new solutions. Language mirrors thought, and different cultures think in different ways. Different cultures also have different institutions, such as legal systems that confuse matters.

Established Versions

For some problems, an answer is provided by tradition. For book and movie titles, someone has already done the work for you, there is an accepted version. When the FBI seizes a Spanish version of a writing by Lenin entitled *"Qué Hacer?"*, the correct English rendition is "What Is to Be Done?", because that is how the essay was translated into English, not the literal "What to Do." There is more time for research on document translation than for spoken interpretation. If you do not know the official translation, simply follow the original as closely as possible.

Idiomatic Expressions

Moving to more fluid territory, certain structures of language, while not equivalent as to construction, are known to mean certain things. To say "It was cold" in Spanish is *hacía frío*, [lit.: It made cold]. When a witness says *Hacía frío*, in answer to a question about the weather, it would be incorrect for the interpreter to say "It made cold." While literal, the rendition is wrong. Even the simple salutation *Buenos Días* [good morning] would be, if rendered literally, "Good Days" in English. These are called idiomatic expressions and represent the particular way something is expressed. Another example, from Spanish, *me duele el estómago*. "I have a stomach ache" would be rendered literally as "The stomach hurts to me". *Me duele la cabeza* "I have a headache," would be, in literal English, "the head hurts to me," and so on. Sometimes, while a literal translation might not be incomprehensible, it would be unnecessarily awkward. For example, while a New York store may "accept" VISA cards, a Spanish store will "admit" VISA cards.

Sometimes there is an expression for which there is a ready equivalent in English, but the interpreter wishes to keep the flavor of the original, to allow the original expression to shine through. The custom of keeping the flavor, and perhaps the word structure of the other language, is something that interpreters who are native speakers of English believe in more than non-native speakers. One does it only occasionally, lest one begin to sound like Hemingway's *For Whom the Bell Tolls* , or Robert Graves' stories of Mallorca (3). Keeping the flavor (being literal) can provide the jury a glimpse into another world, another way of thinking about things. Those who dislike the approach argue that one has not made the full transformation from one language to another that interpreting supposes. At other times when there is no ready equivalent in English, one will have to do a literal rendition which, while perhaps clumsy, will still be exact.

A classic danger in the Spanish language is the structure that deals with who did what. For example, *me robaron* [lit.: they robbed me] means "I was robbed." Even though the verb form in Spanish is plural, the expression does not necessarily go to the issue of how many robbers there were, it usually represents a passive construction in English. The interpreter who hears on the stand, *me robaron*, and says "They robbed me," may immediately hear from the defense attorney "Your Honor, they who? The witness is speaking of two robbers, surely the other robber is escaped, and my client is innocent. I move for a mistrial." The impersonal plural structure in expressions such as *Me robaron, le mataron, le arrestaron* should be interpreted "I was robbed," "he was killed," "he was arrested." Counsel will have to inquire further of the witness to determine who did the robbing, killing, or arresting, and how many robbers, killers, or arresting officers there were. Our colleague Myriam Sigler provides an example that shows what can happen: a witness talks to a policeman and says *Yo hablé con Juan y Pablo y me dijeron que habían matado a Ramón* . Properly translated, this would be "I talked with Juan and Pablo and they told me Ramón had been killed," but at the time it was interpreted as "I talked with Juan and Pablo and they told me that *they* had killed Ramón." The language lends itself to both meanings, and in this case it was the first, Ramón has been killed, that the speaker intended, but it was understood in the second sense.

Another classic danger, as Frank Almeida of Los Angeles has pointed out, is the "no" in Spanish that really means "well, ah," often used as a sort of verbal crutch at the beginning of a sentence. An associated peril is the expression *como no* , which means "of course," or "naturally." With both these expressions, if the court hears a "no" in Spanish but does not hear a "no" in English, it may believe that there has been a misinterpretation, where there may not have been.

False Friends

Other dangers await in false cognates or what the French call "false friends."
A false friend is a word that appears to mean the same thing in both English
and Spanish, but the meanings can be different or the usage reversed. For
example, when an attorney says to a witness "Did you discuss," it is best to
use *conversar* or some verb like it because if you say *discutir* in Spanish, the
first and most common meaning of *discutir* is "argue." If the witness then
answers with *Sí, discutimos*, you are not sure if he is saying "Yes, we
discussed," or "Yes, we argued."

Differing Legal Systems

Spain and Latin America, for example, do not have the grand jury tradition,
neither do they have trial by a jury of ones peers for most cases. Trial is
usually by one judge or by a panel of judges. Further, they do not have all the
constitutional, evidentiary protections that we have. Thus, when we must
refer to grand jury, probation, parole or a plea bargain, we need to use
language that, at least for Spanish, is an artificial construct, because the
concepts do not originate in Spanish-speaking lands. Interpreters continue to
argue over which words best express certain U.S. legal terms.

   Even if you and your colleagues have come up with a wonderful term,
there is no guarantee that the defendant will understand it. A good expression
for grand jury, suggested by Chandler Thompson of New Mexico, is *jurado
superior de instrucción* . You may use this term, but you may wish to tell the
defendant that for the purposes of this case you will be calling it *gran jurado*,
which *El País* of Madrid (March 2, 1991) has used in citing a newsworthy
case pending in a U.S. court. The use of the word *instrucción* in the long
expression reminds the defendant that accusation is part of its function. The
defendant may have heard the expression *gran jurado* out on the street, or in
jail from compatriots.

The Horse in the Sewing Basket

Homilies or little wise sayings are not always equivalent between languages
or cultures; sometimes they simply do not exist in the other language or
culture. Spanish has the wonderful saying *Cura nuevo, santos en danza,*

literally, "A new priest, the saints will dance." When a new priest comes to a parish, the little statues of the saints will be moved to different alcoves in the church, and the ladies who head the altar guild may be changed from their positions, and there will be general uproar in the church for a while. Close to that we have in English "A new broom sweeps clean," but that has the image of sweeping things out, especially corrupt political hacks, whereas the Spanish implies a moving around of what is already there, the displacement of petty satraps.

We say in English, for example, "to call a spade a spade," while in Spanish it is "to call bread bread, and wine wine" [*llamar al pan, pan, y al vino, vino*]. Another way of saying this in Spanish is "to speak without hairs on the tongue" [*hablar sin pelos en la lengua*], which means not to mince words, to speak clearly, since you are not picking those hairs out of your mouth, should you have just chomped down on a little furry animal.

In court a prosecutor may say that the defendant "wants to have his cake and eat it too." In Spain this becomes *querer el oro y el moro* [lit.: to want the Moor and the gold], an impossibility because the Moorish pirate who once roamed the Spanish coasts would defend to the death his booty or gold, so it had to be one or the other. In Argentina that same defendant might be accused of wanting to have *la chancha y los veinte chanchitos* [lit.: the mother pig and her twenty little piglets], which she should presumably defend to the death. In Argentine terms if what one wants is beyond all bounds of imagination, then one also wants the machine to make sausages with.

The danger of using an appropriate rendition of a little saying in the target language is that the speaker may continue with the image in the source language. For example: "The grass is always greener in the neighbor's yard," in Spanish can be *La cabra de mi vecina más leche da que la mía* [lit.: my neighbor's goat gives more milk than mine does], or *la gallina de mi vecina más huevos pone que la mía* [lit.: my neighbor's hen lays more eggs than mine]. Now you have the possibility of grass, on the one hand, and goats, milk, chickens, and eggs on the other. If the speaker continues with the grass, or the eggs, or the milk, and those elements have not been interpreted into the target language, the interpreter is in trouble and the listeners in confusion. Sayings may have the history of a nation and a culture behind them. We say here "It's as easy as falling off a horse." No self-respecting Spaniard with any historical sense would admit to ease in falling off a horse, the very notion is scandalous. When Spaniards find something very easy, for them it is *tan fácil como cantar y coser* [lit.: as easy as singing and sewing]. Such expressions and little sayings are traps that cause the listener to ask just how the horse got into the sewing basket.

Embarrassments in Interpreting

We said earlier that the interpreter must keep out of the case, and that our only concerns are language and meaning. There are times when something is said that will be embarrassing to interpret, but it must be interpreted nevertheless. One category is rudeness to the judge. Mr. Atracabancos, a defendant in an armed robbery, when asked if he has anything to say before the court pronounces sentence, says to the judge: "It may be that you are unfamiliar with the laws of the United States, it may even be illegal to sentence a foreigner to so much jail time." This is rude, it will not help the defendant, and you wonder if the judge, following an old custom of the kings as to messengers who brought bad news, might not say: "Fill her mouth with sand." But, you have no part in the case, and you simply interpret what is said. The emotions that have to be ignored are fear at any anger the judge might feel toward the interpreter, and disbelief that a defendant would gratuitously say something so against his own interest.

Another message one would rather not interpret is a statement that will take someone back to where he does not want to be. For example, on a mental health hearing, where a young man is trying to get out of a mental hospital, he has answered his own attorney's questions well, but the Corporation Counsel says to him: "Do you hear voices?" And the witness says: "Well, no. But I like to go to the horror movies, and after the movies, the vampires come out at me." You know that the young man is going back to the hospital, you know he does not want to go, and you also know that you have to repeat what he said about the vampires without changing one jot or tittle of it.

The last and most common is vulgarity. One hesitates to repeat vulgarity in interpretation because people will think one is not a real lady. Again, what the interpreter thinks or feels is irrelevant, even more irrelevant is what the interpreter thinks others might think of her. Plunge in. Vulgarisms are interesting. What is vulgar varies by culture: what is offensive in one language and culture may be much less so in another. The Spanish culture, for example, believes that the honor of a husband resides in the wife's chastity, so to call a man *cabrón*, [lit: large goat] means that his wife is making a cuckold of him, possibly with his consent. The term *cabrón* in Spanish is a knife-pulling term. To suggest that a man has improper relations with his mother might achieve the same result in English. Indeed, for crimes of violence it is often one insulting word that proves the final straw, resulting in a deep slash to the abdomen, emergency surgery at George Washington University Hospital, and charges of assault with intent to kill, possession of a prohibited weapon, knife, and so on.

The interpreter has choices: she may provide an equally offensive term in English; she may stick with a literal rendition of the original; or she may prefer to repeat the original Spanish word, and allow the attorneys to ask the witness what that word means to the witness. Attorneys working on a case where an insult starts a fight or escalates it do well to ask their witnesses about such terms. If that term has little impact in English but is horribly offensive in the source language, the attorney may wish to ask the witness about the word and its impact in the witness' own culture. It pays to study such words and have them ready. You will be surprised at how often it may be necessary to interpret such words from the witness stand. Don't be embarrassed, just be ready. Being ready means you have to focus on the problem, that is, the nature of the case. When you walk into a courtroom where two men are on trial for having wished, according to the prosecution, to solicit a supposed prostitute, unless you are thinking deeply about prostitution, you may believe you have heard a new English word and jump up saying "What? Will counsel please repeat what he has just said." When counsel repeats, it will become clear what *sokanfok* was. No matter what solution you chose, the rule is always the utmost precision, with no thoughts of looking like a lady, or a gentleman, should it come to that. What a speaker says is his problem: the interpreter is simply a conduit.

Regional Expressions

Regional speech can vary. There are variations in accent as well as vocabulary. Some words have different meanings in different places, and many Latin American jokes depend on horrified reactions to a word that is innocent in one place but shocking in another. In Spain, for example, the word *coger* means to take, take the bus, take the package, etc. But in Argentina, *coger* is a copulative verb, as is *tumbar* [lit: to bring down, to cause to fall] in Peru, and *comer* [lit: to eat] in Cuba. In the Caribbean it is held to be very vulgar to speak the names of certain fruits. When one must speak of them, they must be referred to in another fashion than the immediately obvious one, lest one inadvertently refer to specific male or female anatomy.

Certain phrases may derive from local custom or events. In Argentina, some years ago, a political candidate, when asked if he would do something that he was very much against, said *ni ebrio ni dormido*, literally, "neither drunk nor asleep," which might be somewhat equivalent to "not if you paid me." In Cuba, according to Tony Rivas of Miami, to say someone *quedó en la página dos*, literally, "ended up on page two," means that he died, was killed, was fired from a job, or had some other grave misfortune. Apparently the expression derives from a newspaper in Havana that used to print the most sanguinary news from the police blotter on page two.

As a general rule, the Spanish one speaks in court should be a standard Spanish that will be comprehensible to all Spanish-speaking listeners. We should know the slang and regionalisms, but we should try to avoid using them, unless the witness uses them first. For example, if you have a fork-lift that must be mentioned, while the word *pato* [lit: duck] may be understood in Peru as a fork-lift, it is prudent to use a more generally-understood term, such as *grúa horquilla*, or *montacargas*. If you say *pato* to someone from the Dominican Republic, he may not take it to mean "duck" or "fork-lift," but rather "homosexual." Colleagues tell me that the same word *pato* means a womanizer in Panama. Of course your witness may simply say *folif*, in which case you may ask if he means *montacargas*, which he does. The great variety in regional terms is especially notable in words for certain parts of the body (the genitalia especially), states of drunkenness and their sequelae, machinery, clothing, foods, plants, and animals. They should all to be watched carefully because they have a proclivity to create confusion.

Within a country you have also the language of the different social groups, which may include different generations or trade groups. Jail slang and criminal slang is always changing, in part because certain groups want to disguise the meaning of their speech from the police. In Spain, in the street ten years ago, hashish was *chocolate*, and a small dealer was the *camello* [lit: camel]. After a while, when too many people know what it means when "the camel is bringing in a load of chocolate," the slang will change. For English you may remember Nancy Mitford's work on U (upper class) and Non-U ways of speaking (1). The magazine *Cosmopolitan*, which tries to polish girls moving to the big city, occasionally tells us how we should speak English so as not to be seen to belong to the lower orders. According to *Cosmo*, "sofa" is preferable to "divan," and "curtains" to "drapes," so they had better not catch you sitting on the divan sewing drapes when they come to see if your English is up to snuff so you can get a nice typing job in New York. Some time ago *New York Times* columnist Russell Baker applied to join the Beautiful People (BP), for which he was turned down, partially because of the presence of a scruffy grey cat. Well, it turns out that the Argentines had their own brand of Beautiful People, *la gente como uno* (*La GCU*) [lit.: people like us], a very flattering concept. As life in one country comes to resemble that in another, we may see greater linguistic approximations.

Anglicisms

As to interpreter use of slang and what the purists call barbarisms, which include Anglicisms, the rule is that the interpreter should not start it. We especially see this problem with words adapted from English. In Washington, D.C., for example, many Salvadoreans have adopted certain English words that they use among themselves and are comfortable with. When counsel asks "Were you in the basement when the robbery took place?", the interpreter will ask if the witness was in the *sótano*, the proper word for basement. The answer can look like this: *Sí, yo estaba en el **basemeng**, tomando un **sis-pac**, cuando vino **la manaja**. Ella dijo que le habían **jolopeado** con un **shogún**.* [Yes, I was in the basement, having a six-pack, when the lady manager arrived. She said that she had been held up with a shotgun.] The more correct way to say this might be: *Sí, yo estaba en el sótano, tomando unas cuantas cervezas, cuando vino la administradora, y dijo que le habían atracado con una escopeta.*

   If the witness is more comfortable with certain slang expression or Anglicism, if he uses the word first, then the interpreter may feel free to use it, providing that both interpreter and witness agree as to its meaning. *El basemeng* is fairly clear in Washington, D.C., as is *el bílding* for apartment building [instead of *el edificio*], *el lobby* [instead of *la recepción*], *el güelfare* for welfare [instead of *asistencia pública*]. Adoption of English loan-words will depend on where a person lives in the U.S., how long he has been here, where he comes from, and his educational level. Someone newly arrived in the U.S. may have no English at all, though he will quickly pick up basic survival words from his compatriots.

Spanish-speakers working in construction in the United States use a good many U.S. construction terms in their Spanish vocabulary. The bottom line is that the interpreter will not always hear Spanish on the witness stand and must be ready for non-Spanish words. María Elena Cárdenas recounts the following experience on the witness stand in Miami:

Attorney:	What is your occupation?
Witness:	Yo soy **güeldo**.
Interpreter	¿Cómo?
Witness:	Yo soy güeldo, usted sabe, Señora, soldador.

Here, the witness, upon being asked his occupation, has said *güeldo*, in an attempt to approximate the English "welder," which in Spanish would be *soldador*, the word he finally provides the interpreter. Thus, the interpreter must be ready for the *güeldo* working in the *bílding*, when she was expecting a *soldador* in the *edifício* . In a recent case, when a witness was asked at what speed he had been driving a backhoe [*retroexcavador*], he said that he had been driving the *bekko* slowly. The adaptations of Spanish to English, or any other language to English, represent an entire field of study. There is Miami Cuban Spanish, and there are varieties of Spanish on the West Coast that interpreters there need to be familiar with. Indeed, along the Mexican border there is said to be a third language that itself requires study and experience to use and understand well.

In a recent case in U.S. District Court in Washington, D.C., a Spanish-speaking witness decided to represent himself, and took the opportunity to address the judge on motions. The interpreters working the case noticed that the defendant, who was spending his time in jail studying the law, introduced a number of English legal terms into his Spanish discourse.

Words seem to go into Spanish faster from English, and adhere more to their English forms in Latin America than in Spain. Spain has distance: they have the purity of the language to uphold, and they have relatively few immigrants going back and forth. All the cousins from the same village do not spend six months a year in West Virginia picking apples, subsequently returning home loaded with refrigerators and corrupt U.S. expressions. For example, if someone says "I'll call you back," you may hear a Latin American speaker use the Anglicized or literal expression *te llamo p'atrás* , instead of the more correct *te volveré a llamar* , which a Spaniard might use. Marvellous things can happen with language: new words can be mine-traps in the courtroom, unless it is established just what a person means when he is using them.

When an interpreter stops to ask a witness about a word, it is perhaps such a new word or Anglicism he is asking about, to make sure how the witness understands it. Judges do not like interpreters to stop and ask questions, but it is better to be precise than to accede to the pressure of time and hurry that often pervade a case. All of this, mind you, assumes preparation on the part of the interpreter. Even though we do prepare, there are always words, terms, or situations that one can not predict.

Further Reading

1. Mitford, Nancy, Ed. *Noblesse Oblige: An Enquiry into the Identifiable Characteristics of the English Aristocracy.* New York: Harper & Brothers Publishing, 1956.

2. Berk-Seligson, Susan. *The Bilingual Courtroom: Court Interpreters in the Judicial Process.* Chicago: The University of Chicago Press, 1990.
   • The author, associate professor of Spanish at the University of Pittsburgh, recorded the work of certain court interpreters and describes some interpreter errors in the courtroom. Her thesis is that the interpreter can have an unwonted impact on language and on the jury's perception of the witness.
   Berk-Seligson suggests that the judicial system would prefer that the interpreter be invisible and transparent with no impact at all on the process, other than doing the job at hand. In Appendix 2 of this book you will see comments by Judge Pollack as to why the federal test was originally needed. Berk-Seligson suggests that even after the federal certification exam is in place (she listened to both certified and uncertified interpreters), the earlier concerns of judges and others are still valid.

3. Graves, Robert. *Collected Short Stories.* New York: Viking Penguin Inc., 1971.
   • The short stories set in Mallorca provide literal renditions of Spanish speech into English that show what can happen when the full linguistic transformation is not made, a fine example of "keeping the flavor."

CHAPTER 6

Translation of Legal Documents

In translation as in interpretation the purpose of the communication is paramount. With verbal interpretation the audience and speaker are presumably there, you know the setting, you know if it is a plea, a trial, or a status hearing, and therefore have an idea of the purpose. Setting, purpose, and context will indicate how a communication is to be cast.

Sight Translation

A sight translation somewhat resembles simultaneous interpretation with the text present before you. For sight translation, you are asked to translate aloud into another language a text that is physically present in your hand. When you are given such a document in the courtroom ask the judge for a moment to read it over before starting to read it aloud in English, which would be the sight translation. A silent reading first enables you to become familiar with some of the handwriting and stylistic vagaries of the writer, as well as the matter in question.

Sometimes as you work on a case you can see one of these things coming at you. Mr. Metemanos had been accused of striking an employee and attempting to feel her up. Halfway through his trial he disappeared (he had been free on personal recognizance), but the trial continued. He was acquitted of all charges except misdemeanor assault. But because the original case had been a felony, his subsequent failure to appear, which constituted another offense, could get him 5 years in jail and/or a fine of $5,000. Mr. Metemanos now re-appears, "voluntarily" turning himself in, in the words of his attorney. His excuse is that his mother was sick and he had to return suddenly to his country without informing the court or his attorney. It gradually becomes clear that he has a letter, yes, a letter said to be written by the doctor who treated his mother. The interpreter who is interpreting this explanation finally hears "why don't we ask the court interpreter to translate this letter." Generally a document to be presented in court in a foreign language is presented along with a full written translation, but it was not to be. The interpreter was handed a grimy note on what looked to be a large prescription form, in handwriting of the sort not associated with an educated person.

Had a full written translation been made, the translator would have translated the letterhead as well as the body of the letter. The challenge here was to provide, verbally, a spoken or sight translation as close as possible to what a full written translation would have been. The interpreter began by describing the visual aspects of the document: a printed letterhead followed by handwritten text. The letterhead said "Dr. Raúl Pierdepapeles, Doctor of Medicine with studies in Mexico at the clinic of Dr. Juan Famoso. Specialties: pediatrics, dermatology, and pediatric dermatology." The body of the letter then said that Mr. Eufebio Metemanos (the defendant) had been obliged to come home to take care of his mother, whom Dr. Pierdepapeles was treating for pneumonia. After the sight-translation of the letter, the prosecutor said: "How is it that Dr. Pierdepapeles, a pediatrician and dermatologist, is treating an adult for pneumonia?"

While just about any document may require sight translation, the documents most likely to appear in criminal court requiring sight translation include: the plea-bargain agreement, conditions of release, a stay-away order, a civil protection order, a pre-sentence report, letters in aid of sentencing, indictment, and parts of jury instructions.

The pre-sentence report recounts what the defendant told the pre-sentence writer, the government's version of events, the report writer's recommendations and impressions, and remarks on possible sentencing. If you have interpreted the pre-sentence interview, you may be familiar with most of what is in the report. An interpreter may be asked to sight translate that report to the defendant in the cell-block a few minutes before sentencing.

Letters in aid of sentencing are often hand-written; they may be written by friends of the defendant who are semi-literate and thus will make certain spelling and grammatical errors. These friends may be effusive. If the "friends" are people of authority and position, their prose may be more restrained. The court will learn from such letters just why the man who arrived on the bus from New York carrying 270 rocks of cocaine is such a great family man and why he ought to be spared the over-long concern of the Bureau of Prisons.

When a document appears frequently such as a waiver of trial by jury in the case of a plea agreement, ask if the court has already prepared that document in Spanish. If it has not, you may want to make your own written translation to use when required, so that you do not have to constantly reinvent the wheel.

Written Translation

A variety of documents may require written translation. The court itself may have some standard forms or orders that it wants translated into Spanish for permanent use, such as conditions of probation, waiver of trial by jury, and stay-away order forms. These documents may arrive printed or typed, and the English may be fairly decent.

Or there may be correspondence from the court to a defendant or other party, which would also be well written and legible. Both sorts of documents would be in typed or printed form, and both written by people with some level of schooling.

Then there may be letters from a defendant to a judge, often written by hand and with less than perfect spelling and grammar. This same defendant may have his friends send letters in aid of sentencing to the judge, which the judge would like translated. A defendant may write out a long statement by hand with a view to exonerating himself or a co-defendant. Again, the handwriting may be poor and the grammar and spelling imperfect.

Civil cases may have a great deal of documentation, most of it typed and some of it reasonably written, though some documents are blurry copies made from messy originals. You may also be asked to translate set pieces such as birth certificates, death certificates, marriage and divorce papers, and police reports from other countries in child custody and other cases.

The ideal document comes to you typed double-spaced. Double spacing is easier on the eye and makes it easier to keep your place when translating. Usually, however, documents we receive for translation are single-spaced. It is preferable for us to produce all material double-spaced, because it makes it easier for the client to read, but the client may prefer that one follow the original single-spacing, in which case do so. For your own purposes, when you are preparing a translation, it is best to set up the document double space. This will enable you to make corrections more easily, and for the final draft you can convert it back to single space if necessary.

Written translation is quite different from sight translation. The document that requires a written translation may have been written long ago and far away, with the original writers unavailable to indicate what they really meant, so any answers we can get must come from the people who hand us the document. Try to establish who prepared it and why, and who now wants it translated and for what purpose. Each document may have at least two purposes; the one for which it was originally intended, and the use to which it is now about to be put. When a defendant writes a judge from the jail: "Your Honor, I killed him because he was messing with my wife," the intent of the writer is to justify his action in the context of his own cultural mores that he assumes the judge shares. The judge may ask for a written translation. If the government has examined the court file where this letter resides, it may wish to present the letter as incriminating evidence. If the defense has looked at the court jacket and seen the letter, it will move to keep the letter out of the case. Barring that, it may try to assert, through expert testimony, that the handwriting is not that of the defendant in question.

Civil cases may generate more documents for translation than criminal ones. For this reason, document management becomes a consideration. A law firm may suddenly find that it needs 1,000 pages translated from Friday to Tuesday. Our colleague Stewart Colten says that this happens because a firm suddenly receives a large number of documents as the result of a discovery demand, which the other side naturally hands in as late as possible before trial. For such a project no one at the firm may be available to answer questions about the case or even the documents. You are dealing with junior associates who themselves may be in the dark about their project. The more people who work on a project, the more time it will take to complete. For a series of documents, one will want to decide which words will be used, especially technical words. One large document may be split into sections and the sections assigned to different individuals, or sets of shorter documents may be given to different translators. If a translator works as part of a group, the lead translator (perhaps the one who has the contract for the work), may call all the translators together and determine matters of style, format, and vocabulary, to provide consistency throughout the document. The chief translator may wish to serve as editor, or what at international conferences is called reviewer, to correct the translations and insure uniformity of style and presentation. Both translator and editor are concerned with timeliness and product quality.

Provide the client a careful estimate of the time a translation will take, and build into the estimate extra time for unforeseen emergencies, such as the printer breaking down or extra research time for mystery words.

Meaning and Understanding

While both civil and criminal cases have certain elements of predictability, the interpreter who works a lot of criminal cases will usually understand at the outset what sort of a case a "three-nickle bag case" (of marijuana) will be, what kind of case "assault with intent to kill" will be, and so on. Civil cases, covering as they may the entire spectrum of business and civil life, can be highly unpredictable. For example, one side may be looking at internal correspondence of an agency or agencies, or of a company, to see how conscious a group was of doing something that the plaintiff feels they should not have been doing.

After the translator has studied the background documents on the case, and before beginning the translation, he should read the entire text through, perhaps more than once. A full reading helps see where a document is going, identify its purpose, and reveals words or terms that will need to be researched. Some colleagues believe that one should understand the entire document before beginning a written translation. This is a novel idea, somewhat akin to preparing an outline for a school paper before actually writing the paper. More power to you if you can do it. I personally find that only at the end of the translation do I really understand the whole thing. Reading the document two or three times will give you at least a feeling for the chunks or parts of the document. During the reading of the document, make a list of words you are not sure of, and list also words that recur frequently, even if you think you know what they mean. I remember one legal translation from Portuguese where one word that was used copiously had eight different meanings in English, depending on the context. Some words may be so arcane or regional that one may wish to turn to the attorneys involved, or specialists working with those attorneys, to clarify their meaning. On a large document, the first ten or twenty pages of the document may contain most of the technical terms that you will need for the entire document. Translators believe that a large document is easier to handle than a small one, because once one has the words, one can move with some dispatch through the remainder. Contrariwise, a short text may require relatively more research, whose immediate usefulness then ends after the ten total pages of the document have been translated.

When a translator wishes to speak with the engineer involved, for example, he may be told that the engineer is out of the country for two weeks, while the deadline for the translation is one week away. The responsibility for discovering what is happening, that is, the meaning of words and ideas in a document, belongs to the translator, which is one reason why broad, general reading on all topics is so helpful. It may happen that the original is not very well written. This "not very well written" can cover a multitude of sins. Lack of clarity creates the most trouble. For textual ambiguities, when no one in the originating office can clear up the confusion, we do what we do in interpretation: where the original is ambiguous, the rendition into the target language should be equally ambiguous.

If you have mystery words that are not in your dictionaries or in any source available to you, you may find words close to the meaning, in which case you may provide those possible meanings in brackets. The translator is hired to provide answers, but where we cannot provide the right answer, we owe our clients our best guess as to the possibilities. A mystery word should be retained in italics, and possibilities suggested, if you have them: *mystery word* [might mean: _____, _____, or _____].

Parts That Are Already Done

Extradition requests may begin by quoting paragraphs from the extradition treaty between the two nations involved. Where there is an official treaty translation it must always be used. The translator asks the person who gave her the work to provide her with a copy of the treaty in both languages concerned, and then simply copies the language of the official translation in the appropriate places.

A similar rule applies to quotations of classical matter. As to quotes from the Bible, go to the Bible in the target language, and quote from the appropriate spot. Some classical works such as Cervantes, Shakespeare, Proust, Tolstoy, have already been translated by literary translators, in which case quote those translations and cite in a footnote which translation you are using. If you quote from books that have not yet been translated, or if you dislike the translations already available, make your own, and indicate in a footnote that they are yours.

Fidelity

Fidelity to the text and to the original meaning is what we want. Just as we keep out of the case for spoken interpretation, so too we keep out of the case for written matters. This means not "improving" the level of a text. Stick as close as possible to original grammar, style, and register. There are times when one must use an awkward English to adhere to the original meaning. The preservation of meaning and register is paramount. Remember especially that any "errors" in the original, be they typographical errors, missing punctuation, or apparent illogic, must be preserved in the translation.

This being said, it is possible to be annoyingly faithful to an original text. If the original text is strewn with spelling and punctuation errors, you may wish to punctuate the document correctly to help make it more understandable. You may prefer not to create equivalent mistakes in English lest further confusion result. When you make editorial "improvements," you should preface the translation with a Translator's Note in brackets saying that you have introduced punctuation to make the document easier to read and you have not sought to replicate spelling errors in the original. Whenever you depart from the original, mention this in a note and provide a reason. This will let the reader know what you are doing and avoid needless attacks by attorneys for the other side. At the same time, some errors may be important, so before deciding what to do, consult with the attorney who assigned you the translation.

Just about any document can be litigated. So too, any translation of any document can be litigated. If a law office calls you and says that they want you to translate a document "just for information purposes," do not believe them. They think it is just for information purposes, but you know it could be litigated, that is, your translation could be subject to dispute. This means that every document that crosses your desk should be translated to the best of your ability. Check everything, because a year from the time you translate the document you do not want to see some expert witness for the other side whispering in the ear of an attorney about the poor quality of your written work. Make it good work, always.

Style and Format

The form in which the document is presented is important. Those who say that it is only the idea that counts, that the form on the page is of no importance, reveal thoughtlessness for the potential audience. Much as a writer must make an effort to be accessible to the public, so too a translator must make special efforts to present a clear piece of work that is readily understandable. Format has a great deal to do with clarity on the page.

The client may want the translation to follow the original format, in which case this is what one does. Some writers tend to write in short paragraphs labeled with many numbers and letters. Other writers favor lists, or half-lines:

- to make a point;
- because they assume their readers are none too sharp;
- and because that is the way it has been done from time immemorial.

The formatting of such documents is time-consuming, and the proof-reading laborious.

Certain agencies may have their own style preferences that may be expressed in a written style sheet or book. While style may deal with questions of format, it usually concerns editorial conventions such as the placement of commas, preferences for the use of which or that, capitalization, use of numbers, placement of titles and page numbers. A translator should ask if there is a style sheet, if she is expected to use it, and if she may have a copy of it. General sources of style for English writing include *A Manual of Style* (University of Chicago) (10), and the *U.S. Government Printing Office Style Manual* (13). These have full discussions of proper citation form for footnotes, bibliographies, legal citations, capitalization, how titles of various works are to be presented, as well as helpful ideas for the editorial management of large documents. Both books are worth reading at leisure, and you may refer to them when you have a specific question on proper English editorial style. For Spanish I would suggest Mario Llerena's *Un Manual de Estilo* (9).

You will need to make up some rules, because no style sheet or book will cover all situations, and none may exactly suit your needs. The goal on any document is to be consistent. Having your own standard style sheet, several pages of instructions to yourself, saves time because you do not constantly have to decide the same issue over and over again. Furthermore, when you manage a project where you use subcontractors, you have a document you can modify for the occasion, so that all team members know what is required stylistically, and save you editorial time.

Just as everything in speaking is transmitted, so too in writing. What this means for a legal document is that everything on the original page should be on your translated page. This includes letterheads, logos, time stamps, signatures, underlining, and other marks. What is not translated is described. For example, you may write:

> [Logo: picture of cactus
> on which a bird appears
> clutching a snake;
> (wording)]
> United Mexican States, Ministry of Agriculture.

As part of everything on the page, attend carefully to the use of UPPER CASE and lower case in the original document. Despite the dictates of good English style, you may wish to preserve the use of upper case words in your translation. In olden times writers used to speak about NATURE and SOCIETY and had a point to make with the capitalization. In our days we may see NAMES written in upper case and it may be helpful to put names in upper case in documents with many names.

Some translators add footnotes. The footnote is a mess to type and to read; it distracts the eye of the reader from his place on the page. Try, when possible, to include your own remarks in brackets within the text, and make those remarks brief, a phrase or a few words. If the remark requires several sentences, then you may prefer to use a footnote. For a matter that will reappear in a text, it is possible to create a note in brackets near the top of the page at the beginning of the text.

For administrative law, agency law, and international activities, a text may come littered with "alphabet soup," that is, acronyms or abbreviations of the initials of various agencies. Such initials may refer to the UN, WHO, FAO or their dependent agencies, or country agencies such as OMB, OSHA and the like. Certain international agencies publish glossaries that provide the abbreviated symbols in the working languages of those agencies. When one deals with the abbreviations for specific governmental agencies in one country, what one does with it depends on what one is given. If one has the initials or acronym, say, GR, one must find and provide the full Spanish, Guardia Republicana, and then the full English, Republican Guard, so that the translated text, at the first reference to that institution, would give the initials, then the full Spanish expression, and then the English translation in brackets. After that, the translator may continue to refer to that institution by its Spanish initials. With national governmental bodies, if the text uses a lot of initials, retain those original initials and do not use target language acronyms unless an internationally-accepted acronym exists.

Some medical and technical abbreviations can be tricky, because if there is a medical text in Spanish, you may have either an abbreviation of Spanish words, or perhaps an English abbreviation that has been accepted in the Spanish medical literature. You may see C.A.T. for computerized axial tomography, or perhaps T.A.C., which would be the Spanish abbreviated. Now that the English has shortened the abbreviation further to CT, one would have to see what the Spanish has done. English abbreviations or acronyms are now common in foreign-language texts.

When a document mentions legislation, provide the name of a law in the source language, then, in brackets, a translation of it in the target language. At some point someone may want to go back to the law in the original country, and if we include the original title of a law along with the translation, the client can avoid being the victim of an inaccurate backtranslation in the future. Often laws have numbers, and some countries have different kinds of laws, so that a Decree-Law is different from an Executive Order, for example. If "Decree-Law" [*Decreto-Ley*] is repeated frequently in a text, indicate in brackets [hereinafter cited as D.L.] so that it will not be necessary to spell out the word for the rest of the text, assuming that the source language text does not spell it out. If the source language text spells it out, the translator may also, unless you have instructions to the contrary.

Correct editorial usage in English holds that *foreign language terms are to be rendered in italics* . If the target language is English, check to see if the dictionary provides the word in italics or in English that is not italicized. If the English is not italicized, this means that the foreign word has come to be part of accepted English, and is no longer regarded, at least editorially, as foreign, such as "patio." Other languages may use italics to indicate foreign words, or sometimes use quotation marks. This will depend on standards of good style in whatever your target language is.

A foreign word whose meaning you cannot find is simply to be left in that language, in italics, with suggested meanings in brackets in the target language. People working with a reviewer or editor will want to alert the editor to such words, because the editor may know those words or know how to find them. Some editors provide the technical words they want you to use; they may have researched the vocabulary before assigning you the text. Some international bodies have a person called a **terminologist**, whose function is to find and record new and difficult words in a variety of languages, and to be available for consultation to translators in that agency. If the translation is simply between you and the client, call the client because she or someone in her office may know the word. Don't be afraid to say "I don't know," if you have searched thoroughly for the meaning and cannot find it or anything close. Leave it in italics and alert the client to it.

Punctuation of documents should follow good form in the target language. The translator may have a Spanish text that goes along without punctuation or commas, which may simply be the result of sloppy writing. English needs commas to make sense of matters. However, if the original can be read two ways without the comma, then leave the comma out of the English version, to provide the same ambiguity as the Spanish. Just as for interpretation, so in translation we do not clarify when the original is ambiguous. Stylistically, when the writer is unclear in the original, the translation should reflect that. The physical document you turn in, however, must always be neat and clean.

If, at an international conference, you must translate something which is a stylistic mess in the original and you say "I'm going to fix it," you find the next day the reviewer has changed it all back, so that the translation resembles the original exactly, which it should always have done. It is tempting to "fix" a translation where the text is vague and noncommittal. Such a text uses verbs of nothing happening such as: "to study," "to promote," "to develop," "to encourage," assiduously avoiding the dangerous verb "to do." The presumption that a text is vague because the author was unable to say what he really meant is naive and mistaken. The author intended to be vague because he did not want to commit his government to doing anything. Don't fix it.

Attorneys working on a case may prefer to call certain things by certain names. This is true of administrative agencies, names of companies and such. Ask them if they have a preference. Also, attorneys may feel that a phrase sounds better in good legal English, which is not always the same as good English. If the original text allows for that rendition, you may make the change to conform to the attorney's preference.

Sign the translation that you hand in. Your name and signature on the document indicate that you are responsible for the accuracy of the translation.

Fax and Modem

Some professional translators or court interpreters who do a lot of document translation find it unthinkable to operate without a fax, which transmits documents electronically over the phone wires and prints them out. When you have a fax, people can send documents to you at late hours, over long distances, and avoid waiting and paying for messengers or express mail. One advantage to the translator is that before bidding on a project you can look at a few pages of the document to determine the degree of difficulty and legibility. Also if you have a fax you can deliver a translation quickly without having to wait for or pay a messenger service or overnight mail. Large law firms and large commercial translation companies like to use the fax, because it means they can reach translators quickly, both to send and receive documents, and transmit contracts quickly. The disadvantage to the translator is that if you have a fax, people can get at you very easily, and thus may be tempted to modify the original documents when you are in the middle of the translation. This is extra work for which you will have to bill, but which a law firm may be unwilling to pay. Many colleagues swear by the fax, but it can expose you to great rush demands.

Some commercial translation companies that use a lot of free-lance people want the translator to have a modem, which will connect your computer to their computer, for the sending of documents without having to print them out at each step of the way. If you wish to work for large translation companies you may need to acquire a modem. A modem could be helpful if you are running a large project yourself and want to keep in close touch with your subcontractors and see how the work is going, assuming that your subcontractors also have modems. When you consider a modem, or even the possibility of handing floppy disks back and forth between colleagues, your computers or disks must be able to speak to each other.

Modems connect computers, so that if there is a virus in the sending computer, your computer may receive that virus along with the document transmission. Remember also that viruses can be transmitted by software that someone gives you as a gift to save you the expense of buying your own. This sort of gift you do not want. Anyone who hooks up a computer to an electronic bulletin board may be at risk. Software is sold that is said to seek out and destroy viruses. The best remedy is prevention, sometimes easier said than done. The advice to "Just Say No" may be as effective here as in other situations where it is more commonly suggested.

The Use of Computers

In the past ten years it has become almost mandatory for a translator to use a computer, because the client wants fast copy and he wants it camera-ready. The growing role of computers in our work was reflected at the Thirtieth Anniversary Conference of the American Translators Association, held in 1989 in Washington, D.C. A great deal of time was devoted to computer issues, and a great deal of what was said on the subject is available in the *Proceedings* (7).

Computer to Handle Terminology

Before the computer, translators kept words on 3 x 5 cards, in shoe boxes, and operated with these sacred shoe boxes. This was old-style terminology management, and the advantage was that the words were in alphabetical order. Interpreters kept word lists. Sometimes the contents of the lists overlapped. The list may have been kept in a notebook perhaps by subject, more often by date. If you could remember that explosives were about 2/3 the way through notebook 5, then you could find those words. A term in a notebook is like gold in the garden, you know you buried it, but don't remember where. Today, translators and some interpreters put their words into a computer, and there is terminology management software to help with this, or you may use a data base program. With a word-processing program you may enter the words alphabetically, which will provide a giant word list, but, unlike the data base, it cannot be easily manipulated and you are unable to retrieve a selective list automatically. If you want to push a button and retrieve all words on ballistics, then use a data base or terminology management program. But if all you require is a very large list, then word processing software is acceptable. It is probably better to begin with a data base or terminology management system, otherwise you will find yourself half way through a two-thousand page list on a word processing program wondering what it would take to learn a data base program. In any event, if you save words that took a lot of time to find, you will be all the more prepared for the next manuscript or trial on the same subject. For terminology management and data-base programs, consult colleagues and attend meetings on the subject at the annual ATA Conference. The *ATA Chronicle* carries advertisements for and reviews of such software.

Computer as Word Processor to Prepare the Translation

It is helpful to write a translation on a computer because one can make corrections and revisions easily. The work itself also goes faster on a computer. When one writes a translation on a computer, one uses the computer as a word processor. One wishes to work with one's own computer, one reason being that client documents are to be kept confidential. Some attorneys ask that you put at the top of all your documents "CONFIDENTIAL and PRIVILEGED, ATTORNEY WORK PRODUCT," for every draft until the final draft that you hand in to the attorney.

Some individuals, when they write on the computer, prefer to do their editing on the screen. Others prefer to print out a draft and edit on paper (hard copy), and then key the corrections back into the computer. When I have worked with subcontractors I require that they make their corrections on hard copy, that is, on a printed version, because they seem to catch more errors that way. Having the paper in your hand gives you some physical and spiritual distance from a document and allows you to look at it more dispassionately, to catch errors that you did not catch on the screen. Also, once you have written a translation, you need to do a line-by-line comparison with the original text to make sure that you have skipped no lines, and have no errors of meaning in the translation. Print out the draft translation to study and revise, and compare with the original, and make corrections on paper, which can subsequently be keyed into the computer.

Computers now have spell checkers that will help you make your version more error-free. Spell check programs are available for various languages. If you use a computer, you can show a draft to the attorney in question, and allow him, if it is reasonable, to suggest some changes, which you can then key in fairly simply to produce the final version. Often there will not be time for that extra step, so to the extent you can ask necessary questions before finishing the translation, you will have a clearer idea of what is wanted.

Novice computer users should be reminded to back up or copy their work both onto the hard disk and onto the floppy disk as they go along, and once in a while to print out a fast draft copy. Lost work cannot always be fished out of a computer at 2 a.m.

Computer as Translating Machine

Computer software is available that does do written translations. Some systems are sold with hardware and software together, while others are simply software packages. A machine translation product may need a great deal of **post-editing**. The post editor is like a super English teacher in that she must clean up work produced. For a machine product to be worthwhile, the agency using it would have to constantly up-date terminology, for which one would have to maintain a knowledgeable professional staff. If you feel that such a system would help you translate large volumes of documents, test such a system before purchase. Be physically present yourself to observe the machine scan in your material, and see the product as it is produced. Too much money and time is at stake not to look into such systems personally before purchase. One suspects that the success of machine translation will depend on narrow choice of field, on the machine's having already the words in it, and on constant updating and modification. Mr. Harry Obst, Director of Language Services at the U.S. Department of State, said in a recent speech that:

> The hundreds of millions of dollars wasted on some machine translation projects could have built many schools of interpretation and translation with huge libraries and state-of-the-art equipment.... In the Department of State, machine translation is not used. We have canvassed the market extensively and so far found nothing which meets our standards of translation quality or is even remotely within the range of cost-effectiveness and speed requirements (11).

For Most of Us

The computer that most translators will need is one on which we write our own translation, and perhaps store and recall terminology. Purchase a computer that you can use. Some large commercial agencies that use free-lance people demand that one have a certain kind of machine, often IBM or IBM-compatible. Some translators may prefer a Macintosh. Either way, first look at the software you want to use, and then see which machine runs it best. The most important thing about a computer is that you should be able to use it.

Further Reading

Note: Please see Further Reading at end of Chapter 3 for a more extensive list of Spanish and English dictionaries.

1. Anca, Augusto. *Abreviaturas y Siglas Médicas en Inglés, con su traducción al Español: English Medical Abbreviations with Translation into Spanish,* 1984. Available from: Augusto Anca, P.O. Box 14-5236, Coral Gables, Florida 33114.
   • About 4,300 English acronyms spelled out in English and then translated into Spanish. Most helpful, both for the English and for the Spanish.

2. Burton, William C. *Legal Thesaurus Complete and Unabridged.* New York: Macmillan Publishing Co., Inc., 1980. English.
   • Helpful for legal translations into English.

3. Davis, Neil M. *Medical Abbreviations: 7,000 Conveniences at the Expense of Communications and Safety.* Fifth Edition, 1990. Available from: Neil M. Davis Associates, 1143 Wright Drive, Huntingdon Valley, Pa., 19006. English.
   • Good for medical records or other medical translations or interpretation.

4. De la Cuesta, Leonel Antonio. *Lecciones preliminares de traductología.* Ediciones Guayacán, 1987. Available from Professor Leonel de la Cuesta, 10625 S.W. 112 Ave., Apt 105, Miami, Fla. 33176.
   • Helpful for translators generally, and for court interpreters who do legal translations. Includes a good overview of translation as a profession. Concentrates on the realities of the work.

5. Fowler, H.W. *Fowler's Modern English Usage.* Second Edition Revised by Sir Ernest Gowers. New York: Oxford University Press, 1965.
   • The standard reference work on English usage.

6. García Yebra, Valentín. *Teoría y práctica de la traducción.* Prólogo de Dámaso Alonso. 2 vols. Madrid: Editorial Gredos, 1982.
   • Heavy on theory.

7. Hammond, Deanna Lindberg, ed. *Coming of Age: Proceedings of the 30th Annual Conference of the American Translators Association. Washington, D.C. October 11-15, 1989.* Medford, N.Y.: Learned Information Inc., 1989.
   • Excellent overview of translation and real translators at work. Good information on textual and linguistic considerations, software, computers, and computer-assisted translation.

8. Joly, Jean-François. *Proceedings of the Second North American Translators Congress: Washington, D.C., 1989.* Regional Center for North America. Available from: The American Translators Association.

9. Llerena, Mario. *Un Manual de Estilo: una presentación práctica y fácil de las normas necesarias para el uso correcto y apropiado del idioma español.* Miami: Logoi, Inc., 1981.
    *   The closest book I have seen in Spanish that would almost be the equivalent of the Chicago style manual for Spanish. Indeed, the visual layout of the book recalls that of Chicago, similar topics covered, though less in depth than Chicago might. Perhaps this is because the author devotes a good deal of space to helping the writer avoid what he calls *vulgarismos* and *barbarismos* . Looks to be very useful.

10. *A Manual of Style.* Fourteenth Edition. Chicago: The University of Chicago Press, 1993.
    *   Good general reference for English editorial style and document management.

11. Obst, Harry. "The Ivory Tower of Babel and the Translation Demands of Diplomacy," a speech given at the Intrepretational Association of University Schools of Translation and Interpretation, Monterey, California, May 26, 1990. Quoted by permission from Mr. Obst's original manuscript.

12. Orellana, Marina. *La Traducción del inglés al castellano: guia para el traductor.* Santiago de Chile, 1986. Available from: Waldenbooks, 1700 Pennsylvania Ave., N.W., Washington, D.C. 20006.
    *   Interesting remarks about differing language structures between English and Spanish, the problems those differences pose, and possible solutions. Helpful also to the interpreter going from English into Spanish.

13. *United States Government Printing Office Style Manual, 1984.* Washington, D.C.: U.S. Government Printing Office, 1984.

14. Vanson, George N. and Marilyn R. Frankenthaler. *Spanish-English Legal Terminology: Terminología español-inglés en el área legal.* Cincinnati, Ohio: South-Western Publishing Co., 1982. Spanish-English.
    *   Each word presented in a phrase in Spanish to show correct use, then that phrase translated to English. Useful for document translation, and good study resource to learn Spanish civil law terms. Well done.

CHAPTER 7

Tape Transcription and Translation

Q. Now, in listening to the conversations did you make any effort to write down in Sicilian the words that you believed you heard while you were listening to the tape conversations?

A. No, sir.

Q. Is it your testimony that you listened to the Sicilian and that what you wrote down was directly into English?

A. That's right.

Q. So that you did not at any time memorialize what you believed the sounds you heard on the tape were?

A. In Sicilian?

Q. Yes.

A. No.

Q. Am I correct that Sicilian is a written language?

A. Yes, sir.

[...]

Q. Now, it was your decision, sir, not to write down on paper what you heard on the tapes in the Sicilian language?

A. I speak and understand Sicilian. It's very difficult to write for me....

[...]

Q. Am I understanding you correctly, you find it difficult to write the Sicilian version of what you have heard on the tapes?

A. Yes, sir.

Q. And that difficulty that you had, did you communicate it to any of the prosecutors or the FBI agents that you were working with?

A. Nobody asked me if I could write Sicilian.

Q. Did you ask anybody whether or not it would be appropriate for you to write it down first in Sicilian to determine whether or not what you believed you heard was in fact what was said on the tape?

A. I don't believe I did.

Procedures and Problems

A tape in a foreign language for presentation in court should first be transcribed or written down *in that language*, and then a translation made of the transcription, so that one ends up with one document in a double-column format, with the Spanish transcription in the left-hand column, and the English-language version in the right hand column.

A party to a case may wish to present tape recordings as evidence. When the speech on a tape is in a language other than English, the side presenting the tape may ask an interpreter to transcribe and translate the tape for trial. The tape itself is evidence. Depending on the jurisdiction, the transcription and translation of that tape may represent evidence, or may be aids to help the jury understand the evidence. The interpreter who prepares tapes for trial in this sense is an expert, and his name and appearance should be included on the witness list that the side that hired him submits. If the interpreter's name is not on the list of expert witnesses, the judge may not allow interpreter testimony as to how the work was done, or the fact that it was his work. Indeed, the jury may not be allowed to see the transcription or translation at all.

Transcribing Original Language Allows Attorneys to See What Was Actually Said

One or two tapes may be crucial to a case, or there may be a whole slew of tapes. Large drug conspiracy cases may depend partially on recorded wiretap evidence collected on 50 to 100 tapes where the flow of conversation will reveal the nature of the dealings. An interpreter may be asked to prepare the whole set, perhaps by the government. Or, one may be approached by a member of the defense who wants transcription and translation of a certain number of tapes, where he believes his client is talking. In a case where one tape is important, it may be the tape of the statement to the police, and if the government believes that the defendant admitted to the crime in that statement, it may seek to introduce that tape at trial. Tapes that include an admission to the crime may have a "Miranda problem," wherein a defendant is improperly advised of his Miranda rights. Officer Atropella Derechos (MV_1) is speaking to a suspect (MV_2) (emphasis added):

MV$_1$: Usted tiene el derecho de hablar con un abogado para consultar con él antes que nosotros le interroguemos, y estar con usted durante el periodo del interrogateo. ¿Entiende?

MV$_2$: Sí.

MV$_1$: Si usted no puede, ah, pagar un abogado, desée uno, un abogado será **prohibido**. ¿Entiende? (Pause) Si usted no desea contestá..., si usted no desea contestar las preguntas ahora sin un abogado, usted tiene todavía el derecho de, de parar de contestar en cualquier momento que desée, hasta que consulte con un abogado. ¿Entiende?

MV$_2$: Sí.

MV$_1$: You have the right to talk with an attorney to consult with him before we interrogate you, and to be with you during the period of the interrogation. Understand?

MV$_2$: Yes.

MV$_1$: If you cannot, ah, pay a lawyer, you want one, a lawyer will be **prohibited**. Understand? (Pause) If you do not wish to ans..., if you do not wish to answer the questions now without an attorney, you still have the right to, to stop from answering at any time you wish, until you consult with an attorney. Understand?

MV$_2$: Yes.

Or, on another case, Officer Atropella Derechos explains the Miranda rights to a different suspect:

MV$_1$: Usted tiene el derecho de guar... de hablar con su abogado para consultar con él antes que nosotros lo interrogamos y estar con usted durante el período del interrogativo. Si usted no puede pagar un abogado y desea uno, un abogado será **prohibido**. Si usted no desea contestar las preguntas ahora sin un abogado usted tiene todavía el derecho de parar de contestar en cualquier momento que usted desea, hasta que consulte con su abogado. ¿Usted entiende eso? (Pause) ¡Dígame!

MV$_2$: Porque eso no, no, no, no quiere decir sí o no. No (Unintelligible) a la cabeza. No quiere decir nada.

MV$_1$: You have the right to remai..., to speak with your lawyer to consult with him before we interrogate you and to be with you during the period of the interrogation. If you cannot pay for a lawyer and want one, a lawyer will be **prohibited**. If you do not wish to answer the questions now without a lawyer, you still have the right to stop from answering any time you wish, until you consult with your attorney. Do you understand that? (Pause) Answer me!

MV$_2$: Because that does not, does not, does not mean yes or no. It doesn't (Unintelligible) the head. It doesn't mean anything.

In this second example the suspect is clearly confused, and says that "It doesn't mean anything," it is not understandable, it does not "[enter] the head," which may be what the unintelligible part was saying, though the voice was too low to catch it. The suspect is indicating that what he has just been told makes no sense.

Officer Atropella Derechos told three different defendants that they would be prohibited from having an attorney. For two cases, he denied that he had said "prohibited" (*prohibido*) but on the third case he admitted he had said it, this admission perhaps made to protect the conviction in one of the two other cases. The government sought to show that he was saying *proveído* meaning: "provided." The problem is that *proveído* is not the correct past participle of *proveer* (to provide). The correct past participle is *provisto*. This problem shows why one tape can be crucial to a case. Notice also on the second tape that the policeman talks about "your lawyer." The concept of "your lawyer" is something for the rich, or for those who have not yet fallen out of the bottom of the middle class. Of course you can talk with "your lawyer." But one of the elements of Miranda is that a lawyer will be provided, a lawyer paid by the government which the second suspect here has not understood and has not been told. The Miranda question is only one of many that a proper transcription of the source language will allow an attorney to litigate. Much more common, of course, is if someone did or did not really set up or participate in a drug deal. In any event, the original language must be transcribed side-by-side with an English translation.

Time Constraints

Before trial the government makes tapes available to the defense in the period called **discovery**. If, for example, discovery has been from June to September, and you receive a call in October to review or prepare some tapes for a defendant, ask when discovery ends for that case. While the government may have made the tapes available during discovery, after that time access may become impossible, so that you cannot fulfill your obligation. The first question then is real access to the tapes. If the discovery period has ended it is perhaps too late for an interpreter to accept that piece of work. An attorney may promise access, but later may not be able to deliver. It is in our own interest to avoid working under such conditions because even if access is granted, if there is insufficient time, the job will be rushed, and you may not have all the time necessary to do an accurate and complete job. Be candid in providing an estimate of the time it will take, whether you are working alone or with a team, and whether it is one tape or many. Courts and attorneys tend to be in a hurry, and it is important to provide them accurate time estimates because trial schedules can be affected. Experienced court interpreters are familiar with the fine line between wanting to do a piece of work, and that work being assigned so close to deadline with impossible conditions of access that it will be difficult to finish on time. When in doubt about time or access, walk away from that contract.

The Transcription

Just as in translation one does not work from original documents, so in tape work one should make sure that the requestor has his own original copy of the tape. The people who give you the tape should insure that no change can be made to the sound on your copy, lest there be inadvertent erasing of all or parts of the tape. On a casette, this is normally done by removing the little plastic flaps at the back that have already been pre-cut on three sides to facilitate the process. It is preferable to have the attorney who gives you the copy of the tape do this for you.

Information for the Transcription

The transcriber needs to know what kind of tape it is, for what purpose, how and where it was made, who made it, how many tapes are involved, when discovery ends, and when the work is due. As to the speakers, it is helpful to know their supposed country of origin, how long they have been in the U.S., and the purported subject of their conversation. This material will help provide context and may offer clues to speech of uncertain meaning.

On large projects those who did the recording may have kept a **log** of calls. Each tape may contain 20 calls, but you may be required to find and transcribe only 4 calls on a given tape. Make sure that whoever provides you the tapes also provides a clear way for you to know exactly which calls or segments of the tape you are supposed to deal with, if you are not required to do the whole tape.

The first step, the most lengthy and demanding, is transcription of the original or source language of the tape. Before beginning the transcription, listen to the tape three times or more if the sound quality is poor. After listening several times, one begins the transcription. Some interpreters find it easier to transcribe directly onto a computer for the first draft and all subsequent drafts, while others prefer to work by hand on lined yellow legal pads, leaving a line between each line of writing for additions and corrections. Once one is satisfied with the hand version, one may put it onto the computer, and then use the printed version to review and correct further against the tapes. How many times one must listen to the tape to extract all the sound on it depends on various factors. Certain tapes or portions of tapes may require thirty or forty passes to catch the maximum sound, while for others two or three times may be sufficient. The ideal tape recorder or dictating machine on which to listen to cassettes would be able to play a tape and slow it down at least 20%. Listening for transcription is an art much like fishing. The transcriber sweeps the same area of the ocean with different size nets to catch all the fish of whatever description or size. The alarming part is that when you believe that you have all the swordfish and tuna, and you are going for the mackerel, suddenly a very large swordfish (a five-word phrase) shows up that had been there all along but that you were simply not aware of. One can slow a tape down on a good tape recorder, but doing that distorts the voice of the speaker, so there are diminishing returns.

The parties to the case need a transcript of the source language to be able to follow the speech and to dispute the accuracy of transcription or translation should they so wish. Attorneys, judges, and clerks not familiar with proper tape procedure may say that they only need, want, or will pay for the English version. But eventually there may be questions as to what the original really said. If only an English version of a Spanish tape is prepared, there may come a time when the entire set will have to be re-done, much to the disgust and inconvenience of the court. Interpreters may be pressured to provide only the English, skipping the key transcription step. An interpreter careful of her reputation will not accept such a job, and is better off declining the contract than doing tape work the wrong way.

Even for non-legal work, say, broadcast tapes for a TV or radio program, where an editor will have to cut what is said to fit what he wants to use, or where the translation will be edited into subtitles, provide the editor with the original transcription, so he can see what he has in hand. An editor of a tape for TV may not at first realize that he will need a transcript of the source language to do his job well, and may say that just the English is enough. Also he may think to save some money by requesting just the English. Tell him you have to do the Spanish anyway, you will need to charge for it in any event, so he might as well have a copy. He will be grateful later, because he will then have the Spanish transcription available to synchronize action and subtitles.

Sound Quality

Sound quality varies depending on who makes the recording, how it is made, and where. Wiretaps on a phone may have fairly good sound, unless there is a radio or TV going, or other background noise. Room tapes can be difficult: the windows are open, there is constant traffic outside, and the police microphone is hidden under the couch or in a clock. Moreover, conversation may take place in low tones of voice.

When police interview a witness or suspect, they may not put the microphone close to the person being interviewed. The person being interviewed may be drunk, may mumble, or speak quickly. An entire case may depend on one such tape. This is the sort of tape that may require many passes to transcribe accurately and fully. Some tape recorders that the police use for such interviews are of less than professional quality.

Body tapes, made when an agent or informant wears a receiver and microphone and recorder or transmitter under his shirt, goes into a restaurant, pretends to be the brother-in-law of the kidnapped cocaine dealer and negotiates for the brother's return, such tapes may not be clear either. For body tapes where the microphone is worn on the body, hidden under the clothing, the transcriber gets to hear all the coughs, sighs, and borborygmus that the wiree is heir to.

Representation of Speech on the Page

As with written documents where everything on the page should be included in the translation, so too for transcriptions, every sound on the tape should be transcribed. When the sound is not speech mention it in parenthesis as (Background noise), or (Noise). The transcriber must indicate overlapping, inaudibility, and intelligibility; these situations may be represented in parenthesis, or with a series of dots.

For interruptions, I prefer the three-dot method, as shown in the next example. Speakers naturally interrupt each other, even if only with grunted affirmations such as "uh huh," when someone else is telling a story. For example, if in a statement to the police, we have:

MV$_2$: Yo andaba con un muchacho, buscando la dirección, va, él la sabía, yo no sabía la dirección, va, y cuando vimos, nos anduvimos ahí, va...

MV$_1$: ...uh huh...

MV$_2$: ... el muchacho, yo, yo me adelanté, va, cuando lo vi en problema esa con.....vi, y vi yo que tenía el problema, va, pero y yo oí los disparos, regresé yo...., va...

MV$_1$: ...uh huh...

MV$_2$: ...cuando esta, cuando oí los disparos....

MV$_2$: I was with a fellow, looking for the address, so, he knew it, I did not know the address, and when we saw, we were going there, well...

MV$_1$: ...uh huh...

MV$_2$: ... the fellow, I, I went on ahead, well, when I saw him, in that problem with...I saw, and I saw that he had the problem, so, but, and I heard the shots, I went back...., so...

MV$_1$: ...uh huh...

MV$_2$: ...when, ah, when I heard the shots....

Some interruptions constitute overlaps of the initial talk. When an interruption cuts the sound, the three dots may be sufficient, but in a true overlap were both people speak at the same time and the two speakers are both audible at the same time, one may say (Overlap), thus:

MV$_2$: ...cuando uno está dudando, pues todavía, pero uno está seguro...

MV$_1$: ...Bien...(Overlap) pero tú no lo dudas, tú los sabes exactamente...

MV$_2$: ...(Overlap) yo estoy seguro que él fue.

MV$_1$: O.K., muchas gracias.

MV$_2$: ...when one is doubting, well, then, but one is sure...

MV$_1$: ...Fine...(Overlap) but you do not doubt it, you know it exactly...

MV$_2$: ...(Overlap) I am sure that it was he.

MV$_1$: O.K., thank you very much.

Our colleague Alee Alger-Robbins of San Diego suggests the useful abbreviation (NAR) for No Audible Response, when, in Alger-Robbins' words, "A question is asked in an interview and no audible response is heard but the next question indicates an answer was probably given with the use of a nod or other inaudible gesture."

When the translator herself wishes to make a note [may also mean: _____] she may use brackets. Brackets also serve for words to fill in ellipses in speech, so that the target language version will represent the idea correctly.

There will be some situations where the overlap obscures what one or both speakers are saying, in which case one might put (Overlap-Unintelligible). As for unintelligibility, if we cannot hear the voice, or if it is unclear, it may be labeled as (Inaudible) or (Unintelligible). Other sounds may confuse the issue; water running, a radio or TV going, in which case (Background noise) will be sufficient.

As to presenting (Inaudible) and (Unintelligible) on paper, some interpreters feel that the transcriber should include those words in parenthesis at the appropriate spot. Because stage directions clutter a text and impede reading, it may be preferable to use a series of dots that approximate the length of the inaudible part. When you revise your transcription, re-listening to that part, you have an idea of the amount of time involved and the potential number of words. Another advantage to using dots is that if you miss two lines of speech, and indicate with dots the two lines missed, the other side and its expert cannot come into court and say: "Yes, the interpreter missed some sound but we have caught it, and here is the entire five pages of what was missed." Your dots will testify as to the extent of the missing words. While we wish to transcribe as much of the sound as we can, it also behooves us to be precise as to the portion we cannot hear.

Words that are half-spoken should be indicated. For example, when someone says *No me acuer...*, try to show the equivalent half word "I don't remem...." in English. There will be hesitations, and stops and starts, just as there are on the witness stand, which the transcriber and translator should note. Also there will be filler words such as "well," "ah," "you know," "like," "I mean," which in Spanish might be *va, este, usted sabe, como, quiero decir*. The corresponding word should be provided in English, though sometimes the actual choice may be arbitrary. Each word and each comma should be shown on the page.

Speech Patterns

Much as the mirror does not lie, in terms of appearance, so too, the tape does not lie in regard to speech patterns and language use. Along with the usual hesitations and starts and stops in speech, incorrect usage will stand revealed in all its glory. On a tape where a suspect makes a statement to the police, the police who interview suspects may themselves not speak perfect Spanish. Imperfections in original speech are simply transcribed. They complicate the subsequent translation, because one hopes to find an equivalent sort of error in English, and such errors may not spring readily to mind. If a policemen says *oistes* [for *oiste*](did you hear?) which the dictionaries call a vulgarism, one might put "you hear?", dropping the "did." But the result in English does not quite convey the tone of the Spanish. It suggests informality rather than uneducated speech. One might say "d'ya hear?" where the "d'ya" brings us down a notch on the social scale in English, to the level of the Spanish. Translations expand to fill the time allotted to them, and tape work may have tight deadlines. While it is troublesome to find a good solution for such problems, they may be infrequent and appear only once or twice on a tape. The amount of time one wishes to devote to them can also depend on how much sound one has managed to get from the tape. If time is short and you must choose between getting more sound from a tape or polishing a translation in matters such as this, it is preferable to listen to the tape again, because getting as much sound as possible from the tape is the first priority.

The people being interviewed, while perhaps native speakers of Spanish, may have grown up in circumstances of privation where the enlightened view held that peasants need not learn to read or write because they will always be peasants. Of course the peasants, not sharing the wisdom of their masters, moved to the United States. Native speakers of Spanish, if they are uneducated, depending on their country of origin, may make some typical mistakes in speaking their own language: for example, some speakers may confuse *mirar* [to look] with *ver* [to see], and may use the word *mirar* for both purposes. As on the witness stand, so for tapes: we cannot always expect to hear good Spanish. The purity of a source language on a tape is something one rather hopes for but rarely finds. Where both parties are not efficient speakers of what each assumes to be his first language, the tape may reveal a good deal of unintentional obfuscation. On one tape you may hear one person who speaks Spanish well, another who is "bilingual" but much better in English, so that his speech has a lot of Anglicisms in it, and a third person speaking Spanish whose first language is another Romance language.

Throughout all this the transcriber is, as in court, impartial. It should not matter for which side you prepare the tapes; give it your best, most careful effort. All you care about is the sound and its faithful reproduction, and then, for the translation, the faithful rendering into English.

Who Is Speaking

Beyond what was really meant, we also have who was really speaking. On wiretaps and other tapes an attorney may suggest that it was not his client who threatened to kill the complainant if he testified against the suspect at trial:

"Your Honor, it was not my client, but even if it was, his words have been mistranslated." Irene King-Tomassini, Supervisory Interpreter at the U.S. District Court in Miami, says that one never identifies a voice on a tape, one simply uses: MV_1, MV_2 (First Male Voice, Second Male Voice); FV_1 (First Female Voice); CV_1 (First Child's Voice). The transcriber cannot really know who is speaking, because she was not there. King-Tomassini adds that if an agent tells you who the voices are, the procedure should be to so indicate:

> Voice identification provided by Special Agent Sabelotodo as follows:
> MV_1 = Paco, MV_2 = Paco's Grandfather, FV_1 = Doña Teti.

If the agent has not provided names, the top of an initial page might look like this:

> Transcription and Translation of DEA Tape N-007.
> MV_1 = First Male Voice
> MV_2 = Second Male Voice
> FV = Female Voice
> ... = interruptions
> .... = longer series of dots approximates length of inaudible or
>   unintelligible part
> Case Number [If written on outside of tape]
> Date [If written on outside of tape]
> Time [If written on outside of tape]

Translation of Transcription

Once the final transcription of the source language is completed, one prepares the written translation of the transcription. Put your Spanish into the computer in the left-hand side of a double-column format. For the English translation, you then scroll up and put that translation side-by-side to the right of the Spanish.

There will be times when meaning is determined by the accent or intonation given a particular word, so that one might wish to replay parts of the tape to refresh one's memory for the translation.

Code

Before considering speech that is deliberately coded or veiled, we need to remember that many conversations between close friends, associates or family members may use a natural code of shared references and assumptions. If I talk with a colleague on a joint assignment and say "I will pick up the equipment," both of us know that this means that I am talking about a certain sort of wired interpreting equipment, which I am going to pick up at the Department of State. Not a radio, not a drill, not an electric saw, but wired interpreting equipment. We have abbreviated the reference because we have done it before and both of us know what I'm talking about. We have no reason to veil our speech, we are just abbreviating the reference. If we ask each other "are you going to Cape May?" we refer to a regional translation meeting that was amply publicized. But to someone unfamiliar with that meeting, "Cape May" could be understood as a reference to a beach holiday or a weekend tryst. So it is not just intentional code that makes understanding tapes difficult, but the normal shared assumptions of friends and associates in any conversation. Abbreviated references of this sort present code-like problems, but we must not read erroneous meaning into something incompletely understood. The best approach is great restraint to avoid unwarranted assumptions.

Defendants may purposely talk in their own code or deliberately veiled form of speech. They may use a word that seems innocent enough such as *mercancía* or "merchandise." The government will argue that the "merchandise" was cocaine, but one should only put "merchandise" on the page. On a robbery of an armored truck where bombing was a side issue, the government overheard in wiretaps the word *embutido*, which means a sausage. This *embutido* was springing up all over the case in conversations that ostensibly had nothing to do with eating, cooking, or the food business. Code words often appear out of context, and here the prosecution suggested that the *embutido* was explosives. For the translation the interpreter could provide the word *embutido* in Spanish at the first reference, with the dictionary definition in brackets [sausage], and subsequently continue with the sausage. Of course a stick of a high explosive called Tovex is packaged somewhat like a sausage.

Two Languages on the Tape to Be Transcribed

You may have to transcribe recorded conversations where both English and Spanish are used, or English and another language. In this case you may put the English in **bold** type for both transcription and translation, if the amount of English is small and the number of tapes few, as in the following example:

MV₁: Roberto este es un contrato de trabajo. Cuando vos **hire** y hacés un contrato a alguien y el maje no viene a trabajar, vos simplemente le decís **"I am sorry"**, me entendés, **"I can't sign**, porque no has venido a trabajar". Punto. Y lo corrés. Estamos hablando de premisas normales, Roberto, términos normales.....

MV₂: ..."**can not be terminated or cancelled**", pero esto,...ahí le cambiastes más, vos, Francisco.

MV₁: No, esa es la mismita, loco.

MV₂: No, no. Vos dijistes **"by any reason"**, no me acuerdo dónde.

MV₁: Roberto this is a work contract. When you **hire** and you make a contract with someone and the guy doesn't come to work, you simply say to him **"I am sorry,"** you get my meaning, **"I can't sign** because you have not come to work." Period. And you give him the boot. We are talking about normal premises, Roberto, normal terms.....

MV₂: ..."**can not be terminated or cancelled**," but you, here you made more changes to it Francisco.

MV₁: No. That is the very same, man.

MV₂: No, no. You said **"by any reason,"** I don't remember where.

When a non-native speaker of English misuses or mispronounces English words, retain the faulty English usage in both transcription and translation. If there is a great deal of English on a tape, and if you have many tapes, it may be impractical in terms of time to put the original English in bold type.

End of the Recording

At the end of a recording, especially if it is a wiretap, you may hear "This recording was made by Special Agent Mario Bueno of a conversation between him and Juan Malo, on March 3, 1992, and the recording was finished at 6:34 p.m." This part you may put in **bold** type. After the agent has said who made the tape, if he says it at the end of the tape, you then need to put your own name on the document

--Transcribed and Translated by
María Hotshot, Interpreter,
Certified by the Administrative Office of the U.S. Courts

assuming that you are indeed so certified. Or, if you are accredited by the American Translators Association as a translator from Spanish to English, you might put that accreditation down after your name. You may wish to add a disclaimer, to the effect that "This transcription and this translation have been done to the best of my knowledge and ability." Of course when you sign your work, that in itself should suggest that you have done the best work you are capable of.

Quality Control

The original tape has on it what was said. The transcription is the transcriber's version of what was said, and the translation is the translator's idea of what that transcription means in English.

It can be helpful to have a colleague check your work before you present it to your client. Your colleague must of course agree to keep the contents of the tape secret. Irene King-Tomassini says that no two interpreters will agree totally on exactly what a tape says. Ideally a colleague can check to see if you have caught as much sound as possible, if you have heard the words correctly, and if you have translated them correctly. As to translation, there may be four or five versions of a translation that may differ and are all correct when compared with the source language. A second opinion may be especially helpful on tapes with poor sound quality such as police station interviews or body tapes. The goal is to retrieve 100% of the sound from a tape. For any tape worth doing, one would hope to retrieve 80% to 100% of the sound, assuming there is no background noise. For less than 80% of the tape content, the result might be unconnected phrases so out of context that it might be difficult to extract meaning from those words that are audible. Before accepting a tape assignment listen to the tape or tapes first, to determine their sound quality and duration. One sixty-minute tape could take days to transcribe. A simple rule of thumb is that one minute of recorded sound may require one hour to transcribe, translate, and check. Where sound quality is poor you may perhaps surpass that limit. On a recent case one colleague listened to some wire-tap tapes and declined the assignment because the sound quality was so poor. It makes little sense to put a client to the expense of transcription and translation if the final result will satisfy no one. Only the interpreter involved can determine if a tape is worth working with. It is sometimes best to turn down work one sees no possibility of doing well.

When you do tape work, the safest way to bill is by the hour of your time. If you plan to bill by the hour, keep a time sheet of all the time you work on a tape to substantiate your bill. Per-page billing may initially appear attractive to a client until that client receives the transcriptions and translations, and finds that the contractor who billed per page put only 27 words on each page. Bid honestly and bill honestly.

Further Reading

1. Fishman, Clifford S. *Wiretapping and Eavesdropping*. Rochester, N.Y.: The Lawyers Cooperative Publishing Co., 1978.

2. ——. *Wiretapping and Eavesdropping: Cumulative Supplement Issued December, 1993*. Deerfield, Ill.: Clark, Boardman, Callaghan, 1993.
   • Both books discuss case law dealing with wiretaps and eavesdropping. Helpful to learn about the issue; names some cases that could be mentioned in motions hearings.

CHAPTER 8

The Interpreter as Expert Witness

When the interpreter interprets, she is regarded as an expert. Nevertheless, the expression "expert witness" may be specially emphasized when an interpreter is asked to provide an expert opinion on transcription, translation, or interpretation already done by another; when she is called to describe transcription and/or translation work she herself has done; or when she is asked to inform the court of proper interpretation procedures and methods. Whether you are called as an expert witness to discuss the work of another person, to present and defend your own work, or to inform the court about translation and interpretation standards and methods, certain considerations may be helpful.

Impartiality

You will be a better and more useful expert witness to the extent that you remain impartial, no matter which side calls you on a case. Your opinion should be independent of who has requested your presence and is therefore paying for it. Your expertise is on the subject of language, transcription, translation, and method. Any attorney who consults you as an expert must be told at the beginning of your discussion that you will examine the material and provide your opinion, but that you cannot say to what extent, if any, your opinion will serve his case. If your opinion helps him you may then testify in court if he calls you to do so. Not every expert consulted by an attorney is asked to testify. The expert may find something that the attorney believes does not favor his client, in which case the attorney may not call the expert to court. It may be useful both to you and to the attorney involved to prepare a written report of what you have found, of course marked CONFIDENTIAL. If only a few words are at issue, a verbal report may suffice.

Critique

Let us say you are presented with a wiretap transcription and translation to review, where counsel who called you disagrees with the translation provided, though he believes the transcription is accurate. Obtain the tape and check the transcription, first off. A look at the English version prepared for court may provide some idea as to the accuracy of the original transcription. You may be asked to look at such material where the other side has provided only the English. To properly check that English, the entire tape will have to be first transcribed and then translated, that is, re-done. The need to re-do it may be suggested by the quality of the English presented. An English translation of a foreign language tape transcription with no filler words, a situation not natural to normal speech, suggests that if the transcriber did not write down the filler words, he may also have skipped other, more important words, and that, in any event, the transcriber did not consider those words important. What else did he not consider important, and how is it that he has arrogated to himself what is properly a function of the jury? As with interpreting, we are not to judge what is important or not, it is all important, and every bit of sound that we can hear must be indicated on the page. On the other hand, you may find that the transcription is accurate, but the translation is deficient.

As for written translation work, so too for a translation critique, one should never work from original documents or tapes, because the documents may be subject to damage or loss. When dealing with documents, use of a Xerox copy means you can make light pencil notes on the document as you study it.

In a written critique of a disputed translation, each word or phrase with whose translation you disagree is a separate topic. Present the source language word or phrase in question, present the rendition the disputed translation offers, and present your preferred version in the target language. Some comments are then in order as to why your version is more accurate than or preferable to the original translation. In telling why your version is better, provide reasons. When one argues in court as to why a certain translation is to be preferred, one should show a basis in the authority of dictionaries and glossaries when possible. You may wish to cite five or six dictionaries for each word that you dispute. Those citations may form part of the textual discussion in a report you provide. This we do by telling the reader how a variety of dictionaries define a word or a phrase. Not all dictionaries agree as to permitted uses of a word. Quote the most standard, and work your way down to the slang and regional dictionaries as needed. While citation of reputable dictionaries is a good place to begin, one may also refer to one's own experience with the languages concerned, especially if one is a terminologist or lexicographer. The interpreter as expert here prepares an essay on language, on the words themselves, and their possible meanings. Provide the relevant opinions of the dictionaries you cite, and tell which one you prefer, and why you believe it should be that way.

For a word that is unknown to you, you may discuss the meaning of the root, assuming the root allows itself to be identified. On a tape where an American was speaking Spanish to a native Spanish speaker and used the word *huevoncio*, that word was not found in any dictionary or glossary the expert had available. However, it was possible to discuss the use of the word *huevo* ["egg" or "testicle"] and its derivatives, some of which are less than flattering. The original speaker may not be available for consultation, or even when he is on "your" side, he may have an interest in presenting a certain meaning now that he did not mean at the time he spoke. Your critique will be a short essay and is the work product you give to the attorney who hired you. The attorney may chose to present that report as an exhibit or may use it as the basis for his questions to you on the witness stand.

Even a simple, short document can be important to a case. For example, Juan Gamberro lends a car to friends, who then return it to him. Juan and his friends are subsequently riding around together in Juan's car. The police stop the car and find a machine-gun with a silencer beneath the front seat. Juan is charged with possession of the machine-gun with silencer, but says that the gun appeared in the car when his friends returned the car to him; he knew nothing about the machine-gun until the three of them were stopped by the police. The machine-gun is therefore not his. Fearing trial, Juan flees to Miami, and when he is picked up on a warrant, the police find in his pocket the notice to appear for trial. Asked why he had been arrested, Juan says:

[*Source Language*]	Me arrestaron por tener una ametralladora con silenciador.
[*Target Language*]	I was arrested for having a machine-gun with a silencer.

Both the Spanish and the English are ambiguous. The Spanish version is correctly transcribed by the police, but a jail matron writes down an English version of Juan's Spanish, as follows:

Police English Version: I was arrested because I had in my possession a
machine-gun with a silencer.

Note that the "for having" has become "because I had in my possession," a
statement much more definitive than the original Spanish. The government
fought to keep its version in the record, because the government version
constituted an admission to the crime with which Juan was charged. It was
possible to show the court that if Juan had meant to say exactly what the
government alleged he said, Juan might have said it differently in Spanish,
and in any event, the government's English version had added something not
present in the original Spanish. The government finally begged leave to
withdraw its English version of the statement. Juan was convicted on the
charge of fleeing to Miami to avoid trial, but was acquitted on the machine-
gun charge.

Part of the testimony hinged on the process of what is called **backtranslation**, that is, taking the purported translation and going back to the
source language. The classical example of backtranslation derives from the
old joke about the translating machine. A wonderful new translating machine
is going to put all the real translators out of work; it can translate anything,
say, to and from Chinese. To test the accuracy of the machine, a phrase is put
in: "The spirit is willing, but the flesh is weak," and a Chinese version is
produced. To check the machine, the experts take the Chinese phrase and put
it back in, that is, they backtranslate it. What comes out is: "The wine is good,
but the meat is rotten." Thus, backtranslation is a good way of checking a
version or rendition on a document, and a good way of asking if something
had really been meant in the original.

Presenting Your Own Tape Work or Translation

If you have prepared a tape or a translation for court, you may be asked to tell
that you did it, how you did it, and at whose behest. You may also be
questioned on the accuracy of what you have prepared. Whether you present
your own work or a critique of work done by another, the rules are similar,
accuracy and impartiality being the guidelines. As an "expert" you can be
attacked from any quarter. Some attacks may have a basis in fact, others may
be undertaken in bad faith. Regardless, one should be precise and polite in
answering all questions.

Preparation with Counsel

Conference with counsel should be adequate so that he can conclude what line of questioning will bring out the facts as you see them. Counsel is often in a great hurry before trial, but it is preferable for counsel to make the time to consult with the expert witness, so that he may put the proper questions to that witness on direct and re-direct examination.

On the Witness Stand

The expert witness differs from witnesses of fact in that she may offer an opinion based on her professional knowledge and experience, and on her examination of the work. As an expert, she is allowed to compare that to other work she has done, and to fit it into the general framework of her professional work, experience, and field of specialty. That the expert may offer an opinion is both her glory and greatest danger.

Qualification

Sometimes opposing counsel will **stipulate to** or agree with insulting rapidity to your qualifications, because if you are very well qualified he prefers not to allow too much "qualification" into the record, lest the court or the jury look with excessive favor on what you are about to say. On the other hand, should an attorney wish to discredit you at this stage, he may try to get you to exaggerate your qualifications. For example, he may use the old trick of asking if you have read certain books with plausible-sounding titles:

> Q.   Madame, surely you have read the noted work "Everything You
> Always Wanted to Know about Interpreting but Were Afraid to Ask,"
> by Danika Seleskovitch?

You had better not have read it because it does not exist. Seleskovitch exists and has written other books, but not this book which has just been invented for the occasion. Each of us is a specialist, and because of our different backgrounds and interests, will have different strengths. Stick to yours, know your limits, and present them honestly when questions arise. Just as it is not necessary to know everything, it is not necessary to have read everything.

The first part of your appearance in court would begin with your qualification, and the attorney who called you may review your résumé and basically ask you questions about your education, experience, teaching, publications, prior expert testimony, and so on. Assuming that the other side does not put trick questions to you on qualifications, or otherwise protest them, if the judge believes your background and experience meet the standards, she may say that you are qualified as an expert.

Just because you are formally "qualified" as an expert, however, does not mean you will necessarily be allowed to testify. The judge may ask the attorney who called you for a **proffer** or explanation of what your testimony will be. If she does not like what she hears, the judge may say: "In the exercise of my judicial discretion, I am going to **preclude** this testimony." This precluding has been helped along by the government's immediate objection to your testimony right after you have been qualified. Of course the defense may later tell you that now they have an appeals issue. The lesson here is that just because you are in the courtroom as an expert, and just because you have been qualified, you may not necessarily be allowed to impart your wisdom to the court and tell the court about complete interpreting coverage for a defendant, who properly needs interpretation at each step of the way. The lack of interpretation at his earlier guilty plea is part of an appeals argument on ineffective assistance of counsel.

The Testimony Itself

If you are permitted to testify, there are some traps to watch out for.

Tell the Truth

When we testify, we swear to tell the truth, and it is Peter Dorram (1) who reminds us that the truth is an issue here. It was necessary to be reminded, because unlike engineers and scientists, most of our testimony does not deal with what we might call objective truths, but rather nuances of meaning, what we heard on a tape, what we believe something "really" means. The problem with all this is that different people can hear different things from the same tape. Also, even if experts for both sides heard the same thing on the tape, there are shades of meaning, and there can be valid disagreement among professionals as to the meaning of a given expression. So it is true that we believe that we heard certain words on a tape, and it is true that we believe that a certain word means such and so in this spot.

One can, however, become entangled in lies to protect the self-image. Countless times we have seen defendants tell what they thought were unimportant lies, only to have their more significant testimony impeached. Our own self-image may become involved when we think of how many times we listened to a tape, say 20 times, or perhaps twice. Whatever the truth of the matter is, just speak it. Did you consult with another interpreter as to the meaning of this passage? Did you ask a colleague to do part of the work with you, and if so, which part? Did someone else ask you to review a tape and its transcription and translation, and, if so, did you listen to the entire tape to check the work of the other person? Did you look up a troublesome word, and if so, in how many dictionaries? Whatever the reality of your mode of work on a particular tape or document, just explain it truthfully when asked. The bottom line here is work method. Did you first transcribe the tape? Did you listen to it a sufficient number of times to make sure you could get all the sound possible from it? Where you sure about what you put down? Remember, if you are unsure about a given word or phrase, it is best to use dots....., rather than venture something uncertain. The real issue is were you thorough, did you put everything down that you heard, and were you careful. For us the question of truth boils down to method.

Because we may be asked about method, it behooves us to go the extra step. If we do careful, conscientious work that is not sloppy, we should have no problem with the question of method. There is no set number of times that one must listen to a tape or part of a tape. Some people may do a good job listening two or three times, others may wish to make 5 or 6 passes or more. Some may wish to hire a colleague for consultation on certain parts of a tape or translation, others may not feel it necessary to do so. Each of us evolves a work method to present a product that we believe to be good quality. Because our name is on it and we want our name associated with good work, the extra step never hurts.

The Trap of the Broad Generalization

During cross examination opposing counsel may attempt to discredit you by getting you to **impeach** or contradict yourself, thus: he will offer a broad generalization, hoping that you agree with it unreservedly, and then cite a specific instance in the tape or document that contradicts his generalization. The key words that alert us are words of broad sweep such as "always," "never," "100%." Listen carefully to the question: "Isn't it true that Spanish speakers from the Caribbean always drop the final 'S' on a word?" Not always. It is a speech pattern common to that area, but not everyone will use it all the time, and some may not use it at all. Whatever the issue, think of reality, and remember the exceptions, because the next question, had you agreed with the broad assertion, may deal with the specific line or part of the work that contradicts the sweeping generalization, and worse for you had you agreed with it. The broad generalization is especially dangerous for interpreters because in private life most of us like a good dramatic story. Drama requires nips and tucks to reality, foreshortening, the exaggeration of funny situations, all in the interest of a better story. But the same drama that makes a good story makes terrible testimony. When in court as an expert, imagine that you are at an academic meeting, or teaching a university class, situations where one wants to be precise, and take into account possible exceptions to a given rule in the most scrupulous and thoughtful way possible.

The Trap of the Unwarranted Assumption

Opposing counsel may ask you a hypothetical question, and you may assume that the example he cites has a direct connection with the case in hand. Revisiting the machine-gun case, the government may ask "What would you say about a person who was born in Perdida, had his education there and in the U.S., studied ten years in Spanish, and another 12 years in English, how good a translator would that person be?" You think, when you hear this question, that the government is referring to the person who did the "I had in my possession" translation, you are appalled, and you say "Well, he would not be much good," and continue in that vein with other foolish remarks. The most thoughtful answer would have be "I don't know." Because no matter what a person's background or where they have lived, some have the gift for translation or interpretation, and others, no matter how cultured and bilingual, may not have the gift. And, the person in the hypothetical example you have not met, and have not administered a translating test to, so no judgement can be made. All you have here is vague indicators, but no real facts of having seen the person's work. But, you make the leap of faith, the unwarranted assumption, and believe, from the way the question is posed, that the government is referring to the person who made the translation for the government. Maybe the person cited in the example was a case agent who told the government that the jail matron had provided a valid and accurate translation. We just don't know, we have no idea how this person got into the question. Watch out for unwarranted assumptions. Do not leap in to the auger hole.

The Trap of the Needlessly Long Answer

Much as clients are advised by their lawyers to just answer the question, we too should follow this advice. This is what attorneys call the "KISS" rule, KISS meaning "Keep it Simple, Stupid." That is, we should not get off the track, not begin to answer with a long, involved explanation of some point of language that goes far beyond what the attorney asked. Interpreters can debate endlessly about language, and can think of exceptions to rules, or other related examples that are just plain interesting. So we begin to weave a lovely web of words and discuss their connections, their history, changing use, and the historical reasons behind the changes. Any interpreter can do this for hours, but the courtroom is not the place to do it. Also, do not needlessly introduce exceptions to something you have just said, unless you are asked about those exceptions. Whoever asks you questions on the witness stand should ask for all the information he needs, so all we have to do is stick to the point. If you get off the point, you may inadvertently give the other side ammunition to bop you with. Just answer the question.

The Trap of Getting Smart or Angry

Expert testimony may serve to help inform the court and the jury (if a jury is present), as to the reality of a given content and meaning of a tape or a translated document. You are there to enlighten them. You believe it has a certain meaning, and so does the attorney who called you. You are there to convince, to get your listeners to share your belief, and to explain why you believe as you do about an issue. Opposing counsel, while supposedly looking for the truth, may wish to discredit the expert, so that his questions may be couched in insulting or arrogant tones. His purpose is to get the jury to share his evident scorn for your assertions, whereupon you might show anger, or become confused at the line of argument you are sustaining. No matter how insulting opposing counsel become, that insolence should not induce you to lose your equanimity. Opposing counsel has nothing personal against you, he is just doing his job. His job, however, may be to destroy your credibility, which is a very good reason not to be "snotty" and not to pretend to more knowledge than you have. How many times have we interpreted attorney advice to defendants to always answer: "Yes Sir," "No Sir," not to lose their temper when baited by opposing counsel. The same thing holds true for us. The voice of the attorney may drip with sarcasm. Don't fight back, don't get mad or rattled. Our words and demeanor should be calm and polite.

When we are hired as an expert, by one side or the other, or even by the court, the rule remains the same: to apply our knowledge, without fear or favor, to the question at hand. To the extent that an expert can be impartial, to that extent she will offer more effective testimony.

When Not to Be an Expert

Because language is your field of expertise, attorneys may ask you to serve as an expert in matters not quite within your province, such as accent identification or voice identification.

Accent Identification

An attorney may want testimony as to the origin of an accent of a speaker. The defendant says he is from Cuba, the government says the defendant is from Peru. One of the attorneys wants you to decide where the defendant is from on the basis of his accent. Some interpreters may have the expertise to do this, but many of us do not. Such expertise may be found at a university department of languages or linguistics, from a person specializing in Spanish American dialects. If you are not an expert in such matters, you may suggest that the attorney speak with the chairman of the Romance languages or linguistics department at your local university to determine if there is such a specialist at that school.

Voice Identification

Some attorneys or police may want you to listen to a tape and tell them whose voice is being heard. Because we were not there, it is best to indicate (male voice) MV_1, MV_2, etc. on the transcription and translation. Among voices, when one or more people converse, one may hold a belief as to which voice (MV_1 or MV_2) is speaking on a particular section of a tape. But who was really there we do not know. If anyone is to identify a voice, it is the case agent involved, not the interpreter.

Further Reading

1. Dorram, Peter B. *The Expert Witness*. Chicago: American Planning Association, 1982.

2. Saferstein, Richard, Editor. *Forensic Science Handbook*. Englewood Cliffs, New Jersey: Prentice Hall, Inc., 1982.
   * First cited in Chapter 2.

CHAPTER 9

Continuing Your Education and Enjoying It

Continuing education is in the hands of the individual interpreter. While attendance at professional meetings and seminars is helpful, ongoing effort may focus on broad reading of books, magazines, and newspapers, and observation of and practice with TV shows and certain tapes.

Books

Books cover a continuum from real crime stories all the way to fiction, and introduce us to the world of the police, the lawyer, and the criminal. Books on great scams are helpful, as are books on terrorism. Knowledge derived from such books will make the unexpected less surprising and help the interpreter retain aplomb through a court procedure. A general selection is suggested. You might like to pay special attention to books written by people who already work in your area, or who choose to set a novel there, because they may use the details and language of the local courts. The broad view, however, is the most important, which means wide, general reading.

Some of the best cop books are written by ex-cops. One of the most literate is Joseph Wambaugh, formerly of the Los Angeles Police Department, who has produced a body of work that is refreshingly literary quality (37-43). Wambaugh shows the natural process of mythologizing where *esprit de corps* is created in a team of officers. Each member is a hero, larger than life, with exaggerated attributes.

Lawyer books are an extension of the verbal instant replay attorneys enjoy. After trial attorneys review a case, and certain "good" cases enter the mythology of the courthouse. Older lawyers sometimes write accounts of their careers and most notorious cases, sharing some of the action and imponderables of case preparation and the quick decisions required in court.

Some autobiographical details describe most unpromising circumstances for the start of a great career. The value of these books is the view they provide inside a case, detailing what could not be said when the case was still being tried or appealed. Men such as Louis Nizer (24, 25), have written memoirs of their career and great cases, while John Mortimer (18) retells some famous British cases. Some of the younger lawyers today who work in criminal defense talk about the moral obligation to provide the best defense possible for a client they may not care for or even approve of. Alan Dershowitz' books are excellent because he details the constitutional rationale for his work. Perhaps this is because Dershowitz tends to work more on appeals than on trials, as he has said (4, 5). Some excellent books have been written about cases that were important for constitutional issues, as described in Anthony Lewis' *Gideon's Trumpet* (15). The book is a moving, well-written account of *Gideon v. Wainwright*, the Supreme Court case that said attorneys should be provided at no cost to indigent defendants in felony cases.

Journalists reporting a notorious case will often decide to do a book on it, and the careful, detailed reporting, bolstered by daily transcripts, as well as observation of court testimony, can make such books compelling. Often reporters write about the entire situation that led to a trial, as well as the trial itself, *The Falcon and the Snowman* (17) and *In Cold Blood* (2) being examples.

Understanding context enables you to find the *mot juste* when you want it. As drug crimes and the money-laundering that must follow become more extensive, books on all sorts of financial scams become more useful. Complicated financial transactions, normal business practices and their corruption may be discussed in court. If you have read about such a case, real, or fictional, it will be easier to understand what is going on when you must interpret a similar case. Bank fraud and money laundering are of special importance.

Professional criminologists follow changing fashions to determine why a person might take up a life of crime. Assignment of motivation for criminal activity changes with the style and tone of the times. The emphasis may depend on fashions in sociology, psychology, and politics. Knowing why someone committed a crime could conceivably help in rehabilitation or treatment, if any is to be undertaken. Of course even this statement presupposes that criminal behavior is abnormal, sort of a sickness. Some crimes are crimes of the moment, crimes of passion, self-defense, or fear. Other crimes are the product of a way of life, where the person in question has made a profession of being a criminal. Lewis Lapham has written thoughtfully about the subject (14).

The mind of the criminal has always fascinated mystery novelists. John Clifford Mortimer, the creator of the fictional criminal defense attorney Rumpole of the Bailey (TV and books) is a wonderful writer; his stories come alive in the PBS series, and are delightful to read and re-read (19-23). Rumpole eventually ran into a spot of trouble when he accepted a libel case. At the end of it, he was thinking with nostalgia of the petty crooks he usually defended, and swearing off the more "respectable" clients as much too devious. John Mortimer has himself been an attorney, playwright, and story-teller, and defended Hugh Selby Jr.'s novel *Last Exist to Brooklyn* when it was first published in England. Attorney Barry Reed's novel *The Verdict* (31), was based on a notorious medical malpractice case in Boston, and is excellent reading.

John Dunne of California has written some novels which, if not always about criminal life, skirt quite close to petty crime and the world of the lawyer who is not always able to live up to his trust (6). Edwin Torres, a judge in the N.Y. courts, has written some punchy novels about Puerto Rican crooks in New York (36). The more an author knows of police work and the criminal courts, the better for verisimilitude and terminology. One of the finest practitioners of detective fiction is the British writer P.D. James, whose stories include a woman private investigator who was initially retained by people in her neighborhood to find lost cats. The investigator subsequently graduated from lost cats to murder. P.D. James has given occasional interviews in the Book Review section of *The New York Times* where she has said that U.S. fictional criminals tend to use guns to commit murders, whereas her own characters show more ingenuity in such matters because fewer Britons than Americans carry guns. What this means is that the bad guys, at least in P.D. James books, are less obvious in their methods than their U.S. counterparts (12).

Periodicals

The Wall Street Journal is a fertile source of interesting indictments in business cases, and *The New York Times* can be helpful as well. Business frauds and scams are all there, though perhaps not in the detail one would wish. No matter how far-fetched a newsworthy case seems, how distant from the sort of interpreting you usually do in court, read about it in the papers. Some day a similar case may be yours, and the articles are good source of terminology and concepts. Logic suggests that when people are adept enough in English to pull big wire frauds they know enough English for court, but there can always be a minor figure as witness, victim, or bookkeeper who does not speak English. Any crime reported in the press may be useful. If it happens in English, it can happen in any language. Other countries and other languages produce and have always produced some great criminal minds. As the scope of foreign criminal operations grow, they will reach out and touch the U.S., and interpreters may be needed for court proceedings.

Crime and potential litigation are found beyond the crime pages in the newspapers. The Alaska oil spill might be discussed in the business or science pages. When a tanker from Uruguay goes aground off Delaware, litigation possibilities arise with "damages," "negligence," and possible criminal charges. There could be a trial. When you first read about the case, as general news, the boat is still aground, and next year's muskrat coat being beslimed. An interpreter wishing to work such a case can imagine, from the data in the newspapers, the sorts of terminology that might be pertinent: shore plants and little animals, navigation, weather conditions, sand-bar formations, tide and current behavior, and the seaworthiness or unseaworthiness of the vessel and the crew. There is something to be said for keeping a clipping file of large cases in your area. When you receive a case from a prosecutor or a private party, the attorneys may have little time to provide much detail, thus your own clipping file could be helpful.

The international gossip press is a great and neglected source of information and terminology. In Spain these magazines are called *revistas del corazón*, "magazines of the heart." We have nothing quite comparable here, perhaps in part because of our libel laws and the contingency fee system. These magazines tell us of the great scandals of Europe, and the great crimes of both Europe and the United States. The color photos are great, the paper stock is good, and you can see pictures of the Infanta of Spain falling off her horse, the Prince of Wales falling off his horse, or the room at the palace of Mar i Vent on Mallorca where the King of Spain *might* have kissed Princess Diana except that, as in murder cases, there were no witnesses and no one saw it, but thirty sources who do not wish to be identified can talk about it. In Spain a whole industry has grown up among celebrities and minor aristocrats who, because work is too demeaning and in any event bad for the health, sell their memoirs *en exclusiva*, exclusively, as they say, to the puff press. They sell the wedding, then they sell the divorce. A Spanish celebrity can sell each stage of his life, his face-lift, whatever. It is a great business. Photojournalists, meanwhile, scour the Mediterranean to find an aging movie star sunning herself topless in some cove of the Greek Islands, the star all unaware that the fishing boat cruising in the distance has been rented by the photographers who will come back with blurry evidence of the ravages of age and indiscretion.

One magazine especially good at this is called *Interviú*, a weekly from Barcelona. It has long complicated articles on white-collar crime, and on how the Spanish government has for some time welcomed crooks to Marbella, much as our government gives people visas to Miami. It has crime scene and air crash photos of a sort not published in the U.S. Other good Spanish weeklies are *Revista* and *Semana*, both heavy on the Spanish royal family and rock stars you have never heard of. A drier exposition of Spanish crime appears in the Madrid newspaper *El País*, whose daily edition has a section entitled *"Tribunales"* or court news. *El País* also sells an international edition, a weekly where you can read non-court news. The daily edition is a somewhat better source of medical, legal, and scientific terminology. Some large U.S. cities have international bookstores or news stands where you can occasionally drop by and see what they have from various countries. Some people prefer to purchase magazines and newspapers occasionally, while others prefer a subscription.

Television

Television programs provide useful general information, and special programs on trials and crimes offer unique opportunities to practice simultaneous interpretation.

The program "Cops" allows the viewer to accompany police as they go out on their calls. The violence, incoherence, and fear in the situations that police must respond to help us understand just how difficult police work is, and the fine line between civilized and uncivilized behavior. It also helps us understand why subsequent witness accounts of what happened can be confused.

Close to reality was "The People's Court," with Judge Wapner. The benefit of watching the small claims cases heard in "The People's Court" was that even if you did not learn much about the law, you learned about life and disputes. Many of the disputes arose over verbal contracts, or the ruined hair-do, or the back alley car repair that was less than successful. Judge Wapner operated mainly out of California, asking people with real cases in small claims court to drop their cases there and have them settled by him, on the air. California appears to have a good number of situations where couples planning marriage move in with each other. The man buys an expensive refrigerator, and installs it in the couple's apartment. Later the couple splits up and the ex-boyfriend comes back with some large, quarterback-size friends to retrieve the refrigerator. The ex-girlfriend sues, alleging that the refrigerator was a gift and now is her property. Unfortunately for her, the judge can rule about the deposition of the fridge, but not on who will eventually have possession of the boyfriend. Judge Wapner also heard a case of a wonderful double scam of some rug merchants. The merchant being sued had some damaged carpets for sale, very cheap. The damage was moths and moth eggs embedded in the rugs. A woman bought a whole bunch of these carpets and took them home, which home was promptly invaded by the moths, resident in the rugs. She had hoped to corner the market in these rugs. Meanwhile, it seems that both merchants were both doing business off the books, all cash, no receipts, so it was a case of the biter getting bitten.

Some 47 states allow TV filming of real trials, under certain circumstances, and when such trials run, if they are notorious, they may have a wide audience. The commercial networks have always been loath to interrupt "General Hospital" or "All My Children" or other programs for real sex, violence, and betrayal. It is now no longer necessary to interrupt, one may simply subscribe to the Courtroom Television Network, known as Court TV, to see real trials as they happen. Court TV does some editing, and offers informed commentary. Some reviews have said there is too much commentary and that it is too pompous, but if you pay commentators to comment, then they are not going to sit there like potted plants, they are going to comment. One wishes great success to Court TV, because the ability to see real, live trials allows us to practice to the screen.

Certain documentary/news programs such as "60 Minutes" or "Exposé," while they may not cover current trials, do speak of current scandals that may become cases if prosecutors and regulators become sufficiently embarrassed by those presentations. Also popular are programs we might call "U-Solvems," such as "Unsolved Mysteries" or "America's Most Wanted," which recreate unsolved crimes and depend on a large viewing public for tips that have sometimes led to the solution of those crimes. Such programs follow the recycling principle: first the crime is re-created, and then if the alleged felon is captured, one can go back to court and film the trial that came about because of the viewer tip arising from the first program.

The C-SPAN channel on cable is helpful for congressional hearings; local news programs sometimes take clips from them or even a direct feed if things are exciting. Late at night C-SPAN has lectures on government administration and other such lively topics, which are good practice material. Any technical or scientific program on any channel should be good practice, though the unwanted side-effect of such programs is a tendency to tear your hair out. Talk shows generally may provide good practice. Larry King, for example, on CNN, does interviews with a variety of people and questions them about their lives, their work, their art, all good practice.

There are Spanish language cable services and non-cable networks. You may be able to find a Sunday morning political discussion program that allows good practice if you want to do simultaneous into English. The SUR network from Latin America offers excellent news from a variety of countries. Also on SUR you may see "La Tremenda Corte," which, while fictional, provides a realistic idea of what happens when witnesses explain themselves in court.

You have a broad choice with TV, whether or not you subscribe to cable. News, documentaries, real trials, U-Solvems, are all useful. Look also for programs that I call "trash news," a combination of old and new scandals, almost like a *National Enquirer* televised. The trash news programs tell you tidbits that *The New York Times* and *The Washington Post* have unaccountably overlooked, so there is a real benefit here. The only caveat is that the announcers on such programs intone their descriptions with the moralizing smarminess that U.S. broadcast journalism is so fond of, look how shocking but we're really grooving on it. So, small doses of trash news, but it will make you the first on your block with obscure cases.

Since reality rarely matches up to fiction, and in any event cannot be endlessly repeated, it is good to welcome some fictional characters on the TV, Rumpole and P.D. James' characters usually appearing on PBS stations. They are quite wonderful and one can get obsessive in watching reruns.

Tapes

If you are teaching or studying court interpreting in a formal classroom setting, certain tapes can be helpful for practice.

Court TV has recently begun to advertise tapes of trials that it has filmed. This means that if you missed the original broadcast, you may still purchase a tape and practice with it at some other time. You may purchase audio tapes that the court reporting students use to practice with, tapes of trials and proceedings. Or, professors might wish to obtain some of the videotapes made and rented or sold by the American Bar Association (ABA), which teach attorneys how to try cases. ABA tapes of special interest in the past have included tapes on a trial for second degree murder, tapes on drug cases, and cross-examination of a forensic pathologist. As a professor and court interpreter, your familiarity with cases tried in your area will tell you the sorts of subjects likely to be most helpful. The value of the ABA tapes is that testimony and questions are very much to the point, so that students can obtain a good idea of the main issues likely to come up in a given kind of case. Another sort of tape would be that of presidential speeches. The White House has in the past been generous in providing audio or video tapes for teaching. One might look for tapes of presidential speeches given at international meetings where an interpreter had to put the English speech into another language. The White House press office has tapes of speeches made by the incumbent. If you wish to practice with tapes from speeches made in earlier administrations, contact the presidential library of the ex-president in question to see what is available.

Professors who want students to practice with tapes of jury instructions may record a set of instructions, say of a trial for Murder II, or possession with intent to distribute, cocaine. For any given area it is helpful to make tapes for cases at both state and federal levels, which means different sets of instructions. As to the recording, consult the copyright holder to receive written permission to make the tape. Publishers may be generous in this regard if you are teaching courses at a university, that is, they may not charge a permission fee. In any event, you need permission in writing from the copyright holder to make such a recording.

And in Closing

If it is our duty to constantly educate ourselves to become better interpreters, the process is enjoyable. Books, newspapers, magazines, and television offer new material that helps us better understand changing legal, social, and criminal contexts. Practice with tapes and TV programs helps maintain and improve our simultaneous interpreting skills. Extensive reading will also make us more educated people. Court interpreting might be called one of the learned professions, in which case, the more learning, the better.

Further Reading

The books that follow are both enjoyable and instructive, but represent only a small segment of the literature. They are offered as examples of the sorts of things to look for.

1. Baker, Mark. *Cops: Their Lives in Their Own Words.* New York: Pocket Books, 1985.

2. Capote, Truman. *In Cold Blood: A True Account of a Multiple Murder and Its Consequences.* New York: Random House, 1966.

3. de Borchgrave, Baroness Sheri de. *A Dangerous Liaison: The True Story of a Fairy-Tale Romance Gone Wrong.* New York: Penguin Books, 1993.
   • A compelling demonstration of how marriage, even to a rich, handsome nobleman, can be bad for your health. Somewhat trashy in tone, but good trash.

4. Dershowitz, Alan M. *The Best Defense.* New York: Random House, 1982.

5. ——. *Reversal of Fortune.* New York: Random House, 1986.

6. Dunne, John Gregory. *True Confessions: A Novel.* New York: Dutton,1971.

7. Gilbert, Michael, Ed. *The Oxford Book of Legal Anecdotes.* New York: Oxford University Press, 1989.
   • The book is funny and has a fine bibliography, generally of memoirs of British attorneys before and after World War II.

8. Grafton, Sue. *"C" Is for Corpse.* New York: Bantam Books, 1987.
   • Grafton has a series of books, and in an interview, when asked how she started writing, said that she was very angry at the husband she had just divorced, which anger lead her to the fantasy of murder, and of just how it would be done, which turned out to be her first mystery book. Setting, California. Problem, how to maintain moral standards in the midst of all surrounding temptations.

9. Grant, Michael. *Line of Duty*. New York: Bantam Books, 1991.
    *   The author, a New York police officer for 23 years, has written a sobering novel about how the police work, describing what happens when some police become corrupt.

10. Heilbroner, David. *Rough Justice: Days and Nights of a Young D.A.* New York: Dell Publishing, 1991.
    *   Reportage of work in state courts in New York City, how a prosecutor deals with witnesses, defendants, and an excessive case load. Excellent.

11. Hubner, John and Lindsey Gruson. *Monkey on a Stick: Murder, Madness and the Hare Krishnas.* New York: Penguin Books, 1990.
    *   Shows what religion can do in a modern guise, what good police work can do, and the wisdom of having one man follow a case to be able to help other police departments when the need arises.

12. James, P.D. *A Taste for Death.* New York: Warner Books, 1987.
    *   In this book, as in most of James' books, the people who get murdered have created more than one enemy, so the culprit is not always immediately apparent. James is a keen observer of the British social scene. In James we tend to see a second murder used to cover up the first, so that her readers know that her investigators should get busy.

13. Kane, Peter. *The Bobbitt Case: You Decide!* New York: Windsor Publishing Corp., 1994.
    *   Transcripts of the Lorena Bobbitt trial. Excellent study book because it provides the real landscape of the courtroom in a notorious case. It would be wonderful if publishers decided to publish trial transcripts in book form for other cases.

14. Lapham, Lewis H. *Money and Class in America: Notes and Observations on the Civil Religion.* New York: Ballantine Books,1988.
    *   Lapham argues that the criminal mentality is pervasive and begins with the higher scams practiced by bankers, stock traders, and captains of industry, showing a Wild West mentality all the way from the slums to boardrooms and palaces of government. Excellent background reading for any court work, and a cautionary tale. May be read with *The Bonfire of the Vanities* (44) as a gloss on that book. Suggests that crime is a venerable American tradition.

15. Lewis, Anthony. *Gideon's Trumpet.* New York: Random House, 1966.

16. Lindsay, Paul. *Witness to the Truth: A Novel of the FBI by an FBI Agent.* New York: Random House, 1992.
    *   Life as an FBI Special Agent where all the "good guys" are not necessarily good.

17. Lindsey, Robert. *The Falcon and the Snowman: A True Story of Friendship and Espionage.* New York: Simon & Schuster, 1979.

18. Mortimer, John Clifford. *Famous Trials*. New York: Penguin Books, 1984.
   • An excellent re-telling of some famous trials. Good bibliography.

19. ———. *The Trials of Rumpole*. New York: Penguin Books, 1979.

20. ———. *Rumpole and the Golden Thread*. New York: Penguin Books, 1983.

21. ———. *Rumpole à la Carte*. New York: Penguin Books, 1990.

22. ———. *Rumpole for the Defense*. New York: Penguin Books, 1983.

23. ———. *Regina v. Rumpole*. London: A. Lane, 1981.
   • Mortimer's main character Rumpole is the model of an irascible defense attorney with an abiding belief in what he calls the "golden thread" of British justice, the concept of reasonable doubt.

24. Nizer, Louis. *My Life in Court*. Garden City, N.Y.: Doubleday, 1961.

25. ———. *The Jury Returns*. Garden City, N.Y.: Doubleday, 1966.

26. Paretsky, Sara. *Blood Shot*. New York: Dell, 1989.

27. ———. *Indemnity Only*. New York: Ballantine Books, 1982.

28. ———. *Killing Orders*. New York: Ballantine Books, 1986.
   • Paretsky's heroine, private investigator V.I. Warshawski, is virtuous to the point of running about five miles every morning. She keeps a reassuringly messy apartment, and after the style of such fiction, does not get home but that the phone rings, with another revelation. New punch to an old form. Setting, Chicago.

29. Parker, Don. *You're Under Arrest: I'm Not Kidding*. 1988 Available from Caroldon Books, 1075 Farmington Rd., Pensacola, Fla. 32504.
   • Amusing account of life as a policeman in the Florida panhandle. In contrast to the Wambaugh books, the policeman, Mr. Parker, shows himself to be somewhat unsure, wistful, and concerned with doing the right thing rather than proving how macho he is.

30. Pienciak, Richard T. *Deadly Masquerade: A True Story of High Living, Depravity and Murder*. New York: Signet, 1991.
   • Careful reconstruction of a murder and the subsequent investigation, pre-trial maneuvering, and trial. Instructive account of police and legal work as well as effective defense tactics. Good reminder that police work and the law do not always function as quickly or as well as one would wish, but that prosecutorial persistence pays off. Excellent.

31. Reed, Barry. *The Verdict*. New York: Simon & Schuster, 1980.
   • A well-told fictional tale of a medical malpractice case. Good demonstration of what can happen when a client lies to his attorney, which can happen, strange to say, even when the case is not called criminal and the client not poor. The attorney Galvin attains a professional and personal victory.

32. ———. *The Choice*. New York: St. Martin's Paperbacks, 1992.
   • A bigger and better case where lawyer Galvin, now ensconced in a fancy Boston law firm, must defend a powerful if distasteful client. Makes you think twice about taking any kind of pill touted as "good" for you.

33. Simon, David. *Homicide: A Year on the Killing Streets*. New York: Fawcett Columbine, 1991.
   • Superb account of the work of Baltimore homicide detectives over a one-year period by a journalist who obtained permission to be a "police intern" to observe the work of homicide detectives. Of all the books cited here, most realistic account of how a detective works a murder case. Persistence and imagination are the traits that good detectives display.

34. Tannenbaum, Robert K. *Material Witness*. New York: Penguin, 1994.
   • Tannenbaum, who has practiced as an Assistant District Attorney in New York City, creates a story of one D.A. trying to do the right thing where crooks are both inside and outside the prosecutor's office. Good reading.

35. Thompson, Thomas. *Serpentine*. Garden City, N.Y.: Doubleday, 1979.
   • Thomas Thompson, may he rest in peace, wrote about real crimes and infused them with the suspense of excellent fiction. The protagonist here was a talented con man and seducer whose methods included murder. Watching him operate is like being fascinated by a cobra. Setting: India and Southeast Asia. Victims: tourists and others.

36. Torres, Edwin. *Carlito's Way*. New York: Saturday Review Press, 1975.

37. Wambaugh, Joseph. *The Black Marble*. New York: Delacorte Press, 1978.

38. ———. *The Blooding*. New York: William Morrow and Company, Inc., 1989.

39. ———. *The Blue Knight*. Boston: G.K. Hall, 1972.

40. ———. *The Choirboys*. New York: Delacorte Press, 1975.

41. ———. *Finnegan's Week*. New York: Bantam Books, 1994.

42. ———. *The Glitter Dome*. New York: Morrow, 1981.

43. ———. *The New Centurions*. Boston: Little, Brown, 1970.
   • The setting is usually California, and the world as seen from the point of view of a group of cops. Items (37-43) are novels, with the exception of (38), which is reportage of a murder case in Britain solved with DNA evidence.

44. Wolfe, Tom. *The Bonfire of the Vanities*. New York: Farrar, Straus Giroux, 1987.
   • *Bonfire* is Wolfe's first novel, and he was chewing over it for years, making New York City the subject. An admirer of Balzac and Zola, Wolfe believes that a good novelist must go out to look at the world around him as a reporter does, and

chronicle that world. This is what he has done here, and the scene is the Bronx criminal courts, as well as the high life with which he as a reporter had been more familiar. Vanity and greed get his characters into trouble. Once they fall into the toils of the judicial system, they are ground down.

Bibliography

Bell, Susan J., compiler. *Full Disclosure: Do You Really Want to Be a Lawyer?* Princeton, N.J.: Peterson's Guides, 1989.

Bergman, Paul. *Trial Advocacy.* 2d ed. St. Paul, Minn.: West Publishing Company. Nutshell Series, 1989.

Berk-Seligson, Susan. *The Bilingual Courtroom: Court Interpreters in the Judicial Process.* Chicago: The University of Chicago Press, 1990.

Bowen, David and Margareta, eds. *Interpreting - Yesterday, Today, and Tomorrow.* American Translators Association Scholarly Monograph Series, Vol. IV. Binghamton, N.Y.: State University of New York at Binghamton (SUNY), 1990.

Carper, Kenneth L., Editor. *Forensic Engineering.* New York: Elsevier, 1989.

Civil Jury Instructions: District of Columbia. 3d ed. Young Lawyers Section of the Bar Association of the District of Columbia. Washington, D.C., 1981. Supplement, 1985.

Conway, J.V.P. *Evidential Documents.* Springfield, Ill.: Charles C. Thomas, 1959.

Criminal Jury Instructions: District of Columbia. Edited by Barbara E. Bergman. 4th Edition. Young Lawyers Section of the Bar Association of the District of Columbia. Washington, D.C., 1993.

Criminal Practice Institute: Trial Manual. Young Lawyers Section Bar Association of the District of Columbia, Public Defender Service for the District of Columbia. 2 vols. Washington, D.C., 1993.

Crump, Ted. *Translations in the Federal Government: 1985.* Privately printed. Out of print.

Cunningham, Lynn E., Esq. *Neighborhood Legal Services Program Manual of Landlord and Residential Tenant Court Practice and Procedure, March, 1978 Edition.* Washington, D.C.: District of Columbia Neighborhood Legal Services Program. 1978. Bound manuscript.

de Jongh, Elena M. *An Introduction to Court Interpreting: Theory and Practice.* Lanham, Md.: University Press of America, Inc., 1992.

De la Cuesta, Leonel Antonio. *Lecciones preliminares de traductología.* Ediciones Guayacán, 1987. Available from Professor Leonel de la Cuesta, 10625 S.W. 112 Ave., Apt 105, Miami, Fla. 33176.

Devitt, Edward J., and Charles B. Blackmar, Michael A. Wolff, and Kevin F. O'Malley. *Federal Jury Practice and Instructions, Civil and Criminal.* Fourth Edition. 3 vols. St. Paul., Minn.: West Publishing Co., 1992.

Di Maio, Vincent. *Gunshot Wounds: Practical Aspects of Firearms, Ballistics, and Forensic Techniques.* New York: Elsevier, 1985.

The District of Columbia Practice Manual, Third Edition. The District of Columbia Bar and The Young Lawyers Section of the Bar Association of the District of Columbia. 2 vols. Washington, D.C.: 1994.

Dorram, Peter B. *The Expert Witness*. Chicago: American Planning Association, 1982.

"Federal Court Interpreters Manual, Policies and Procedures." Administrative Office of the U.S. Courts, Washington, D.C. In press.

Fishman, Clifford S. *Wiretapping and Eavesdropping*. Rochester, N.Y.: The Lawyers Cooperative Publishing Co., 1978.

_____. *Wiretapping and Eavesdropping: Cumulative Supplement Issued December, 1993*. Deerfield, Ill.: Clark, Boardman, Callaghan, 1993.

García Yebra, Valentín. *Teoría y práctica de la traducción*. Prólogo de Dámaso Alonso. 2 vols. Madrid: Editorial Gredos, 1982.

Genetic Witness: Forensic Uses of DNA Tests. Congress of the United States, Office of Technology Assessment. Washington, D.C.: U.S. Government Printing Office, 1990.

Goffman, Erving. *The Presentation of the Self in Everyday Life*. New York: Doubleday, 1959.

González, Roseann, Victoria Vásquez and Holly Mikkelson. *Fundamentals of Court Interpretation: Theory, Policy, and Practice*. Durham, N.C.: Carolina Academic Press, 1992.

Graves, Robert. *Collected Short Stories*. New York: Viking Penguin Inc., 1971.

Gray's Anatomy of the Human Body. 30 Edition. Ed. Carmine D. Clemente. Philadelphia: Lea & Febiger, 1984.

Hammond, Deanna Lindberg, ed. *Coming of Age: Proceedings of the 30th Annual Conference of the American Translators Association. Washington, D.C. October 11-15, 1989*. Medford, N.Y.: Learned Information Inc., 1989.

Handbook of Forensic Science. U.S. Department of Justice, Federal Bureau of Investigation. Washington, D.C.: U.S. Government Printing Office, 1994.

Herbert, Jean. *The Interpreter's Handbook: How to Become a Conference Interpreter*. Second Edition Revised and Enlarged. Geneva: Librarie de l'Université, 1968.

Hilton, Ordway. *Scientific Examination of Questioned Documents*. Revised Edition. New York: Elsevier Science Publishing Co., Inc. 1982.

Jaffe, Frederick. *A Guide to Pathological Evidence*. Toronto, Canada: The Carswell Company Limited, 1976.

Joly, Jean-François. *Proceedings of the Second North American Translators Congress: Washington, D.C., 1989*. Regional Center for North America. Available from: The American Translators Association.

Llerena, Mario. *Un Manual de Estilo: una presentación práctica y fácil de las normas necesarias para el uso correcto y apropiado del idioma español*. Miami: Logoi, Inc., 1981.

A Manual of Style. Fourteenth Edition. Chicago: The University of Chicago Press, 1993.

Mitford, Nancy, Ed. *Noblesse Oblige: An Enquiry into the Identifiable Characteristics of the English Aristocracy*. New York: Harper & Brothers Publishing, 1956.

Mlyniec, Wallace J. and John Copacino. *Juvenile Law and Practice in the District of Columbia: Representing Children and Parents in the Juvenile and Intra-Family and Neglect Branches of the District of Columbia Superior Court Family Division*. Washington, D.C.: The District of Columbia Bar, 1988.

Murray, Katharine Maud Elisabeth. *Caught in the Web of Words: James A.H. Murray and the Oxford English Dictionary.* Preface, R.W. Burchfield. New Haven: Yale University Press, 1977.

Obst, Harry. "The Ivory Tower of Babel and the Translation Demands of Diplomacy," a speech given at the Intrepretational Association of University Schools of Translation and Interpretation, Monterey, California, May 26, 1990.

Orellana, Marina. *La Traducción del inglés al castellano: guía para el traductor.* Santiago de Chile, 1986. Available from: Waldenbooks, 1700 Pennsylvania Ave., N.W., Washington, D.C., 20006.

Park, William M., *Translator and Interpreter Training in the USA: A Survey,* Second Edition, Arlington, Va.: American Translators Association, 1993.

Saferstein, Richard, Editor. *Forensic Science Handbook.* Englewood Cliffs, New Jersey: Prentice Hall, Inc., 1982.

Second Annual Neglect/Delinquency Practice Institute, March 30 and 31, 1990. Washington, D.C.: Young Lawyers Section The Bar Association of the District of Columbia. Spiral bound.

Seleskovitch, Danica. *Interpreting for International Conferences: Problems of Language and Communication.* Translated by Stephanie Dailey and E. Norman McMillan. Washington, D.C.: Pen and Booth, 1978. Available from: Pen and Booth, 1608 R St., N.W., Washington, D.C. 20009.

Trabing, M. Eta. *Manual for Judiciary Interpreters English-Spanish 1979.* Houston, Texas: Agri-Search International Inc., 1979. Out of Print.

United States Government Printing Office Style Manual, 1984. Washington, D.C.: U.S. Government Printing Office, 1984.

Wellman, Francis L. *The Art of Cross-Examination: With Cross-Examination of Important Witnesses in Some Celebrated Cases.* Fourth Edition, Revised and Enlarged. New York: Collier Books, 1962.

Wantanabe, Tonio, and Michael M. Baden and Milton Helpern. *Atlas of Legal Medicine.* Philadelphia: Lippincott, 1968.

The Court Interpreters Act of 1978

The 1978 law is the legislation that mandates certification of interpreters for the federal courts, and says that certified people should be used in federal proceedings once those people are certified.

The examination on which certification is based is mentioned and is further considered in Appendix 2.

92 STAT. 2040   PUBLIC LAW 95-539 OCT. 28, 1978

COURT INTERPRETERS ACT

Public Law 95-539
95th Congress

An Act

To provide more effectively for the use of interpreters in courts of the United States, and for other purposes.

Be it enacted by the Senate and House of Representatives of the United States of America in Congress assembled , That this Act may be cited as the "Court Interpreters Act".

Sec. 2. (a) Chapter 119 of title 28, United States Code, is amended by adding at the end thereof the following new sections:

"§ 1827. Interpreters in courts of the United States

"(a) The Director of the Administrative Office of the United States Courts shall establish a program to facilitate the use of interpreters in courts of the United States.

"(b) The Director shall prescribe, determine, and certify the qualifications of persons who may serve as certified interpreters in courts of the United States in bilingual proceedings and proceedings involving the hearing impaired (whether or not also speech impaired), and in so doing, the Director shall consider the education, training, and experience of those persons. The Director shall maintain a current master list of all interpreters certified by the Director and shall report annually on the frequency of requests for, and the use and effectiveness of, interpreters. The Director shall prescribe a schedule of fees for services rendered by interpreters.

"(c) Each United States district court shall maintain on file in the office of the clerk of court a list of all persons who have been certified as interpreters, including bilingual interpreters and oral or manual interpreters for the hearing impaired (whether or not also speech impaired), by the Director of the Administrative Office of the United States Courts in accordance with the certification program established pursuant to subsection (b) of this section.

"(d) The presiding judicial officer, with the assistance of the Director of the Administrative Office of the United States Courts, shall utilize the services of the most available certified interpreter, or when no certified interpreter is reasonably available, as determined by the presiding judicial officer, the services of an otherwise competent interpreter, in any criminal or civil action initiated by the United States in a United States district court (including a petition for a writ of habeas corpus initiated in the name of the United States by a relator), if the presiding judicial officer determines on such officer's own motion or on the motion of a party that such party (including a defendant in a criminal case), or a witness who may present testimony in such action—

"(1) speaks only or primarily a language other than the English language; or
"(2) suffers from a hearing impairment (whether or not suffering also from a speech impairment)

so as to inhibit such party's comprehension of the proceedings or communication with counsel or the presiding judicial officer, or so as to inhibit such witness' comprehension of questions and the presentation of such testimony.

"(e) (1) If any interpreter is unable to communicate effectively with the presiding judicial officer, the United States attorney, a party (including a defendant in a criminal case), or a witness, the presiding judicial officer shall dismiss such interpreter and obtain the services of another interpreter in accordance with this section.

"(2) In any criminal or civil action in a United States district court, if the presiding judicial officer does not appoint an interpreter under subsection (d) of this section, an individual requiring the services of an interpreter may seek assistance of the clerk of the court or the Director of the Administrative Office of the United States Courts in obtaining the assistance of a certified interpreter.

"(f) (1) Any individual other than a witness who is entitled to interpretation under subsection (d) of this section may waive such interpretation in whole or in part. Such a waiver shall be effective only if approved by the presiding judicial officer and made expressly by such individual on the record after opportunity to consult with counsel and after the presiding judicial officer has explained to such individual, utilizing the services of the most available certified interpreter, or when no certified interpreter is reasonably available, as determined by the presiding judicial officer, the services of an otherwise competent interpreter, the nature and effect of the waiver.

"(2) An individual who waives under paragraph (1) of this subsection the right to an interpreter may utilize the services of a non-certified interpreter of such individual's choice whose fees, expenses, and costs shall be paid in the manner provided for the payment of such fees, expenses, and costs of an interpreter appointed under subsection (d) of this section.

"(g) (1) Except as otherwise provided in this subsection or section 1828 of this title, the salaries, fees, expenses, and costs incident to providing the services of interpreters under subsection (d) of this section shall be paid by the Director of the Administrative Office of the United States Courts from sums appropriated to the Federal judiciary.

"(2) Such salaries, fees, expenses, and costs that are incurred with respect to Government witnesses shall, unless direction is made under paragraph (3) of this subsection, be paid by the Attorney General from sums appropriated to the Department of Justice.

"(3) The presiding judicial officer may in such officer's discretion direct that all or part of such salaries, fees, expenses, and costs shall be apportioned between or among the parties or shall be taxed as costs in a civil action.

"(4) Any moneys collected under this subsection may be used to reimburse the appropriations obligated and disbursed in payment for such services.

"(h) In any action in a court of the United States where the presiding judicial officer establishes, fixes, or approves the compensation and expenses payable to an interpreter from funds appropriated to the Federal judiciary, the presiding judicial officer shall not establish, fix, or approve compensation and expenses in excess of the maximum allowable under the schedule of fees for services prescribed pursuant to subsection (b) of this section.

"(i) The term 'presiding judicial officer' as used in this section and section 1828 of this title includes a judge of a United States district court, a United States magistrate, and a referee in bankruptcy.

"(j) The term 'United States District court' as used in this section and section 1828 of this title includes any court created by Act of Congress in a territory which is invested with any jurisdiction of a district court of the United States established by section 132 of this title.

"(k) The interpretation provided by certified interpreters pursuant to this section shall be in the consecutive mode except that the presiding judicial officer, with the approval of all interested parties, may authorize a simultaneous or summary interpretation when such officer determines that such interpretation will aid in the efficient administration of justice. The presiding judicial officer on such officer's motion or on the motion of a party may order that special interpretation services as authorized in section 1828 of this title be provided if such officer determines that the provision of such services will aid in the efficient administration of justice.

"§ 1828. Special interpretation services

"(a) The Director of the Administrative Office of the United States Courts shall establish a program for the provision of special interpretation services in criminal actions and in civil actions initiated by the United States (including petitions for writs of habeas corpus initiated in the name of the United States by relators) in a United States district court. The program shall provide a capacity for simultaneous interpretation services in multidefendant criminal actions and multidefendant civil actions.

"(b) Upon the request of any person in any action for which special interpretation services established pursuant to subsection (a) are not otherwise provided, the Director, with the approval of the presiding judicial officer, may make such services available to the person requesting the services on a reimbursable basis at rates established in conformity with section 501 of the Act of August 31, 1951 (ch. 376, title 5, 65 Stat. 290; 31 U.S.C. 483a), but the Director may require the prepayment of the estimated expenses of providing the services by the person requesting them.

"(c) Except as otherwise provided in this subsection, the expenses incident to providing services under subsection (a) of this section shall be paid by the Director from sums appropriated to the Federal judiciary. A presiding judicial officer, in such officer's discretion, may order that all or part of the expenses shall be apportioned between or among the parties or shall be taxed as costs in a civil action, and any moneys collected as a result of such order may be used to reimburse the appropriations obligated and disbursed in payment for such services.

"(d) Appropriations available to the Director shall be available to provide services in accordance with subsection (b) of this section, and moneys collected by the Director under that subsection may be used to reimburse the appropriations charged for such services. A presiding judicial officer, in such officer's discretion, may order that all or part of the expenses shall be apportioned between or among the parties or shall be taxed as costs in the action.".

(b) The table of sections for chapter 119 of title 28, United States Code, is amended by adding at the end thereof the following:

"1827. Interpreters in courts of the United States.
"1828. Special interpretation services.".

Sec. 3. Section 604 (a) of title 28, United States Code, is amended—

(a) by striking out paragraph (10) and inserting in lieu thereof:

"(10) (A) Purchase, exchange, transfer, distribute, and assign the custody of lawbooks, equipment, supplies, and other personal property for the judicial branch of Government (except the Supreme Court unless otherwise provided pursuant to paragraph (17)); (B) provide or make available readily to each court appropriate equipment for the interpretation of proceedings in accordance with section 1828 of this title; and (C) enter into and perform contracts and other transactions upon such terms as the Director may deem appropriate as may be necessary to the conduct of the work of the judicial branch of Government (except the Supreme Court unless otherwise provided pursuant to paragraph (17)), and contracts for nonpersonal services for pretrial services agencies, for the interpretation of proceedings, and for the provision of special interpretation services pursuant to section 1828 of this title may be awarded without regard to section 3709 of the Revised Statutes of the United States (41 U.S.C. 5);";

(b) by redesignating paragraph (13) as paragraph (17); and

(c) by inserting after paragraph (12) the following new paragraphs:

"(13) Pursuant to section 1827 of this title, establish a program for the certification and utilization of interpreters in courts of the United States;

"(14) Pursuant to section 1828 of this title, establish a program for the provision of special interpretation services in courts of the United States;

"(15) (A) In those districts where the Director considers it advisable based on the need for interpreters, authorize the full-time or part-time employment by the court of certified interpreters; (B) where the Director considers it advisable based on the need for interpreters, appoint certified interpreters on a full-time or part-time basis, for services in various courts when he determines that such appointments will result in the economical provision of interpretation services; and (C) pay out of moneys appropriated for the judiciary interpreters' salaries, fees, and expenses, and other costs which may accrue in accordance with the provisions of sections 1827 and 1828 of this title;

"(16) In the Director's discretion, (A) accept and utilize voluntary and uncompensated (gratuitous) services, including services as authorized by section 3102 of title 5, United States Code; and (B) accept, hold, administer, and utilize gifts and bequests of personal property for the purpose of aiding or facilitating the work of the judicial branch of Government, but gifts or bequests of money shall be covered into the Treasury;".

Sec. 4. Section 604 of title 28, United States Code, is amended further by inserting after subsection (e) the following new subsections:

"(f) The Director may make, promulgate, issue, rescind, and amend rules and regulations (including regulations prescribing standards of conduct for Administrative Office employees) as may be necessary to carry out the Director's functions, powers, duties, and authority. The Director may publish in the Federal Register such rules, regulations, and notices for the judicial branch of Government as the Director determines to be of public interest; and the Director of the Federal Register hereby is authorized to accept and shall publish such materials.

"(g) (1) When authorized to exchange personal property, the Director may exchange or sell similar items and may apply the exchange allowance or proceeds of sale in such cases in whole or in part payment for the property acquired, but any transaction carried out under the authority of this subsection shall be evidenced in writing.

"(2) The Director hereby is authorized to enter into contracts for public utility services and related terminal equipment for periods not exceeding ten years.".

Sec. 5. Section 602 of title 28, United States Code, is amended to read as follows:

"§602. Employees

"(a) The Director shall appoint and fix the compensation of necessary employees of the Administrative Office in accordance with the provisions of chapter 51 and subchapter III of chapter 53 of title 5, relating to classification and General Schedule pay rates.

"(b) Notwithstanding any other law, the Director may appoint certified interpreters in accordance with section 604 (a) (15) (B) of this title without regard to the provisions of chapter 51 and subchapter III of chapter 53 of title 5, relating to classification and General Schedule pay rates, but the compensation of any person appointed under this subsection shall not exceed the appropriate equivalent of the highest rate of pay payable for the highest grade established in the General Schedule, section 5332 of title 5.

"(c) The Director may obtain personal services as authorized by section 3109 of title 5, at rates not to exceed the appropriate equivalent of the highest rate of pay payable for the highest grade established in the General Schedule, section 5332 of title 5.

"(d) All functions of other officers and employees of the Administrative Office and all functions of organizational units of the Administrative Office are vested in the Director. The Director may delegate any of the Director's functions, powers, duties, and authority (except the authority to promulgate rules and regulations) to such officers and employees of the judicial branch of Government as the Director may designate, and subject to such terms and conditions as the Director may consider appropriate; and may authorize the successive redelegation of such functions, powers, duties, and authority as the Director may deem desirable. All official acts performed by such officers and employees shall have the same force and effect as though performed by the Director in person.".

Sec. 6. Section 603 of title 28, United States Code, is amended by striking out the second paragraph thereof.

Sec. 7. Section 1920 of title 28, United States Code, is amended by striking out the period at the end of paragraph (5) and inserting a semicolon in lieu thereof and by inserting after paragraph (5) the following new paragraph:

"(6) Compensation of court appointed experts, compensation of interpreters, and salaries, fees, expenses, and costs of special interpretation services under section 1828 of this title.".

Sec. 8. Section 5 (b) of the Act of September 23, 1959 (Public Law 86-370, 73 Stat. 652), is repealed.

Sec. 9. There are authorized to be appropriated to the judicial branch of Government such sums as may be necessary to carry out the amendments made by this Act.

Sec. 10. (a) Except as provided in subsection (b), this Act shall take effect on the date of the enactment of this Act.

(b) Section 2 of this Act shall take effect ninety days after the date of the enactment of this Act.

Sec. 11. Any contracts entered into under this Act or any of the amendments made by this Act shall be limited to such extent or in such amounts as are provided in advance in appropriation Acts.

Approved October 28, 1978.

_____

LEGISLATIVE HISTORY:
SENATE REPORT No. 95-569 (Comm. on the Judiciary).
CONGRESSIONAL RECORD:
   Vol. 123 (1977): Nov. 4, considered and passed Senate.
   Vol. 124 (1978): Oct. 10. H.R. 14030 considered and passed House; passage vacated and S. 1315, amended, passed in lieu.
   Oct. 13, Senate concurred in House amendment.

Seltzer & Torres Cartagena v. Foley et al., 1980

Seltzer & Torres Cartagena v. Foley et al. represented a challenge to the federal Spanish certification exam itself. In upholding the examination, Judge Milton Pollack provides an excellent discussion of why and how the examination was put together, and just what it seeks to test.

UNITED STATES DISTRICT COURT
SOUTHERN DISTRICT OF NEW YORK

```
-------------------------------------x
```
NORMA SELTZER and   :
MARGARITA TORRES-CARTAGENA,

                                     :

          Plaintiffs,

                                     :   80 Civ. 6496 (MP)

          v.   :

WILLIAM E. FOLEY, et al,

                                     :

          Defendants.

```
-------------------------------------x
```

OPINION
And
SUPPLEMENTAL FINDINGS

APPEARANCES:

BUCHWALD & KAUFMAN
Attorneys for Plaintiffs
530 Fifth Avenue
New York, N.Y. 10036
By: Don D. Buchwald, Esq.

JOHN S. MARTIN, JR.
UNITED STATES ATTORNEY FOR THE
SOUTHERN DISTRICT OF NEW YORK
1 St. Andrews Plaza
New York, N.Y. 10007
By: William Hibsher, Asst. U.S. Attny

MILTON POLLACK, District Judge

The plaintiffs seek a declaratory judgment and an injunction against the Director of the Administrative Office of the United States Courts to prevent him from certifying Spanish/English interpreters for the United States Courts on the basis of the written examinations he utilizes to determine the qualifications of applicants for such certification. The nub of the plaintiffs' claim is that the examination administered, tests applicants on language proficiency unrelated to anything encountered normally in a courtroom by bilingual interpreters, uses inaccurate and invalid criteria, and fails to take into consideration the statutory obligation to consider "education, training and experience". Plaintiffs, two independent consultants, who have for many years performed Spanish/English interpreting services to the satisfaction of judges and lawyers, have taken the written examination twice and failed to pass it.

An application for a temporary restraining order was denied on November 14, 1978 and a hearing for a preliminary injunction as well as a trial of the merits has been held.[1] The Director presented evidence which established that the test was soundly formulated by experts, suitable for the statutory purposes sought to be achieved and rationally related thereto and fairly administered; that in carrying out his statutory mandate under the Court Interpreters Act of 1978, 28 U.S.C. § 1827, et seq., his procedure was neither arbitrary nor capricious.

At the conclusion of the hearing and trial, the Court made basic findings of fact pursuant to Rule 52 (a) on the substance of the claims and denied the requested injunction and ordered the complaint to be dismissed and judgment entered pursuant to Rule 58, leaving it to a later supplement and opinion to be filed to deal with other matters.

Jurisdiction

At the threshold, the Director moved to dismiss this suit for lack of subject matter and personal jurisdiction. The relief sought herein is neither certification nor money damages, but only a declaration that the Director's actions have not comported with the

---

1.   Pursuant to Fed. R. Civ. P. 65(a) (2) the Court ordered the trial of the action on the merits to be advanced and consolidated with the hearing of the application

statute, an injunction undoing the certifications made to date under the examinations conducted and a mandatory injunction to establish a new certification program in conformity with the Act.

Judicial immunity and sovereign immunity urged by the government against proceeding with this suit, appear to be inapplicable concepts here. There is no real interference with or questioning of any judicial function or act. Moreover, even as to judges, it has been held in numerous cases, that immunity does not extend to injunctive relief. *Person v. Association of the Bar of the City of New York*, 554 F. 2d 534, 537 (2d Cir. 1977). Sovereign immunity has two exceptions which could apply in this case if the terms of the complaint could be factually sustained. "Those exceptions are (1) action by officers beyond their statutory powers and (2) even though within the scope of their authority, the powers themselves or the manner in which they are exercised are constitutionally void." *Dugan v. Rank*, 372 U.S. 609, 620 (1962).

Plaintiffs' allegations in the complaint that a government official had acted unconstitutionally to deprive them of a liberty interest of procedural due process, thereby raised a substantial federal question within the subject matter jurisdiction of the federal courts. 28 U.S.C. § 1331 (Supp. 1980); *Bell v. Hood*, 327 U.S. 678 (1976).[2]

The government further contended that there is an absence of personal jurisdiction over the Director and that 28 U.S.C. § 1391 (e) does not avail plaintiffs herein to establish the Southern District of New York as a permissible venue for this suit. The government relied by analogy on *Liberation News Service v. Eastland*, 426 F. 2d 1379, 1384 (2d Cir. 1970), a suit against 10 United States Senators and the Senate Committee's Chief Counsel, none residents of New York. The Court of Appeals concluded that Congress intended Section 1391(e) to apply only to the executive branch. The Court stated:

> [T]he officers and employees of the United States who were made reachable by § 1391(e) were the same types of officers or employees who could be compelled to perform a duty to the plaintiff under § 1361. (*Id.* at 1384).

The government argued that this holding that Section 1391(e) is inapplicable to congressional officials applies also to officials of the judiciary as was held by the Fifth Circuit in *Duplantier v. United States*, 606 F. 2d 654, 661 (5th Cir. 1979). In that case a suit was dismissed for lack of personal jurisdiction as to the Judicial Ethics Committee of the Judicial Conference, Judge Edward Allen Tamm, the committee chairman and clerks

---

2.   Plaintiffs' claims of jurisdiction under the Tucker Act, 28 U.S.C. §1346-(1) (2) (Supp. 1980) are misplaced; that statute does not authorize claims for anything other than money damages. Likewise, their claims to jurisdiction under the Administrative Procedure Act., 5 U.S.C. §701 et seq., and the Mandamus and Venue Act of 1962, 28 U.S.C. §1361 will not serve to authorize this suit. Those statutes apply to matters arising in the executive branch and its administrative agencies.

of all United States courts, on the ground that Section 1391(e) is inapplicable to such judicial personnel who were performing a "judicial administrative function".

The response of the plaintiffs to the holding in *Duplantier* was two-fold. They called attention to the fact that the Fifth Circuit nonetheless permitted the suit to be continued against the United States and the Attorney General for a ruling on the merits. Plaintiffs said that a ruling rejecting personal jurisdiction under § 1391 (e) "would likely be fatal to plaintiffs' lawsuit because plaintiffs' limited resources make pursuit of the action in Washington unlikely."

The second point made by plaintiffs on the issue of personal jurisdiction was that the role of the Director and his office is purely administrative and non-judicial.

It cannot fairly be urged that we are not dealing with an arm of the judiciary. The office of which Mr. Foley is the Director is the "Administrative Office of the United States Courts"; it was so constituted and entitled by the Congress, 28 U.S.C. §§ 601, 604. The interpreters who are to be certified by the Director are to be used "in courts of the United States". 28 U.S.C. §1827(a). The interpreters certified are not divorced from direct involvement in the disposition by the courts of their judicial business. Clearly the Director is called upon to perform a judicial administrative function in certifying interpreters for the disposition of judicial business by the federal courts, in the same sense of judicial administration that the designee of the Judicial Conference of the United States, Judge Tamm, performed his function in developing reporting forms and promulgating necessary regulations and receiving the financial reports of members of the federal judiciary, pursuant to the Ethics in Government Act of 1978, 28 U.S.C. App. I, § 301 et seq.

The objection of the government of lack of personal jurisdiction of the Director was, during the trial, withdrawn and waived but solely for the purposes of this suit and without prejudice in any other matter.

The Propriety of the
Certification Procedure

Plaintiffs' challenge to the Court interpreters certification procedure falls into three areas:
1. they attack the decision to screen out candidates based on the first part of the test, the written proficiency test;
2. they attack the written examination itself as designed to test archaic and esoteric matters that do not confront bilingual interpreters in federal court proceedings; and
3. they assert that certain individuals improperly received preferred treatment and status.

The Statute Involved

Passed in 1978, the Act sought to systematize the selection and appointment of Court Interpreters and directed the Administrative Office to devise a certification procedure;

a. The Director of the Administrative Office of the United States Courts shall establish a program to facilitate the use of interpreters in courts of the United States.

b. The Director shall prescribe, determine, and certify the qualifications of persons who may serve as certified interpreters in courts of the United States in bilingual proceedings and proceedings involving the hearing impaired (whether or not also speech impaired), and in so doing, the Director shall consider the education, training, and experience of those persons. The Director shall maintain a current master list of all interpreters certified by the Director and shall report annually on the frequency of requests for, and the use and effectiveness of, interpreters. The Director shall prescribe a schedule of fees for services rendered by interpreters.

28 U.S.C. § 1827.
The procedure which the Director followed in prescribing, determining and certifying the qualifications of persons who may serve as certified interpreters in courts of the United States in bilingual proceedings was substantially the following.

Mr. Jon Leeth, the Chief of the Court Interpreters Unit of the Director's office, undertook a broad scale study of the problem of interpreting needs of the federal courts. The purpose was to identify the manner in which interpreting was being conducted, the capabilities in use, the needs of the federal courts in this regard and how to qualify persons to fill those needs.

Mr. Leeth visited with about 80 persons including: Chief Judges of federal courts; the leaders, presidents and vice presidents of the major interpreting associations in the United States; people in the professional interpreting departments at the Department of State, United Nations; and directors of interpreting programs of various universities around the country. He interviewed State of California officials who were developing tests for interpreters and met with representatives of the City of Los Angeles to see what kind of tests they had.

A point that emerged from these interviews was that there was a mistaken belief abroad that if one was bilingual he or she could interpret; but that just does not follow.

The other thing discovered was that judges insisted that the people to be certified should be able to render what is said in the court as it was said, not to short-circuit what was being said *or* to change the level of the language that was being used; that it was not the role of the interpreter to simplify the language of the courtroom to a level *believed by the interpreter* to represent the level of a witness' understanding.

He found as he did job audits and interviewed interpreters that in fact many interpreters believed that they should short-circuit the judicial proceedings; that it is their job to make certain that the individual for whom they are interpreting understands what is being said and that if the lawyers and Judges use elaborate vocabulary, they were to reduce it to very simple terms so that a peasant, for example, could understand. Another thing he found on his job audits was that many interpreters simply do not have the command of the language, either Spanish or English, to know what is being said in the courtroom. Not knowing English they couldn't get it across in Spanish. He sat in one magistrate's courtroom in Texas where the interpreter completely changed the motive of the accused although she had no idea that she was changing his motive; but she didn't know what he said.

Mr. Leeth also found that interpreters were asked to do a very difficult job and were not remunerated for the kind of effort and skills and abilities that they had to have. Mr. Leeth recommended to the Director that he approve an upgrading of interpreting jobs from Grades JSP 5, 6 and 7 to JSP 10, 11 and 12 which while it didn't quite double the salary it did increase it considerably and put employed interpreters on the same level as the State Department and international interpreting.

In the course of the study, six outstanding professional people were identified and enlisted to help the Director set up a proper test for language proficiency and oral interpreting skill, namely:

1. Dr. Roseann Gonzalez a professor of English at the University of Arizona who had done a PhD dissertation on the level of language used in courtrooms. She made an extensive examination of transcripts of court proceedings and had analyzed them in a major study of the language used in the courtroom.
2. Dr. Maria Theresa Astiz, a professor of Spanish at the State University of New York, who is also a former interpreter for the United States Department of State and who has done intensive study of court interpreting throughout the United States at the local, state and federal levels.
3. Etilvia Arjona, who is a graduate of the Geneva School of Interpreting, an ex-director of the Monterey Institute's Department of Interpreting and Translation which is the only school in the United States that gives a Master's Degree in interpreting and translation; she is now a PhD student at Stanford University in Education and Testing.
4. Ellie Weinstein, the President of the California Court Interpreters Association, who for 15 years has been a practicing court interpreter in the Superior Court System in Los Angeles.
5. Alvaro Galvan, who is the head Spanish/English interpreter at the Organization of American States.
6. Dr. Eugene Briere, a professor of Linguistics at the University of Southern California and a specialist in setting up these kinds of tests; he has done a major analysis of the Miranda Rights language.

This team was brought to Washington for a two week conference at which it was decided that a test was needed. The test would have to indicate a good vocabulary, wide range for criminal and civil cases; actual interpreting skills; and an ability to interpret with precision and in such a manner that the style and the tone of the language that was being used in the court could be conserved without changing the meaning of what was going on. Test words were taken out of actual trial transcripts. Vocabulary lists that the California Court Interpreters Association had prepared for their members to study from in anticipation of the State of California test were studied and selections made therefrom.

A whole series of cases had been brought to the conference together with reference material, text books, language guides and word frequency books to determine the level of difficulty of the words that were taken out of the transcripts so that the conferees could match and make equally difficult words on the test. Dr. Gonzalez' study had shown that it was necessary to have a minimum of 14 years of education (equivalent to 2 years of college) to understand what goes on in a criminal trial and they all believed that it was necessary to have more than that to understand what goes on in a civil trial.[3]

After the group had finished developing a proposed test three judges came to review it with them: Judge Rinaldo Garza of Texas, Judge Juan Perez Gimenez of Puerto Rico, and Judge Jose Gonzalez of Fort Lauderdale. They were shown what had been done and why it had been done and the judges were asked whether the conferees were on track and going where the judges wanted them to go and they all replied "yes". One of the judges commented that "this is good and if interpreters don't pass this test they should not be in my courtroom".

All of the consultants who are specialists in test development said that a pilot test would have to be run for the result produced. The group wanted to pilot test it around the country so that they would have people who had different backgrounds in Spanish taking the test. Accordingly, they went to the southwest, to Texas, to Los Angeles, to Chicago, came to New York and went to Miami to have people take the pilot test.

Twenty-four people participated in the pilot test. They were requested to answer every question and make any comments they wanted about each item and furnish their global assessment of the test. The test was open-ended without a time limit on it because for statistical analysis the group wanted to be sure they answered the questions and wanted their comments on every question.

The results of the test were then shipped to the University of Southern California where Professor Briere ran them through a computer for a statistical analysis to see how the pilot test had come out. For validity and reliability purposes the statistics were very good and better than one would expect on a first run of a test of this kind. The test had an English section and a Spanish section each of which had five parts to it; antonyms, synonyms, a sentence completion section, a reading comprehension section, and a language usage section to test those things that the experts said were needed to gauge language proficiency.

As a result of the analysis of the pilot test responses, the questions were revised and improved. Thereafter the whole group of people mentioned above met in Brownsville, Texas to work on the oral portion of the test and there were added to the group Theodore Fagen, Chief Interpreter of the United Nations, and Dr. David Gerver, who

---

3.   The language level in the courts is high due to the fact that lawyers, expert witnesses and judges represent groups of professionals who have had at least 15 to 20 years of formal classroom education. This calls for interpreters with an essential comprehension at the college level of language proficiency and precision in each language

was from the University of Stirling in Scotland; he had done major work identifying interpreter aptitudes.

It was thought that for practicality of testing on the oral examination that it would be done in a simulated courtroom format. Trial transcripts were obtained from the archives in Brownsville and sections were taken out that would determine whether a person could handle the frozen language that occurs in court, the formal language, the slang, and the colloquialisms. A charge to the jury and an opening statement by defense counsel were utilized.

Dr. Astiz and Mrs. Arjona and Judges Gonzalez and Perez Gimenez wrote the direct testimony, the direct examination and cross-examination questions that would be in a courtroom format. Simulated probation reports were prepared and used. Dr. Carlos Astiz wrote a power of attorney and these were used as testing instruments to see if the person in fact had skills in interpreting in addition to having the vocabulary needed.

One of the interesting things that was done in the oral tests was to develop a way for the first time in interpreter testing to objectify a scoring system for interpreters. Every other test that had been heard of for interpreters was just a subjective reaction of a panel to how the person did, but this group wanted an objective portion and that was put in. A subjective part was also put in. This covered: how adaptable is the person to the language used; how well does the interpreter deliver the material that the interpreter is hearing; what is the level of fluency and pronunciation: it was all graded pass-fail.

Each candidate was reviewed by a panel of three people; an active court interpreter as a peer rater; a specialist in the Spanish language; and an international conference interpreter for interpreting techniques. The names of these raters were obtained through the State Department, the test development team and others who were helpful.

A group of 15 test raters was assembled and they were trained for three days in how to apply the oral test so that everybody would be tested exactly the same way throughout the United States.

The written and oral tests were then administered to the candidates for certification and the people who passed the tests were recommended to the Director for certification.

Some on the certification list took neither the oral test nor the written test nor the pilot written test. But those were people who helped develop those tests, had been professional interpreters with the Department of State, or graduated the Geneva School of Interpreting, or were professionals with the United Nations or the Organization of American States. Each of those who was certified had qualifications at least equivalent and probably superior to the level of certification.

It will be useful to detail here also, some of the testimony of Professor Roseann Duenas Gonzalez, another member of the team of experts engaged to develop the examination for certification status.

Dr. Gonzalez is a professor of linguistics and teaches applied linguistics at the University of Arizona where she is the Director of the Graduate Program. Her doctoral dissertation was on the subject of the courtroom register of English, a work that she was commissioned to do beginning in 1975 by the Superior Court in Tucson, Arizona. Her project was to come up with an instrument that would test the English language proficiency of a defendant in the justice system and also to find the appropriate time when to test a defendant's knowledge of English so that an interpreter could be called at the right times so that he would have total due process. Dr. Gonzalez found that the language of the law was not common everyday English and that it was something unto itself.[4]

This idea of the language of the law is an old idea. Courtroom language is something unto itself; English is not the official language of the court and this is what she began studying; what exactly are the parameters of courtroom English. Her study is the first to have looked at it in a very objective way.

She looked at transcripts of records from the Superior Court in the criminal field and covered a group of more than 10,000 words which she looked at for vocabulary, the difficulty of the vocabulary, its complexity, its breadth, and the precision of the kind of vocabulary that was used in the courtroom area. She looked at courtroom language from the point of view of readability which is a study of the complexity of the concepts of the language that takes into consideration the syntax, the structure and the complexity of the vocabulary. She also looked at courtroom language according to what kind of structure was used, the verbs, the circumlocutions, the indirect uses of language and other idiosyncrasies.

Her conclusion was that it was appropriate to talk of courtroom language as a separate register of English, a separate brand of English which had its own characteristics, its own set of vocabulary which repeated through many, many transcripts. It has an overall difficulty level, according to her readability study, of the fourteenth grade which means that a person has to have competence of understanding language, an intellectual understanding of the fourteenth grade level which is a sophomore in college level.

Dr. Gonzalez used a readability formula called the Yoakam formula, to measure the complexity of language of textbooks so that when she measured the complexity of the language in the courtroom sample that she studied it came across the board as fourteenth grade.

She emphasized that the important thing to remember is that we are not just talking about the ability to comprehend the language at a minimal level but to comprehend it to the point where the interpreter would be able to give a meaningful, accurate equivalent of that language, conserving the language level, style and tone.

---

4.   Dr. Gonzalez had found that words used in simple hearings never appeared or appeared three times or less in a normal million words of print.

Dr. Gonzalez emphatically rejected the notion that an interpreter's role is to simplify the fourteenth-grade language used in the courtroom so that a defendant who does not have a fourteenth-grade education can understand it.

Describing the Washington conference of the experts she testified that they came to the distillation of what is the function of an interpreter, how best to test it, a decision to have a two-part examination and each part was to have equal importance. The first part had to be a written examination because they had to get at the basic command that a person has of both languages and that was where her work really came into play. In the choosing of the vocabulary, the reading passages were geared to the fourteenth grade level. She has worked continually on college board examinations and educational testing service and the level mentioned is not considered to be a very rigorous examination of language. It is basic command of language, vocabulary and reading. The reading passages are in the test because there is a very high correlation between the ability to extract information from a reading passage and the proficiency of one's language. So when the antonym and synonym and sentence completion sections were chosen the group constantly had in mind this readability level.

The experts selected 23 out [of] 48 English words from her list compiled from courtroom records.

Those who were involved in the preparation of the test had made up enough tests so that the content validity and the face validity of the test prepared vindicated their expertise and established it to be a good test of what it was wanted to measure.

When the three judges mentioned previously spoke to the group they emphasized that the interpreter had to have precision in language and in order to have this a person had to have a wide range of vocabulary and had to have the subtleties and the nuances of the language really down pat.

The pass–fail score was determined computationally at the point where the minimal competency should be drawn. That happened to be lower than what the group of experts intuitively felt should be the cut-off point but they went along with the lower figure. It was a computational analysis based on standard deviation.

Dr. Gonzalez called attention to one of the greatest misperceptions that there is in this whole field. That is that if a person is bilingual it is believed that that person is able to interpret. She gave examples of experiences in Arizona and New Mexico where janitors were called into the court to interpret; where secretaries of judges or clerks of libraries were called in to interpret; and that, she explained, was the problem with the justice system and why it was necessary to have this certification process. Dr. Gonzalez pointed out that language competency is not a static monolithic entity. Language competency is a developing area, a knowledge that unless it is developed can stagnate, or can stay at the same level. And so when a person has daily expanded his or her language ability, learned more precise vocabulary, learned more nuances and subtleties of language, then, this kind of training and learning and experience and education is reflected most definitely on a proficiency test of their language command and their language.

Counsel for plaintiffs viewed the Court's function in this case to be the determination of the Director's reasonableness, not necessarily agreeing with every choice of question — his reasonableness in setting up the certification examination. It was testified by Dr. Gonzalez, that the experts employed here were of outstanding quality who had the expertise and who had the experience in writing these tests, people who were Geneva School graduates. "You just don't find people like that. I think there is one to a continent. You don't find people like that very often." To make the best test possible the Director had used the best possible input available; "they were the six best in the country," she said.

The other experts called by the government corroborated the opinions and advice given by Dr. Gonzalez and the procedures used by Mr. Leeth. They testified that the language used in the test that had been formulated was neither arcane, esoteric or archaic as charged by the plaintiffs.

It was further established that the test used for certification was evaluated before the test was given by a psychometrician who was entirely outside of the group of experts. Psychometrics is metrics from mathematical measurement; it is the psychology of measurement. The procedures in setting up the test were thus reviewed and found to be of the highest quality.

The Court finds on the totality of the evidence that the tests given by the Director were in all respects reasonable and not beyond his statutory powers, not an abuse of his discretion and represented a constitutional exercise of those powers to achieve the use of interpreting personnel in the courts of the United States having language proficiency and oral interpreting skill.

The Court has heretofore filed basic findings hereon which are hereby supplemented and the foregoing shall constitute further findings pursuant to Rule 52 (a) Federal Rules of Civil Procedure. (A copy of the findings previously filed is annexed hereto as an Appendix).

SO ORDERED.
December 8, 1980   Milton Pollack
                          _____

                                          U.S. District Judge

APPENDIX

FINDINGS
Made at the Close of the Trial December 2, 1980

THE COURT: I find and decide as follows on the substance of the claims herein, leaving it to a later supplement and opinion to be filed to deal with other matters presented, namely:

1. The examinations and the parts thereof in the content and manner in which they were given for certification of interpreters for the United States courts were fairly, reasonably and comprehensively developed and prepared under outstanding expert guidance, and properly, fairly and reasonably administered.

2. The said tests and/or the criteria used by the Director bore a rational and proper relation to skills appropriate, necessary and required for requisite precision interpretation by bilingual interpreters in courtroom settings and were valid and reliable in purpose and effect.

3. The written portions of the examination administered, tested candidates on language proficiency rationally related to matter normally encountered in a courtroom by bilingual interpreters, and presented proper, reasonable, and valid criteria, and necessarily and in fact took into consideration the education, training and experience of courtroom interpreters, and of the applicants for certification as such under the statute being considered.

4. The objections to the written portion of examinations that have been asserted have not been shown to relate to the precision of the bilingual performance of interpreters heretofore used in the United States courts and elsewhere.

5. The forensic qualities and prior extended use in court of interpreters are not to be equated with the performance of precise interpretations of the meaning and level of the matter and of the individual being translated.

6. There was no improper or preferential treatment of any persons or improper selection of or undue advantages afforded to any candidate who was certified or tested under the statute for interpretative work, and the methods of rating of performance on the tests were fair, reasonable, and appropriate, and rationally related to the object thereof.

7. The certification program and the examinations therefor, devised and used, satisfied the express and implied terms and intent of the Court Interpreters Act of 1978, 28 USC, Section 1827, et seq., and of the consideration to be given thereunder to the education, training and experience of persons seeking to qualify for the statutory certification.

8. The tests to which applicants for certification were subjected were neither arbitrary nor capricious in any aspect thereof.

9. The Court finds the evidence of the government's witnesses to be credible and unimpeached.

The foregoing shall constitute the findings of fact r[e]quired by Rule 52 (a) on the substance of the claims herein, which will later be supplemented by findings on peripheral matters, and judgement thereon shall be entered pursuant to Rule 58, Federal Rules of Civil Procedure.

In view of the foregoing, the motion for a preliminary injunction is in all respects denied, and since only a narrow issue is here presented which would not involve the matters on which the plaintiffs' counsel has indicated he has not had the opportunity to address himself, there seems to be no further reason for the maintenance of this suit.

The complaint will accordingly be dismissed, without costs.

It is so ordered December 2, 1980.

The Judicial Improvement and Access to Justice Act; Court Interpreters Amendments Act (1988)

Ten years after the Court Interpreters Act of 1978, certain amendments to that law were enacted in Public Law No. 100-702. The Judicial Improvements and Access to Justice Act (H.R. 4807, Title VII, Sections 701-712, amending 28 U.S.C. §1827), effective November 19, 1988 [Source: Circular letter of May 12, 1989 from the Administrative Office of the U.S. Courts]

TITLE VII - COURT INTERPRETERS
AMENDMENTS

SEC. 701. SHORT TITLE
This title may be cited as the "Court Interpreter Amendments Act of 1988".

SEC. 702. AUTHORITY OF THE DIRECTOR
Section 1827 (a) is amended to read as follows:
"(a) The Director of the Administrative Office of the United States Courts shall establish a program to facilitate the use of certified and otherwise qualified interpreters in judicial proceedings instituted by the United States.".

SEC. 703. CERTIFICATION OF INTERPRETERS; OTHER QUALIFIED INTERPRETERS.
Section 1827 (b) is amended to read as follows:
"(b)(1) The Director shall prescribe, determine, and certify the qualifications of persons who may serve as certified interpreters, when the Director considers certification of interpreters to be merited, for the hearing impaired (whether or not also speech impaired) and persons who speak only or primarily a language other than the English language, in judicial proceedings instituted by the United States. The Director may certify interpreters for any language if the Director determines that there is a need for certified interpreters in that language. Upon the request of the Judicial Conference of the United States for certified interpreters in a language, the Director shall certify interpreters in that language. Upon such a request from the judicial council of a circuit and the approval of the Judicial Conference, the Director shall certify interpreters for that circuit in the language requested. The judicial council of a circuit shall identify and

evaluate the needs of the districts within a circuit. The Director shall certify interpreters based on the results of criterion-referenced performance examinations. The Director shall issue regulations to carry out this paragraph within 1 year after the date of the enactment of the Judicial Improvements and Access to Justice Act.

"(2) Only in a case in which no certified interpreter is reasonably available as provided in subsection (d) of this section, including a case in which certification of interpreters is not provided under paragraph (1) in a particular language, may the services of otherwise qualified interpreters be used. The Director shall provide guidelines to the courts for the selection of otherwise qualified interpreters, in order to ensure that the highest standards of accuracy are maintained in all judicial proceedings subject to the provisions of this chapter.

"(3) The Director shall maintain a current master list of all certified interpreters and otherwise qualified interpreters and shall report periodically on the use and performance of both certified and otherwise qualified interpreters in judicial proceedings instituted by the United States and on the languages for which interpreters have been certified. The Director shall prescribe, subject to periodic review, a schedule of reasonable fees for services rendered by interpreters, certified or otherwise, used in proceedings instituted by the United States, and in doing so shall consider the prevailing rate of compensation for comparable service in other governmental entities.".

SEC. 704. LISTS OF INTERPRETERS; RESPONSIBILITY FOR SECURING SERVICES OF INTERPRETERS.

Section 1827 (c) is amended to read as follows:

"(c)(1) Each United States district court shall maintain on file in the office of the clerk, and each United States attorney shall maintain on file, a list of all persons who have been certified as interpreters by the Director in accordance with subsection (b) of this section. The clerk shall make the list of certified interpreters for judicial proceeding available upon request.

"(2) The clerk of the court, or other court employee designated by the chief judge, shall be responsible for securing the services of certified interpreters and otherwise qualified interpreters required for proceedings initiated by the United States, except that the United States attorney is responsible for securing the services of such interpreters for governmental witnesses.".

SEC. 705. SOUND RECORDINGS.

Section 1827 (d) is amended by—

(1) redesignating paragraphs (1) and (2) as subparagraphs (A) and (B), respectively;

(2) inserting "(1)" after "(d)"; and

(3) adding at the end thereof the following:

"(2) Upon the motion of a party, the presiding judicial officer shall determine whether to require the electronic sound recording of a judicial proceeding in which an interpreter is used under this section. In making this determination, the presiding judicial officer shall consider, among other things, the qualifications of the interpreter and prior experience in interpretation of court proceedings; whether the language to be interpreted is not one of the languages for which the Director has certified interpreters, and the complexity or length of the proceeding. In a grand jury proceeding, upon the motion of the accused, the presiding judicial officer shall require the electronic sound recording of the portion of the proceeding in which an interpreter is used.".

SEC. 706. AUTHORIZATION OF APPROPRIATIONS; PAYMENT FOR SERVICES OF INTERPRETERS.

Section 1827 (g) is amended—

(a) by amending paragraphs (1), (2), and (3) to read as follows:

"(g)(1) There are authorized to be appropriated to the Federal judiciary, and to be paid by the Director of the Administrative Office of the United States Courts, such sums as may be necessary to establish a program to facilitate the use of certified and otherwise qualified interpreters, and otherwise fulfill the provisions of this section and the Judicial Improvements and Access to Justice Act, except as provided in paragraph (3).

"(2) Implementation of the provisions of this section is contingent upon the availability of appropriated funds to carry out the purposes of this section.

"(3) Such salaries, fees, expenses, and costs that are incurred with respect to Government witnesses (including for grand jury proceedings) shall, unless direction is made under paragraph (4), be paid by the Attorney General from sums appropriated to the Department of Justice.";

(b) by redesignating paragraph (4) as paragraph (5) and by inserting between paragraph (3) and paragraph (5), the following:

"(4) Upon the request of any person in any action for which interpreting services established pursuant to subsection (d) are not otherwise provided, the clerk of the court, or other court employee designated by the chief judge, upon the request of the presiding judicial officer, shall, where possible, make such services available to that person on a cost-reimbursable basis, but the judicial officer may also require the prepayment of the estimated expenses of providing such services.".

SEC. 707. APPROVAL OF COMPENSATION AND EXPENSES.

Section 1827(h) is amended to read as follows:

"(h) The presiding judicial officer shall approve the compensation and expenses payable to interpreters, pursuant to the schedule of fees prescribed by the Director under subsection (b) (3).".

SEC. 708. DEFINITIONS.

Subsections (i) and (j) of section 1827 are amended to read as follows:

"(i) The term 'presiding judicial officer' as used in this section refers to any judge of a United States district court, including a bankruptcy judge, a United States magistrate, and in the case of grand jury proceedings conducted under the auspices of the United States attorney, a United States attorney.

"(j) the term 'judicial proceedings instituted by the United States' as used in this section refers to all proceedings, whether criminal or civil, including pretrial and grand jury proceedings (as well as proceedings upon a petition for a writ of habeas corpus initiated in the name of the United States by a relator) conducted in, or pursuant to the lawful authority and jurisdiction of a United States district court. The term 'United States district court' as used in this subsection includes any court which is created by an Act of Congress in a territory and is invested with any jurisdiction of a district court established by chapter 5 of this title.".

Sec. 709. SIMULTANEOUS INTERPRETATION.
Section 1827 (k) is amended to read as follows:
"(k) The interpretation provided by certified or otherwise qualified interpreters pursuant to this section shall be in the simultaneous mode for any party to a judicial proceeding instituted by the United States and in the consecutive mode for witnesses, except that the presiding judicial officer, sua sponte or on the motion of a party, may authorize a simultaneous or consecutive interpretation when such officer determines after a hearing on the record that such interpretation will aid in the efficient administration of justice. The presiding judicial officer, on such officer's motion or on the motion of a party, may order that special interpretation services as authorized in section 1828 of this title be provided if such officer determined that the provision of such services will aid in the efficient administration of justice.".

SEC. 710. TECHNICAL AMENDMENTS.
(a) Section 1872 (d) is amended—
    (1) by striking out "competent" and inserting in lieu thereof "qualified";
    (2) by striking out "any criminal" and all that follows through "relator" and inserting in lieu thereof "judicial proceedings instituted by the United States"; and
    (3) by striking out "such action" and inserting in lieu thereof "such judicial proceedings".
    (b) Section 1827 (e) (2) is amended by striking out "criminal or civil action in a United States district court" and inserting in lieu thereof "judicial proceedings instituted by the United States".

SEC. 711. IMPACT ON EXISTING PROGRAMS.
Nothing in this title shall be construed to terminate or diminish existing programs for the certification of interpreters.

SEC. 712. EFFECTIVE DATE.
This title shall become effective upon the date of enactment.

Suggested Interpreter Oaths

On January 22, 1979 the Administrative Office of the U.S. Courts in "Temporary Regulations to Implement the Court Interpreters Act" suggested an oral oath and a written oath.

The Oral Oath (I) or a similar oath is frequently administered to interpreters before the start of a proceeding.

The Written Oath (II), which I have seen only as a suggestion by the Administrative Office, provides a succinct definition of the duties and responsibilities of court interpreters.

I SUGGESTED INTERPRETER'S ORAL OATH

Do you swear (or affirm) that in the case now in hearing you will interpret truly the testimony you are called upon to interpret, so help you God?

II SUGGESTED INTERPRETER'S WRITTEN OATH

ON MY WORD OF HONOR, AS OFFICIAL COURT INTERPRETER AND OFFICER OF THE _____, I _____,

       (Name of Court)   (Interpreter's Name)

swear (or affirm) to be true to the Code of Ethics of my profession, and to discharge faithfully the following solemn duties and obligations:

I WILL interpret accurately and faithfully to the best of my ability. I will convey the true meaning of the words, phrases, and statements of the speaker, and I will pay special attention to variations of the target language due to educational, cultural and regional differences.

I WILL never interject my own words, phrases, or views, and if the need arises to paraphrase any statements in order to convey the proper meaning, will do so only after the presiding judicial official has granted permission.

I WILL familiarize myself with the case as much as possible prior to going into the courtroom. I will inquire whether the language in the case will involve terminology of a technical nature or a particular vernacular that would require special preparation. I will study the indictments or charges to avoid possible interpretation problems during formal court proceedings.

I WILL speak in a clear, firm, and well modulated voice, and when using inflections, I will be particularly careful not to allow them to be interpreted as partiality. I will employ the techniques of interpretation best suited to the situation at hand or according to the needs or wishes of those utilizing my services.

I WILL maintain an impartial attitude during the course of interpreting and will guard any confidential information entrusted to me. I will not discuss the testimony or the merits of the case under any circumstances, with anyone, particularly not with those for whom I interpret.

I WILL attempt to establish rapport with the persons needing my services and will explain to them my position as an impartial officer of the court, serving both the court and the individuals involved in the case. I will also inquire whether any person involved suffers from a hearing impairment or any physical or psychological problem that could interfere with the effectiveness of my services, and I will make adjustments accordingly.

I WILL adopt a conservative manner of dress and conduct in upholding the dignity of the Court and of my profession, particularly when attention is upon me in the courtroom. I will familiarize myself thoroughly with all the local court rules and I will abide by them.

I WILL strive constantly to improve my knowledge of legal terminology in English and in the language I interpret, and to be familiar with general courtroom procedures, so that in addition to interpreting, I may, when time and conditions permit and with the permission of the presiding judicial officer, explain to those for whom I interpret what is occurring in the courtroom.

I WILL be personally responsible for having the proper dictionaries and other linguistic reference materials readily available for consultation when needed.

So Help Me God.

_____

(Signature)

Index